T0301530

Women, Family and Family Businesses Across
Entrepreneurial Contexts

Women, Family and Family Businesses Across Entrepreneurial Contexts

Edited by

Séverine Le Loarne – Lemaire

Professor of Strategic Management and Head of the Female Entrepreneurship for a Renewed Economy Research Chair, Grenoble Ecole de Management, France

Candida G. Brush

Franklin W. Olin Distinguished Chair of Entrepreneurship, Babson College, USA and Visiting Adjunct, Nord University, Norway and Dublin City University, Ireland

Andrea Calabrò

Professor of Family Business and Entrepreneurship, IPAG Business School, France

Adnane Maâlaoui

Professor of Entrepreneurship, IPAG Business School, France

IN ASSOCIATION WITH THE DIANA INTERNATIONAL PROJECT

 Edward Elgar
PUBLISHING

Cheltenham, UK • Northampton, MA, USA

Published by
Edward Elgar Publishing Limited
The Lypiatts
15 Lansdown Road
Cheltenham
Glos GL50 2JA
UK

Edward Elgar Publishing, Inc.
William Pratt House
9 Dewey Court
Northampton
Massachusetts 01060
USA

A catalogue record for this book
is available from the British Library

Library of Congress Control Number: 2022946669

This book is available electronically in the **Elgar**online
Business subject collection
http://dx.doi.org/10.4337/9781800375178

ISBN 978 1 80037 516 1 (cased)
ISBN 978 1 80037 517 8 (eBook)
Printed and bound by CPI Group (UK) Ltd, Croydon, CR0 4YY

Contents

Figures

Tables

Contributors

Stacy Brecht is Assistant Professor of Marketing and Entrepreneurship at Azusa Pacific University in the United States and is pursuing her Doctorate in Business Administration from Grenoble Ecole de Management in France. She also owns and operates a public relations company in the Los Angeles area.

Candida G. Brush is the Franklin W. Olin Professor of Entrepreneurship at Babson College. She is one of the early pioneers in entrepreneurship research, and conducted one of the first and largest studies on that subject in the US. She has co-authored reports for the OECD, the Global Entrepreneurship Monitor and the Goldman Sachs Foundation, and has presented her work at the World Economic Forum in Davos and the US Department of Commerce. Professor Brush has authored more than 160 publications in entrepreneurship, including 15 books, and is one of the most highly cited researchers in the field. Her current research investigates angel capital funding of nascent ventures, venture capital funding of women entrepreneurs, healthcare entrepreneurship and entrepreneurship education.

Andrea Calabrò is Director of the IPAG Entrepreneurship & Family Business Center and Professor of Family Business & Entrepreneurship at IPAG Business School, France. He is Global Academic Director of the STEP (Successful Transgenerational Entrepreneurship Practices) Project Global Consortium (www.thestepproject.org). He has published journal articles on family firms, internationalization and corporate governance in leading international journals such as *Strategic Management Journal, Entrepreneurship Theory & Practice, Journal of International Business Studies, Family Business Review, Harvard Business Review,* and *Journal of Business Ethics.* His latest book, *A Research Agenda for Family Business: A Way Ahead for the Field,* is published by Edward Elgar Publishing and sets the stage for a shift in the family business debate. His research has appeared in different practitioner-oriented outlets such as *The Wall Street Journal.* He is the author of several practice-oriented family business reports. He serves as an advisor to family businesses and coaches next-generation members.

Didier Chabaud is Full Professor of Entrepreneurship and Strategic Management at the IAE Paris – Sorbonne Business School, University of Paris I Pantheon Sorbonne, France; Director of the Chair ETI (Entrepreneurship

Territory Innovation, http://chaire-eti.org/); and Honorary President of the French Academy of Entrepreneurship and Innovation. His research focuses on the processes of entrepreneurship, family business and social business and entrepreneurship, and he has published more than 100 articles, chapters and books.

Cinzia Colapinto has a PhD in Business History and Corporate Finance (University of Milan, Italy) and is Associate Professor at the Department of Management and Member of the AgriFood Management & Innovation Lab, Ca' Foscari University of Venice (Italy), and Senior Researcher in Strategy and Entrepreneurship at IPAG Business School (France). Her research interests focus on entrepreneurship, innovation and strategy. In particular, she is interested in the role played by digital technologies in business model transformations and their impact on the achievement of sustainable development goals by SMEs. Her main publications are in *Management International Review, Management Decision, European Journal of Operational Research* and *Annals of Operations Research*. She is the author of several monographs, including *Adaptive Decision Making and Intellectual Styles* (Springer).

Rola El Ali is currently a DBA candidate at Grenoble Ecole de Management. She previously worked as a training manager and instructor at the American College of the Middle East and the Australian College of the Middle East. Her research focuses on women's entrepreneurship in developing countries; their emancipation process, entrepreneurial practices and support system; and the strategies they develop to achieve their entrepreneurial objectives.

Soumaya El Hayek Sfeir holds a PhD in Management Sciences from Grenoble Alpes University (France). She is Assistant Professor at Excelia Group (La Rochelle, France) and has an MSc in Entrepreneurship and Business Innovation. Her research focuses on the diversity of directors on boards of family-owned businesses, paying attention to their behaviours and beliefs that guide the choice of successor, but also to emotions and any other non-economic aspects that can explain succession in family businesses.

Luz Marina Ferro-Cortes is Associate Professor at Universidad de los Andes (Colombia). She is a research professor in female entrepreneurship, international marketing and entrepreneurship at UASM. Her PhD in Management with a specialization in Entrepreneurship comes from HEC, Montreal-Canada. Her research focuses on the entrepreneurship process (opportunity-formation process, trust-building process, networking) in female entrepreneurship and international entrepreneurship in contrasting contexts such as Canada, Colombia and other emerging countries in Latin America. She leads a project with colleagues from Uniandes, ESCP Europe and ESAN Peru on Research on

Latin American Female Entrepreneurship, and a research group with undergraduate and doctoral students on innovative female entrepreneurship.

Vladi Finotto has a PhD in Management and is Associate Professor in Entrepreneurship and Strategy at the Department of Management, Ca' Foscari University of Venice. He has been working on themes such as business model reconfiguration and strategic innovation induced by changes in consumer preferences and behaviours since 2008. He has published on this topic in international management, innovation and strategy journals and in an edited Oxford Handbook on creative industries (with a chapter on the strategic implications of consumer community dynamics). His research has focused on a variety of industries, paying particular attention to mature, medium-tech ones, with an increasing focus on the food industry. He coordinated the local unit in a EU/FP6 project, has taken part in a number of national high-impact projects and is involved in international research networks on innovation and strategy. Currently he teaches strategy and innovation for the agri-food industries in Ca' Foscari's Masters programme in Food and Wine Culture. At Ca' Foscari he is the delegate for technology transfer, entrepreneurship and industrial liaisons and coordinates a variety of industry-university initiatives.

William B. Gartner is the Bertarelli Foundation Distinguished Professor of Family Entrepreneurship at Babson College. He is recognized as a leading scholar in the field of entrepreneurship by such awards as the 2005 Swedish Entrepreneurship Foundation International Award for outstanding contributions to entrepreneurship and small business research; the 2013 Academy of Management Entrepreneurship Division Foundational Paper Award; the 2016 Academy of Management Entrepreneurship Division Dedication to Entrepreneurship Award, and he was recently selected as a 2022 USASBE Justin G. Longenecker Fellow which is the highest recognition that the United States Association for Small Business and Entrepreneurship (USASBE) gives to individuals who have made an outstanding contribution to the development, furtherance, and benefit of small and medium businesses. His scholarship spans a wide array of topics in the entrepreneurship field: entrepreneurship as practice, the social construction of the future, varieties of value creation and appropriation, translating entrepreneurship across cultures and countries, the poetics of exchange, the demographics of entrepreneurial families, and the influence of legacy on family entrepreneurship.

Mónica Grau-Sarabia is a Marie Sklodowska-Curie Individual Fellow at CARE Netherlands and the International Institute of Social Studies at the Erasmus University of Rotterdam. She is currently working on the project Women's Economic and Psychological Empowerment – EMPOWER. The project is bringing together feminist economics, gender and development concepts and social psychology to understand better how to ensure personal empowerment processes through the promotion of women's access to economic resources in specific contexts. She holds a PhD in Philosophy (University of Barcelona), an MSc in Human Resource Development (IDPM, UK), a Degree in Psychology (Valencia University, Spain), and a Postgraduate in French Studies (Montpellier University, France). Dr Grau-Sarabia has international experience in the fields of gender equality, women's economic empowerment, and sustainable development. Her research disciplines are social psychology, management and entrepreneurship, feminist theory, and feminist economics. She is a policy adviser for an international development agency on programming, management and measuring the impact of gender equality projects and policies. She has recently published, with her co-author M. Fuster-Morell, an article in *Humanities and Social Sciences Communications*, 8(1).

Mona Haug supports individuals, teams and organizations in gaining insight into sought-after solutions for the world of tomorrow and strategies for overcoming current challenges in society, culture and career. Dr Haug draws on tailored knowledge from scientific areas such as leadership, management, team, and power and gender diversity theory. In addition, clients benefit from 20 years of Dr Haug's international practice as an executive coach in major companies, several countries and more than 16 nations. This gives her clients an edge in global competition. Her PhD research focuses on career development for female executives: what barriers as well as supporting circumstances affect women in top leadership positions?

Jasmine Jaim completed her PhD in Management at the University of Nottingham, UK. Currently she serves as Professor at the Institute of Business Administration, Jahangirnagar University, Bangladesh. Professor Jaim also has consultancy and university teaching related experiences in the UK and USA. In addition to book chapters, she has published articles in some top-tier ABS-ranked journals, including *Journal of Business Ethics*, *Journal of Small Business Management* and *Gender Work & Organization*.

Séverine Le Loarne – Lemaire is Full Professor at Grenoble Ecole de Management (France) and holds the FERE (Female Entrepreneurship for a Renewed Economy) Research Chair. Her research focuses on strategizing practices of women middle managers in big organizations and of women entrepreneurs. In that regard, her work focuses on the role of spousal support and the dynamic of the couple on women's entrepreneurial practices. She has published many books and peer-reviewed research articles on these subjects and has also been published in managerial journals.

Adnane Maâlaoui is Head of the Department for Disadvantage & Entrepreneurship and co-director of the IPAG Entrepreneurship and Family

Business Center at IPAG Business School (France). His research mainly focuses on issues of entrepreneurship, and in particular on disadvantaged entrepreneurs (such as elderly, immigrant and disabled entrepreneurs). He works on topics such as entrepreneurial intention and the cognitive approach to entrepreneurship. He mainly applies those questions to cases of diversity and social entrepreneurship.

Nancy Matos is Associate Professor at Esan Graduate Business School, Lima-Peru and President of the Academic Committee at the Latin American Council of Management Schools-CLADEA. Her research and publications focus on innovation, intellectual property rights, female entrepreneurship, and innovation in SME. She is the former Vice-president of Academic Affairs and Director of the doctoral programme at Esan University. She realizes mentoring for new ventures for the Council of Science and Technology – CONCYTEC in Peru; teaches innovation and entrepreneurship, marketing and negotiation skills; is a member of various journals' editorial review boards; and provides consulting services on the development of SME to the government and diverse international organizations such as PNUD, BID, USAID, GIZ and ACDI.

Christine Mauracher is Full Professor of Agricultural Economics at the Department of Management, Ca' Foscari University of Venice. She is Director of Agrifood Management and Innovation Lab and Co-director of the Masters in Culture of Food and Wine. Her current research interests include agri-food economics and marketing, consumer behaviour, fishery economics and wine tourism. More recent research is focused on digitalization of SMEs in the food industry. She has published on these topics in international journals such as *Wine Economics and Policy*, *Food Quality and Preference* and *International Journal of Globalisation and Small Business*.

Gry Osnes is an independent researcher and a clinically trained psychother-apist, cand.psychol, MSc HEC and PhD from University of Oslo, with 20 years of coaching and consultant experience and several published books and articles. Osnes works with new and old business owners on the intersection between the individual, the family dynamics and the emotional foundation for strategy capability. Osnes' work and writing focuses on organizational and individual psychological aspects of strategy capability. It has focused on suc-cession as strategy practice and group dynamic (PhD), the role and leadership of the chair of the board (forthcoming) and applying affect neuroscience, or the Emotional Brain, to organizational dynamics and interpersonal dynamics.

Florence Pinot de Villechenon is Emeritus Professor and Academic Director for Latin America at ESCP Business School, where she teaches on interna-tional business, international relations and geopolitical issues. Her research and publications focus on business dynamics and cooperation between Europe and Latin America, SMEs' internationalization, female entrepreneurship and big events as soft power tools. She has headed the CERALE research centre (Centre d'Etudes et de Recherche Amérique latine Europe) at ESCP Business School since 2001. She taught at IHEAL (Institut des Hautes Etudes d'Amérique latine)-Université Sorbonne Nouvelle between 2005 and 2016, and is a member of the Strategic Council of IHEAL. She was also a member of the Scientific Council of the Institute of the Americas until 2019. She is President of ALFA Business Forum Argentina France and a member of the boards of Maison de l'Amérique latine and Forum de l'Universel. She is in charge of the French Section of Marianne Asociación de Mujeres Francoargentinas.

Kim Poldner is Professor of Circular Business at The Hague University of Applied Sciences and serial entre-searcher in sustainable fashion. Kim has published in top academic journals, such as the *Journal of Business Venturing*, *Organization* and *Business & Society*, and has written award-winning case studies on sustainable fashion pioneers, such as Veja and Osklen.

Hedi Yezza is Assistant Professor of Entrepreneurship & Family Business at the Business School of Sherbrooke – Université de Sherbrooke, Québec (Canada) and affiliate researcher of the academic chair 'Entrepreneuriat Territoire Innovation' at IAE Paris-Sorbonne Business School – France (http://chaire-eti.org/). His current research focuses on family businesses, particularly the succession process, strategic renewal, conflict management and social capital. His publications on these topics include book chapters and academic journal articles and he has spoken at national and international conferences. He received the Best PhD Award in entrepreneurship from the French-speaking international association *Association Internationale de Recherche en Entrepreneuriat et PME (AIREPME)*. Since 2020, he has served as Editorial Assistant of *Revue de l'Entrepreneuriat/Review of Entrepreneurship*.

Introduction to *Women, Family and Family Businesses Across Entrepreneurial Contexts*

Séverine Le Loarne – Lemaire, Candida G. Brush, Andrea Calabrò and Adnane Maâlaoui

Family firms have a prominent role across countries and industries and are the main organizational form for most ventures worldwide. Family firms are organizations characterized by intertwining of the family and business systems, which gives a special flavor to how decision-makers act and react and to how strategic decisions are taken. In fact, economic and non-economic objectives co-exist in such types of organization, where the family is attached to the stock of affect-related value—also labeled as socioemotional wealth (Gómez-Mejía et al., 2007)—that has been invested in the firm. The tendency to preserve family control and influence, family identification with the firm, and emotional attachment, and the desire to transfer the business to the next generation, are characteristics that make family firms different from other organizational forms. Moreover, those features can vary depending on contexts (Welter, 2011) and cultures (Hofstede et al., 2001). There is indeed a great heterogeneity among family firms due to different degrees of family involvement in ownership and management, business and family governance, organizational size and international scope (ranging from small ventures to multinational enterprises), and industries. Several themes have been investigated within the family business research field, such as leadership succession, business and family governance, innovation, internationalization, role of siblings, corporate entrepreneurship, and the role of women as mothers, daughters, and sisters (Martinez Jimenez, 2009). With specific reference to the role of women in family business, research has suggested that this context gives a special flavor to the legitimation process of women's leadership (Calabrò et al., 2022). The role of women belonging to a family business is different than that in other types of organizations: on the one side they are legitimized as being part of the business as they belong to the owning family (Campopiano et al., 2017), and on the other they might be exposed to challenges, when entering the corporate world, such as entry barriers, the glass ceiling, and stereotypes (Chadwick &

Dawson, 2018). They often face additional challenges such as struggles with their male siblings, usually considered the natural heirs (Akhmedova et al., 2020; Calabrò et al., 2018). And, even if they make it to the top, they could face double stereotyping; in addition to stereotypes aimed at women, they face the judgment that they attained their role only because they are part of the owning family.

Research suggests that the role of women within these types of businesses is often minimized; they are present but contribute "in the shadows" to the growth and sustainability of the family firm (Haberman & Danes, 2007). Despite some studies revealing that women should have a more official presence on boards of directors starting with the second or third generation of family owners (Sonfield & Lussier, 2004), others indicate that only 23 percent of succession of family firms in developed countries involves women (Ahrens et al., 2015). Further studies also suggest that, within the family firm context, firstborn sons (male primogeniture) are often preferred as natural heirs and thus CEOs of the family business, with a systematic exclusion of daughters. Unfortunately, there is as yet a lack of understanding of the process that leads to the legitimization of women in family firms and of women's roles within family businesses.

Women within family firms might indeed be exposed to several challenges, especially when it comes to the decision as to who will be the next leader, whether having a female successor is considered an option, and whether they are in fact willing to take over (Calabrò et al., 2018). The familial, social, cultural, and institutional dynamics which take place often lead those "family business women" to renounce their original desire to lead the family firm in order avoid tension within the family, leaving the firm to their brothers or perhaps exiting it and starting an entirely new type of entrepreneurial activity (Hamilton, 2006).

At the same time, women entrepreneurs running ventures while managing family commitments have become a global phenomenon (Elam et al., 2019). But women face different challenges than their male counterparts, as they are the primary caregivers for children and their families (Shelton, 2006). This can cause work–family conflict, including job–spouse conflict, job–homemaker conflict, and job–parent conflict, which can create even more challenge as women entrepreneurs grow their businesses (Kim & Ling, 2001; Nikina et al., 2013). The ways in which women entrepreneurs manage work and family are understudied to date. Increasingly, women are starting businesses with their spouses or family members, a phenomenon referred to as "copreneurship." This could ultimately be considered a preliminary phase in the constitution of a family business, where business ownership and operations are shared by dual-career couples (Marshack, 1994). Yet the ways in which these businesses are structured and how they perform is not well understood.

In sum, there is a lack of systematic knowledge about women in the context of family businesses, and about how women as entrepreneurs are managing their families.

This book marks the 12th volume resulting from the Diana Project, established in 1999 to engage in research activities focusing on women entrepreneurs. The book builds on the dialogue catalyzed by scholars working on the field of women entrepreneurship per se and scholars whose work is in the field of family business, and who focus on the role of women in that context. As a starting point, we take the position that the term family can take different meanings depending on the angle of investigation. It could refer, for example, to the original "social bubble" which the woman comes from and in which she might feel secure. It can also refer to the "bubble" created by women getting married. Beyond this distinction, family structure changes across context and cultures; for instance, in North American and North European cultures the family is generally composed of parents and children, while elsewhere, for instance in South European, African, and Asiatic cultures, the frontiers of the family are much broader, including cousins and parents-in-law—often also labeled as extended family.

Therefore, in this introduction we revisit the two sets of literature, proposing a rapid overview of the state of the art provided on respective family impact on women entrepreneurship and women's place in family businesses, and also showing the research gaps they perceive. In that respect, we also seek to explain how the two sets of literature can nourish each other. We also introduce some selected chapters originally presented to the 2021 meeting of the Diana Project, as well as others that were collected to propose a fresh insight of current research debates on the topic. Most of the chapters suggest that women are still trapped in traditional roles within their own patriarchal families, with emancipation still to come. While working on business ventures, women still note children and education duties as their top priority, far higher up the list than meetings with financers and clients. In addition, there is evidence that women still find it difficult to establish a place in male-dominated family businesses. Women do succeed in pursuing their entrepreneurial goals, but only in some specific contexts. For instance, in contexts where social welfare differs across countries, women have to strategize with their spouses to pursue their entrepreneurial objectives. Further, in other less developed contexts, for example in Lebanon and Syria, women refugees who become entrepreneurs may have to "strategize" against their spouses to pursue their entrepreneurial objectives.

We conclude that further research is needed to better understand many of the challenges and opportunities emerging from these chapters. In particular, we are calling for a better study of what emancipation means for women from different contexts. Second, we are calling for more studies on the impact of the "meso" level (Brush et al., 2009) and on the context (Baker & Welter, 2020) of these results.

1.   RE-EXPLORING THE ACTUAL IMPACT OF THE FAMILY ON WOMEN'S ENTREPRENEURSHIP AND DEFINING WOMEN'S PLACE IN FAMILY BUSINESSES

1.1   Re-exploring the Actual Impact of the Family on Women's Entrepreneurship

Since the presentation of the first paper on women's entrepreneurship, in 1977, research has considered women entrepreneurship as a set of practices (Bruni et al., 2004) that are conducted by women, as individuals, who are leading companies, alone or with partners. In that attempt, and because they are women, they face constraints. Primary among the 5Ms identified as characterizing women's entrepreneurship is the mother role (Brush et al., 2009), which inhibits both optimal levels of involvement in networks that are helpful to ensure the growth of their venture, and investment of the necessary time into their business. Thus, research tends to consider that the family is a burden that prohibits women from pursuing their own careers and expressing their leadership in established organizations (Benschop & Doorewaard, 1998; Merluzzi & Phillips, 2022). In that respect, entrepreneurship tends to be presented as key for combining self-professional achievement and family, especially motherhood (Goss et al., 2011). On the other side, and once the venture has been created, research also shows that family, especially when women are also mothers, reduces women's ability to network properly and to invest the requested amount of time in achieving the ideal level of performance of the new venture (Shelton, 2006).

In such circumstances, spousal support plays a great role (Nikina et al., 2013). However, perceived support differs across women themselves, depending on the role they want to have in society: either being equal to their spouse in role-sharing or choosing to embrace a more traditional role (*mumpreneurship*) and therefore developing their activity as they please, with their own rhythm (Nikina et al., 2013).

The greatest concern and limitation of this research lies in the fact most studies have been conducted in western societies, specifically in rich clusters of innovation. However, following the call in the second special issue of *Entrepreneurship Theory and Practice* (Hughes et al., 2012), which was devoted to women entrepreneurship, there is a need to better explore women entrepreneurship across cultures and contexts. This seems relevant if we want to generalize any result that refers to the family's role in women entrepreneurship, since family structure differs across cultures (d'Iribarne, 2009;

Sharma & Manikutty, 2005). Moreover, taking into consideration the five components of the construct of "context" (Welter et al., 2016), there is also a need to better consider different family contexts and their impact on women entrepreneurship within the same country, and how family operates on women entrepreneurship across contexts.

1.2 The Role of Women in Family Businesses: How Can the Literature on Women in Family Business Contribute to the Understanding of Women's Entrepreneurship?

The multiple roles that women play in the family and in the business environment have constantly evolved in the past decades. These roles are embedded in a complex network of family and social relationships and reflect individual expectations as well as social norms. Women who are part of a family business might face advantages and disadvantages in legitimizing their leadership role within the firm. Indeed, women who are part of the owning family generally have more advantages than men in family firms in relation to flexibility in work schedules and job security for maternity leave (Salganicoff, 1990). Some studies also show that being part of a family business provides women with better access to managerial positions in relation to their non-family counterparts (Ramadami et al., 2017). Moreover, parental support and mentoring for leadership are key factors that facilitate daughter succession, as is sharing a vision for the future of the business (Overbeke et al., 2015). Nevertheless, disadvantages arise too, especially when it comes to being promoted in top managerial roles within the family firm. The competition with male siblings often puts them in a subordinate role where mother, sisters, and daughters are supposed to contribute to the family firm by taking care of and nurturing the next generation of family successors. Moreover, they often face barriers in accessing top managerial roles in family firms that are in traditional masculine industries (such as construction and transportation), where male family members are preferred for the leadership post. They are also preferred over male family members in cultures where inherited social norms and overall cultural and historical norms, such as primogeniture, are followed in selecting the firstborn son as the next CEO of the family firm, even if this will be detrimental for post-succession firm performance (Calabrò et al., 2018). It is especially when they experience this glass ceiling effect and systematic exclusion from top leadership roles within the family firm that female family members may give up, in order to avoid escalation of possible conflicts with male family members that could undermine overall family harmony and balance. This is also seen among women belonging to family firms who seek to take over the family firm. Recent research indeed shows that children's early exposure to a family firm increases intention to take over the family firm, by increasing the level of their affective commitment. However, this mechanism is valid for sons and not for daughters, suggesting that there is a gendered perspective in the investigation of succession intentions when it comes to family firms (Gimenez-Jimenez et al., 2021).

In sum, while women in family firms might have a privileged position in accessing managerial positions, they still face several challenges in finding a balance between what is best for the family and what is best for their own career plans. They are often seen as being "chief emotional officers" and playing a shadow and/or supporting role for the other family members within the family and the firm. Furthermore, even when they reach top managerial roles, they might be exposed to judgment and stereotyping—both within and outside the organization, they might be seen as "privileged" and as being in such positions only because they are "daughters of," "sisters of," "mothers of." More research and practice-oriented studies are surely needed to overcome these barriers that women in family firms still face.

2.　PURPOSE OF THIS BOOK: PROVIDING AN OVERVIEW ON THE IMPACT OF FAMILY ON WOMEN WHILE ENTREPRENEURING

In seeking to start a dialogue between the literature on women entrepreneurship and the literature on family business, we selected 11 chapters that reflect complementary approaches to a common phenomenon: the ways in which women, while entrepreneuring (Rindova et al., 2009), win their emancipation as individuals and, in such an attempt, manage with or without their family. Therefore, the book falls into four different parts, described as follows.

Part I, "Women and Family Business in a Paternalist Context," is the starting point of the journey. Whatever the country, and even beyond capitalistic contexts, family business remains the dominant entrepreneurial practice. However, the literature states that, whatever the nature of the family business—whether the business is driven by a couple or an extended family—women have long remained in the shadows, with these ventures largely dominated by males. But what does "in the shadows" mean? And how might women take the lead of a family-owned company?

The first two chapters focus on a particular context, which reflects on women's place in family businesses in a time of succession. The first chapter, by Soumara El Hayek Sfeir, is located within the subject matter of established family businesses but describes how women attending boards of a company held by a family are not necessarily members of that family. In that respect, the author thus first confirms that women who are present in these boards impact strategic decisions of the company, but also reveals that impactful women in these boards do not often come from within the family per se. Women who come from the family tend to have been overprotected, and therefore lack experience. Other women are taking the lead, especially during succession phases. Chapter 2, co-written by Hedy Yezza and Didier Chabaud, notes that what is happening inside a venture during the succession process is strongly influenced by some aspects of the context, especially the macro-level, and, moreover, the religion of family members. Focusing on a longitudinal analysis on a very long succession process in a Tunisian company that operates in a "female" industry—the nailcare industry—the authors show how the brother uses religious beliefs to justify his legitimacy to take the lead in the venture and how the sisters, who are also seeking to take the lead in the venture, face difficulty in asserting a legitimacy that does not come from "God" and have to refer to different interpretations of the Qu'ran to keep their place.

Part II is titled "Women's Autonomy and Distance from the Family." Addressing the difficulty of being better considered among the leaders of a family business, the second part of the book seeks to enter a dialogue. It reveals that women deciding to develop their own venture, not involving their spouse or family, still have to cope with the family, whose members can become a real burden. In that respect, Jasmine Jaim, focusing on the context of Bangladesh, reveals the strong role of the spouse, whose support and adhesion to the project is almost compulsory for a woman to access loan finance for her business. In that respect, the results are consistent with those presented in Part I, revealing the strong role of the patriarchs who often refuse to give a lead role to women either in family business or in stand-alone businesses developed by women. In another context, in Lebanon, Rola El Ali sheds light on the situation of women refugee entrepreneurs. In terms of the support received from NGOs, which claim to support their efforts at emancipation, women are officially the head and the leader of their small venture. However, this hides the fact that such women are often enslaved by their family. In the best case, they carry the entire responsibility for the survival of the family. In the worst case, their entrepreneurial activity is controlled by the spouse or by the spouse's family.

Looking beyond spousal control, then, Luz Marina Ferro-Cortes, Nancy Matos, and Florence Pinot de Villechenon, considering the case of women entrepreneurs in Latin America, confirm that family environment conditions the innovation capacity of women entrepreneurs: beyond moral support, the extended family environment (spouses, siblings, children) regulates decision making (W/F balance, push/pull) and leverages tangible and intangible resources (knowledge, networking) as the entrepreneurial process progresses.

While the authors have revealed a common pattern among conditions for women in family businesses and for those developing their own ventures, Part III is titled "Leading a Business Within a Family or Making Up with the Family while Leading a Business: Same Fight?" and investigates these similarities more deeply. Do they definitely exist? The previous cases refer to situations in developing countries, but do we note similar results in other contexts? Considering different contexts and countries, Mona Haug and Gry Osnes sketch a comparison between women leaders in family businesses and women in top positions in big organizations that evolve through male-dominated activity. They reveal that, beyond contexts, these women are trapped in a similar fight: in all these cases, embedded gender images (acting as a proxy for stereotypes and bias) have a significant impact and are partly detrimental. Catalysts built on a sense of autonomy enable a solid experience of authority in challenging obstacles. This experience is facilitated and supported through formal or informal coaching or mentoring.

Focusing on one extreme context of women entrepreneurs evolving in the male-dominated wine industry in Italy, Cinzia Colapinto, Vladi Finotto and Christine Mauracher partly confirm these results. Thus, the boundaries between the post of leadership within an established company and entrepreneurship are thin. These women—who do not have familial connections with the industry—successfully entered the male, family-dominated field by following one of three following strategic paths, namely: geographical displacement as a trigger of the entrepreneurial idea; generational change leading to the use of technology; or generational change leading to a focus on local wines.

Part IV considers "Women's Practices to Realize Themselves while Entrepreneuring." Setting aside the two extreme contexts discussed in Part III, in Chapter 8 Kim Poldner, Mónica Grau-Sarabia and William B. Gartner explore the three types of practices which women entrepreneurs develop across contexts, especially in Southern Europe: reconnecting the entrepreneur's own aspirations with the needs of others; resourcing their human, social, and financial capital by staying close to their origins; and recharging themselves, personally, through reflection and ownership of their situations.

The book concludes our journey by considering how women entrepreneurs manage their entrepreneurial emancipation with their family by reconsidering and reopening the debate on the work–life balance of women entrepreneurs. In that respect, Stacy Brecht investigates entrepreneurs who were working remotely before Covid-19 and, focusing on home-based entrepreneurs in California, highlights that home-based entrepreneurship has different meanings depending on the identity of the entrepreneur: for some males, working from home refers to a temporary situation in place until the venture has sufficient funding to have its own business location. For some males and females, working from home can reflect a lifestyle and willingness to live in a place that offers "fun" and "liberty." Last, for many women, working from home still refers to the possibility to have both time for children's education and time for the business, while reducing the costs of the small venture. Among these three categories of entrepreneur, the "life-stylers" are the single category that manage their time in a different manner; the two other categories adopt the same method of time management as if they were working from a "place of business."

3.   PERSPECTIVES

Each of the contributions in this volume call for further research. First, each chapter sheds light on specific insights that emerge from particular contexts; there is thus a need to better investigate other contexts, not only to generalize identified results but also to gain a better understanding of differences across contexts. For instance, there is a need for better understanding of the signs of spousal control identified in the extreme case of Syrian women refugee entrepreneurs in Lebanon. So far, the real reasons behind such control are underexplored, but there is also a need to better question the extent to which women can really become emancipated through entrepreneurship.

Second, some chapters contain innovative research designs, such as the study of calendars and diaries. The robustness of such research designs should be better grounded and applied to other entrepreneurial contexts.

Third, and last, this book mostly reflects on the traditional family; it would be interesting to consider less standardized cases, focusing on how women who educate their children alone combine it with entrepreneurship in practice. Studying the dynamic of women entrepreneurship within polygamist families, which represent the great majority in some Muslim countries, could also complete existing results and provide a better understanding on the dynamic of women's self-emancipation. In such an attempt, other less common cases, such as looking at tribal families or considering how women lesbian entrepreneurs develop their family while doing entrepreneurship, could also revel interesting insights to better understand the dynamic that exists between women entrepreneurship and the family.

REFERENCES

Ahrens, J.P., Landmann, A., & Woywode, M. (2015). Gender preferences in the CEO successions of family firms: family characteristics and human capital of the successor. *Journal of Family Business Strategy*, *6*(2), 86–103.

Akhmedova, A., Cavallotti, R., Marimon, F., & Campopiano, G. (2020). Daughters' careers in family business: motivation types and family-specific barriers. *Journal of Family Business Strategy*, *11*(3), 100307.

Baker, T., & Welter, F. (2020). *Contextualizing Entrepreneurship Theory*. Routledge.

Benschop, Y., & Doorewaard, H. (1998). Covered by equality: the gender subtext of organizations. *Organization Studies*, *19*(5), 787–805.

Bruni, A., Gherardi, S., & Poggio, B. (2004). Doing gender, doing entrepreneurship: an ethnographic account of intertwined practices. *Gender, Work & Organization*, *11*(4), 406–29.

Brush, C.G., De Bruin, A., & Welter, F. (2009). A gender-aware framework for women's entrepreneurship. *International Journal of Gender and Entrepreneurship, 1*(1), 8–24.

Calabrò, A., Minichilli, A., Amore, M.D., & Brogi, M. (2018). The courage to choose! Primogeniture and leadership succession in family firms. *Strategic Management Journal, 39*(7), 2014–35.

Calabrò, A., Conti, E., & Masè, S. (2022). Trapped in a "golden cage"! The legitimation of women leadership in family business. *Journal of Family Business Strategy*, forthcoming.

Campopiano, G., De Massis, A., Rinaldi, F.R., & Sciascia, S. (2017). Women's involvement in family firms: progress and challenges for future research. *Journal of Family Business Strategy, 8*(4), 200–212.

Chadwick, I.C., & Dawson, A. (2018). Women leaders and firm performance in family businesses: an examination of financial and nonfinancial outcomes. *Journal of Family Business Strategy, 9*(4), 238–49.

D'Iribarne, P. (2009). National cultures and organisations in search of a theory: an interpretative approach. *International Journal of Cross Cultural Management, 9*(3), 309–21.

Elam, A.B., Brush, C.G., Greene, P.G., Baumer, B., Dean, M., Heavlow, R., & Global Entrepreneurship Research Association. (2019). *Women's Entrepreneurship Report 2018/2019*.

Gimenez-Jimenez, D., Edelman, L.F., Minola, T., Calabrò, A., & Cassia, L. (2021). An intergeneration solidarity perspective on succession intentions in family firms. *Entrepreneurship Theory and Practice, 45*(4), 740–66.

Gómez-Mejía, L.R., Haynes, K.T., Núñez-Nickel, M., Jacobson, K.J., & Moyano-Fuentes, J. (2007). Socioemotional wealth and business risks in family-controlled firms: evidence from Spanish olive oil mills. *Administrative Science Quarterly, 52*(1), 106–37.

Goss, D., Jones, R., Betta, M., & Latham, J. (2011). Power as practice: a micro-sociological analysis of the dynamics of emancipatory entrepreneurship. *Organization Studies, 32*(2), 211–29.

Haberman, H., & Danes, S.M. (2007). Father–daughter and father–son family business management transfer comparison: family FIRO model application. *Family Business Review, 20*(2), 163–84.

Hamilton, E. (2006). Whose story is it anyway? Narrative accounts of the role of women in founding and establishing family businesses. *International Small Business Journal, 24*(3), 253–71.

Hofstede, G., Nijnatten, C.V., & Suurmond, J. (2001). Communication strategies of family supervisors and clients in organizing participation. *European Journal of Social Work, 4*(2), 131–42.

Hughes, K.D., Jennings, J.E., Brush, C., Carter, S., & Welter, F. (2012). Extending women's entrepreneurship research in new directions. *Entrepreneurship Theory and Practice, 36*(3), 429–42.

Kim, J.L.S., & Ling, C.S. (2001). Work–family conflict of women entrepreneurs in Singapore. *Women in Management Review, 16*(5), 77–88.

Marshack, K.J. (1994). Copreneurs and dual-career couples: are they different? *Entrepreneurship Theory and Practice, 19*(1), 49–69.

Martinez Jimenez, R. (2009). Research on women in family firms: current status and future directions. *Family Business Review, 22*(1), 53–64.

Merluzzi, J., & Phillips, D.J. (2022). Early career leadership advancement: evidence of incongruity penalties toward young, single women professionals. *Organization Studies*, 01708406221081619.

Nikina, A., Shelton, L.M., & Le Loarne, S. (2013). Does he have her back? A look at how husbands support women entrepreneurs. *Entrepreneurial Practice Review*, *2*(4), 17–35.

Overbeke, K.K., Bilimoria, D., & Somers, T. (2015). Shared vision between fathers and daughters in family businesses: the determining factor that transforms daughters into successors. *Frontiers in Psychology*, *6*, 625.

Ramadani, V., Memili, E., Palalić, R., & Chang, E.P. (2020). *Entrepreneurial Family Businesses*. Springer International Publishing.

Rindova, V., Barry, D., & Ketchen Jr, D.J. (2009). Entrepreneuring as emancipation. *Academy of Management Review*, *34*(3), 477–91.

Salganicoff, M. (1990). Women in family businesses: challenges and opportunities. *Family Business Review*, *3*(2), 125–37.

Sharma, P., & Manikutty, S. (2005). Strategic divestments in family firms: role of family structure and community culture. *Entrepreneurship Theory and Practice*, *29*(3), 293–311.

Shelton, L.M. (2006). Female entrepreneurs, work–family conflict, and venture performance: new insights into the work–family interface. *Journal of Small Business Management*, *44*(2), 285–97.

Sonfield, M.C., & Lussier, R.N. (2004). First-, second-, and third-generation family firms: a comparison. *Family Business Review*, *17*(3), 189–201.

Welter, F. (2011). Contextualizing entrepreneurship—conceptual challenges and ways forward. *Entrepreneurship Theory and Practice*, *35*(1), 165–84.

Welter, F., Gartner, W.B., & Wright, M. (2016). The context of contextualizing contexts. In F. Welter and W.B. Gartner (eds), *A Research Agenda for Entrepreneurship and Context*. Edward Elgar Publishing.

PART I

Women and family business in a paternalist
context

1. The influence on succession of women's involvement in the boards of directors of family firms, through the lens of neuroscience

Soumaya El Hayek Sfeir

1.   INTRODUCTION

Emile Zola wrote: "We are like books. Most people only see our cover, the minority read only the introduction, many people believe the critics. Few know our content." This quote invites us to discover what a superficial reading cannot reveal. It calls us to go beyond what we see and to go deeper to discover the richness of the content of human beings.

Thus, the purpose of this chapter is to delve into the secrets of the women who are part of the governance bodies of family firms (FF). These persons make choices and interact within the governance body of the FF. We aim to discover what they have experienced and how their personal identity and their actions are inspired by such experiences. We consider it essential to gain a better and more complex understanding of gender diversity due to the insights into behavior, motivations, and actions that it can offer (Maseda et al., 2021). These persons contribute to the sustainability of an FF.

Therefore, the involvement of women in FF boards is an important theme to explore (Bettinelli et al., 2019). This chapter aims to contribute to this debate by investigating the experiences of women directors on FFs' boards. We explore the past experiences of these women, whether members of the owner-family or not, and examine if they influence the way the women accompany and guide successors in the FF, given that women directors' experiences shape their behavior (Hambrick, 2007). This will allow us to understand "how individual-level factors impact organizations; and to understand the processes that aggregate individual actions into resultant firm behavior outcomes" (De Massis and Foss, 2018, p.387).

We propose to ground our study on neuroscience, and particularly on mental time travel. The latter refers to "the faculty that allows humans to mentally project themselves backwards in time to re-live, or forwards to pre-live, events" (Suddendorf and Corballis, 2007, p.299). This theory is relevant in explaining women directors' behavior because they "can draw on their wealth of lived experiences to aid them in making decisions" (Picone et al., 2021, p.125), particularly in supporting a successor. Therefore, the cornerstone of our research is a focus on women directors' experiences. We highlight the importance of women directors' past experiences and argue that they allow them to prepare the future of the FF by guiding a successor. This leads us to answer in this chapter the following research question: How can women directors' past experiences contribute to support for a successor in FFs?

There have been several recent calls for FF scholars to provide new empirical evidence on interdisciplinary approaches in the FF field (Nelson and Constantinidis, 2017; Nordqvist and Gartner, 2020; Maseda et al., 2021). Our aim here is to contribute to the discussion about the suitability of interdisciplinary approaches, using the field of neuroscience and, in particular, mental time travel to understand the outcomes of women directors' past experiences.

This chapter is organized as follows. We begin by providing a literature review. We then set out the theoretical framework. After this, we present our cases and our methodology in relation to case studies, before discussing and theorizing our results and their implications. We conclude by mentioning limitations and outlining possibilities for future research.

2.   LITERATURE REVIEW

The key topic related to our research question is the contributions of board gender diversity in FFs.

2.1   Board Gender Diversity in Family Firms

The literature on women's involvement on FF boards offers various outcomes. Many articles have focused on women economic contributions in FF boards (Amore et al., 2014; Cruz et al., 2012). However, the findings do not show clear outcomes regarding the impact of women's presence on FF boards. While some studies identify a positive relationship between gender and financial outcomes, others find no significant relationship, or even a negative one (Maseda et al., 2021).

Still, many studies highlight the effects of board gender diversity on non-economic outcomes. Hence, women have a key role in reducing conflict and increasing shared meaning, collaboration and integration among family members involved in the FF (Haberman and Danes, 2007). Women directors also contribute female leadership qualities (Post and Byron, 2015). Thus, they are considered more supportive than their male counterparts (Ali et al., 2014).

In addition, women directors are usually considered less risk-averse and make less radical decisions (Croson and Gneezy, 2009); this tends to support sustainable investments (Charness and Gneezy, 2012). Women directors' inputs focus on their unique knowledge capabilities (Adams and Ferreira, 2009), marketing abilities and networks (Ali et al., 2014), and support of entrepreneurial initiatives (Post and Byron, 2015).

Some studies suggest that having women on boards exerts a greater influence on corporate social responsibility (CSR) and philanthropic engagement (Angelidis and Ibrahim, 2011; Galbreath, 2011; Zhang et al., 2013; Campopiano et al., 2017, Maseda et al., 2021). Women's participative and communicative style within the board improves sensitivity toward socially responsible activities, supporting a broader perspective on stakeholder needs (Bear et al., 2010; Rodríguez-Ariza et al., 2017). Indeed, women are often appointed as directors due to their sensitivity. As to philanthropy, FFs with women involved on the board are more philanthropic (Burgess and Tharenou, 2002) and particularly committed in the areas of community services and the arts (Williams, 2003). Women directors bring different perspectives into board discussions, which encourages open conversations (Campopiano et al., 2017). Furthermore, empirical findings outline a positive relationship between women on boards and firms' charitable donations, corporate social responsibility initiatives (Bear et al., 2010), and environmental performance (Elmagrhi et al., 2019). These contributions are dependent on their knowledge, experience, and values, which are different from those of their male counterparts (Post and Byron, 2015; Kanadlı et al., 2018).

Finally, Faraudello et al. (2017) paid particular attention to women's representation in ownership and governance bodies and their key role in the succession process. We therefore see that a number of studies suggest that women often play a crucial role in FFs, especially in succession processes (Barrett and Moores, 2009; Kubíček and Machek, 2019).

However, we still ignore the uniqueness of women members of FF boards, as well as a number of other contributions they make (Al-Dajani et al., 2014). It should be kept in mind that the literature highlights that "the survivability of many family businesses in the future will depend on more awareness of, and more options for, women" (Gersick, 1990, p.119).

Analysis of the literature on board gender diversity in FFs allowed us to identify the gap we aim to fill in this chapter. Indeed, we answer this need by going beyond women's resumes and deepening our knowledge by exploring if women directors' past experiences matter for succession. We use the mental travel theory to analyze the impact of women directors' previous experiences. The core of the mental travel approach is that decision-making in FFs is driven by past experiences of the women directors (Ernst, 2019). In this regard, we suggest that their past experiences will influence preparation for the future of the FF by ensuring support and assistance is provided to the successor.

2.2   The Theoretical Framework of Mental Time Travel

Mental time travel is a form of memory which allows us to mentally relive events in our past and imagine those in our future. It is indispensable in planning future actions and longer-term life projects (Berthoz, 2012). A fundamental component is the fact that past events, or judgments, must be taken from memory, selecting those that are relevant to the present (Berthoz, 2012). The human mind has the remarkable ability to detach itself temporarily from the immediate present to mentally travel into the past or future (Ernst, 2019). This ability, known as mental time travel, combines the concepts of autobiographical memory and future thought, which allow us to mentally re-experience or pre-experience past or future personal events when they are evoked (Ernst, 2019).

Hence, a previous experience is a memory. The ability to recall past events or to project oneself into the future is based on information stored in memory (Tulving, 1985, 2001). This is why we mobilize autobiographical memory in order to study the impact of past experiences. It preserves the memory traces of each individual's past (Tulving, 1985; Conway and Pleydell-Pearce, 2000). Tulving (1985) distinguishes, within autobiographical memory, episodic memory, which contains memories of personally experienced events situated in a precise spatiotemporal context. It allows the individual to travel mentally in time by becoming aware of himself in the present as a continuity of what they were in the past and a prelude to what they will be in the future (Tulving, 2001). Semantic memory works with episodic memory to compose the autobiographical register. It brings together the general knowledge that an individual has about himself and the world (Tulving, 1985). Conway and Pleydell-Pearce (2000) take up Tulving's work (1985) and consider that memories are not exact copies of events experienced. On the contrary, they evoke—by modifying them—past experiences. When a memory is reconstructed, it corresponds as well as possible to the lived experience (principle of correspondence) while being coherent (principle of coherence) with the individual, his aspirations, his current beliefs, and the image he has of himself.

From a cognitive science perspective, autobiographical memory has three functions (Cohen and Conway, 2007). The first, or identity, function informs an individual about him or herself through past experiences. The second, known as the social function, allows us to communicate and create or maintain social relationships. The third, orientation or adaptation, function helps the individual to use his past experiences to make decisions or anticipate future scenarios. Pillemer (2001) observes that a specific event can redirect a life course. The important thing is not the episode experienced as such but its reconstruction in the form of a memory and the interpretation that the individual makes of it in order to achieve the act (Pillemer, 2001).

Addis et al. (2007) suggest a constructive episodic simulation hypothesis which offers a theoretical framework to explain the links between autobiographical memory and future thought on a cognitive and brain level. This hypothesis proposes that both past and future mental representations are based on information stored in the memory that is flexibly retrieved and recombined into a new coherent event.

Pursuant to studies by several authors (Suddendorf et al., 2009; Schacter et al., 2012; Addis, 2018), the constructive nature of the autobiographical memory results from the fact that its primary function is not so much to preserve exact copies of past events, but rather to provide the basic "ingredients" necessary for anticipation, reflection, and imagination of future events. The memory would therefore be a kind of reservoir where information is stored and can be reused to form new future representations (Suddendorf et al., 2009; Schacter et al., 2012; Addis, 2018).

These thoughts about the past usually come in the form of remembering events that women directors have experienced and that they apply to the choices they want to make in the present in order to prepare the future. For women, the memories associated with life transitions are, according to Pillemer (2001), particularly vivid and lasting. Since a memory can shape a career, it is quite possible that it can contribute to the guidance of a successor.

3. METHOD

We have followed an interpretive approach under the broader umbrella of qualitative methods. The interpretive paradigm aims to understand how the researcher constructs the meaning he or she gives to reality. The position of the interpretive approach in relation to epistemology is that interpretive researchers believe that reality is multiple and relative (Cherkaoui and Haouata, 2017). Therefore, the goal of interpretive research is to understand and interpret the meanings of human behavior rather than to generalize and predict cause and effect (Cherkaoui and Haouata, 2017). For an interpretive researcher, it is important to understand motives, meanings, reasons, and other subjective experiences related to time and context (Neuman, 2007). Interpretive approaches give research the opportunity and freedom to address issues of influence and impact and to ask questions such as why and how particular technological trajectories are created (Avenier, 2011).

Our qualitative approach is based on abductive reasoning—reaching a probable conclusion based on what we know. Abduction is defined as "any proposition added to observed facts, tending to make them applicable in any way to other circumstances than those under which they are observed" (Aguinis et al., 2011, p.150). This approach was chosen for two main reasons. First, this research is part of an exploratory process aimed at improving the understanding of complex phenomena and the specificity of their contents (Huberman and Miles, 1991). Second, we are not situated in a knowledge-free context, since we already have a theoretical basis to assist us. We approach the gender diversity phenomenon in family business boards via abductive reasoning so that we may carry out the study with few preconceived ideas and "let the field speak"; that is to say, we try to be as receptive as possible to the reality that emerges from our observations.

The case study research method has been defined by Flyvbjerg (2011) as "an intensive analysis of an individual unit (as a person or community) stressing developmental factors in relation to environment" (p.103). This research method provides an in-depth analysis of the phenomenon in context, and our observations are authentic representations of the studied reality. In short, it is a method that is appropriate for capturing the specific complexity and dynamics unique to family businesses. Thus, case-based exploratory methods are suitable for our study (Eisenhardt, 1989; De Massis and Kammerlander, 2020).

In seeking potential cases, the first condition to be met was the size of the FF. We chose medium-sized FFs because of the gap in the literature related to this category of FFs (Gabrielsson and Huse, 2005). In the European Union, medium-sized companies are those with 50 to 250 workers and annual revenues of less than €50 million (about $56 million as of mid-2019).

The context of private medium-sized FFs is particularly suitable for studying and observing the impact of gender diversity in boards. Private medium-sized FFs correspond to the definition adopted by the literature. They are typical FFs with a concentrated shareholder base and family member insiders who are active in management and on the board (Lane et al., 2006). We focused on boards with a gender-diverse composition and including mainly family members. An additional criterion for case selection was that the FF was preparing for or thinking about the succession process and/or trying to choose a successor, or had designated a successor to be in place within two years. The final sample consists of four medium-sized cases with family and/or non-family women on their boards and is consistent with the four-to-ten case scale proposed by case study methodology (Eisenhardt, 1989), considered appropriate to reach theoretical saturation (Eisenhardt, 1989). These four medium-sized family businesses operate in different economic sectors.

3.1   Description of the Cases

Case 1 is a third-generation French FF, founded in 1946 by the grandfather of the current chair. The company operates in the distribution sector, and is a national leader in the rental and leasing of industrial vehicles and trucks with drivers. The family holds approximately 92 percent of the capital. In October 2019 the current chair of the board of directors stepped down as CEO, and his son succeeded him in this position. The board comprises three independent members (unrelated to the family or the company), two family members working in the company (the chair and the CEO/son), and two family members not working in the company (two daughters). The board meets four to five times per year.

Case 2 is a fourth-generation French FF founded in 1884. Its database helps customers to navigate the complex world of transport prices and regulations. It specializes in the business of debt collection agencies and customer financial information companies. It has experience in business information, finance, and risk management. The family owns 100 percent of the company. The board is composed of three family members who work in the company and two family members who retired after working in the company for several years. It meets formally four times per year and is preparing for the succession process.

Case 3 was born in 1985 with a leveraged management buyout by the CEO, the main managers of the company, and some financial organizations. It is a French FF operating in the design and manufacture of custom design interconnect. The firm interconnects electronic devices provided by different suppliers into one system. As an expert in cabling engineering, Case 3 is able to design the whole cabling network. Its engineers assist customers with the most appropriate tools, including simulation software and co-design in all the development stages: idea, concept, prototypes, industrialization, volume ramp-up, and mass production. It is a family business with a diverse management team of two family members. In 1998, the current chairman of the board of directors stepped down as CEO. His daughter succeeded him in this position. She has been designated as the successor to her father.

Case 4 is a French food company. It was founded in 1905. In France, this FF mainly markets ham, cured ham and other cured meats, poultry products, various meat products (pâtés and so on), surimi, and ready-made meals. The service business consists of three strands: the delivery of boxes and meal trays to companies; airline catering; and hospital catering. The company remains independent and family owned. The chairman belongs to the fifth generation. He joined the family business in 2001 and was Vice President in charge of strategy and investments. He has been chairman of the board of directors since the beginning of 2009. The board of directors is responsible for reviewing and approving the direction of the business. It is made up of five independent directors, five directors representing the founding families, and two directors representing employees. The presence of independent directors is due to the FF's desire to reconcile good management, security, and sustainability. The board of directors meets five times per year. Within the board, specialized committees are responsible for improving operations and helping to make decisions.

Table 1.1 summarizes the characteristics of the four firms and the gender diversity in their boards of directors. It also shows the number of interviews completed in each case.

3.2   Data Collection

We collected data via interviews. According to Picken (2017), the interview is a common data collection method that can obtain a high standard of qualitative data. Our interviews, which were recorded and transcribed, enabled us to support our argument and recommendations.

We used an interview guide to ensure that all elements of the conceptual framework were covered. The guide was inspired by our literature review on the composition of boards of directors in FFs, particularly on gender diversity within the board; it was also used in a larger research project. The interview guide is composed of five parts: (1) general questions about the firm, history, number of generations, shareholders, governance, and composition of the board of directors; (2) specific questions about the board of directors' role and their discussions and decisions; (3) specific questions about the personality and the behavior of each director, as viewed by the other directors; (4) questions to enable directors to introduce themselves, which cover age, professional and personal experiences, motivations, decisions, choices, interests, and behavior; and (5) questions covering emotions experienced by directors during board meetings, including how these were managed and what influence they had.

The first part highlights the history of the FF, its evolution with time, its governance, and so on. Through the stories told by the interviewees, we aimed to establish their perception of the events. They remembered past events in detail and tried to describe the path taken to reach their present situation. They were coherent and authentic in their discourses, and no variance in the content of stories was noted (Kammerlander et al., 2015).

The second part focuses on the board of directors. We aim to know the real functions of the board, if there is any real discussion or debate, and how decisions are taken. The relationships among directors and between the board and the chief executive were relevant to permit full and frank discussions of the crucial issues facing the firm (Astrachan et al., 2020).

The third part contains questions about the directors in the boardroom, their behavior, and their personality as perceived by the other members. Our objective was to underline the importance of the directors of the board for an FF's strategic behavior and choices (Hambrick, 2007), and particularly when choosing a successor.

Table 1.1   *Characteristics of the four firms and their boards*

Case	Nationality	Activity	President	Board members	Male interviewees	Women on the board	Female interviewees
1	French	Transportation	Family president	Four family members Three non-family members	Two family members: **Steven** **Anthony** One non-family member: **Marc**	Three women: two family member (one interviewed) One non-family member	**Helen:** family member **Victoria:** non-family member
2	French	Business information	Family president	Five family members	Two family members: **John** **Mike**	Two women: two family members (one interviewed)	**Mary:** family member
3.	French	Cabling; Engineering	Family president	Two family members	One family member: **Charles**	One woman: family member	**Vicky:** family member
4.	French	Food company	Family president	Five family member; seven non-family members	One family member: **Richard**	Three women: one family member (one interviewed; two non-family members (one interviewed)	**Ana:** family member **Lena:** non-family member

The fourth part aims to gain a deeper knowledge of each interviewed director. We sought to encompass information such as demographic and cognitive diversity. These diversities have the potential to provide the directors with different types of knowledge and decision-making styles and a greater variety of professional perspectives (Koryak et al., 2018). Each director was invited to talk about herself, her identity, and how that identity is linked to her perception of the succession process.

The last part is devoted to emotions. FFs are concerned with emotions (Cohen and Sharma, 2016). We aimed to enhance our understanding of emotions and their influence among directors, between the board and the chief executive, and on the succession planning process (Randerson and Radu-Lefebvre, 2021).

We conducted 13 semi-structured interviews by phone or Skype with the CEO and some members of the board. Each respondent was interviewed once, and the interviews lasted between 40 minutes and 2 hours. These interviews allowed us to benefit from the interviewees' knowledge of the organization, their attitudes toward governance diversity in the company, and the contributions of each board member, especially women board members. These interviews provided subjective perceptions, which is consistent with other qualitative research in family businesses (Nordqvist et al., 2009), delivering points of view that offer explanatory potential regarding women's experiences. Interviews were transcribed and the data was coded according to categories. We compiled these categories according to key variables to facilitate interpretation of results. In total, 13 semi-structured interviews were completed. For confidentiality, names have been modified.

3.3   Data Analysis

All interviews were conducted by us, were registered, and delivered points of view that allowed us to highlight some elements of the research question. As previously mentioned, our aim was to discover women directors' experiences and how they shape their behavior and actions. Some respondents limited themselves to answering the questions set out in the interview guide while others provided more details about themselves. In addition, we wanted to obtain a deeper knowledge about the contributions of each women director.

We transcribed the interviews in order to examine the information obtained and identify its relevance in the context of our research. We began by reading the transcripts. Then, in order to identify concepts that might explain the phenomena under observation, we coded the relevant items according to actions, activities, choices, experiences, personal backgrounds, and differences. We tried to counter any possible bias by not deviating from the transcript data. The next step was to create categories by amalgamating several codes. Manual codification of the mass of information collected allowed us to classify, compile, thoroughly analyze, and cross-check the data, thereby facilitating the interpretation of results. When we coded data on experiences, we identified several types of experiences: personal and professional. The structure of our data is shown in Figure 1.1. First-order concepts were drawn from the most representative quotes from our interviews to shed light on the personal and professional experience of women board members. Next, we organized the quotes into second-order themes. Finally, we developed aggregate dimensions. In "reaching closure," we went back and forth between our coded data and the literature on gender diversity on boards of directors in FFs (Gioia et al., 2013); in this way, our model builds on and extends the literature.

4.   FINDINGS

This section presents our findings regarding women's experiences in the FF boardroom. This research was carried out with multiple informants per firm (see Table 1.1). Thus, it is necessary to understand the vision, priorities, and values of women on the board and to see if their past experiences lead to the desired outcome, which is support of the successor. It is relevant to specify that we consider experiences at the individual level, not from the corporate perspective.

As our objective is to shed light on the previous experiences of women in the boards of directors of FFs, we focus on their personal and professional experiences, personality, values, behavior, and priorities as described by them and as seen by other members of the board. It is worth noting that we did not make any comparison between the female family business directors and the female non-family business directors because the latter acted as "pseudo-family" members.

Regarding the methodological approach used in our empirical study, the analysis of the four cases allows us to identify the diversity of experiences of women directors on the FF boards in our sample. In the following, we explain women directors' personal and professional experiences and present their outcomes related to the succession process and particularly to the way they support and guide the successor. We theorize the relation between women directors' experiences and support of the successor (see Figure 1.2). We identify that women directors' identities are past experience-dependent and that the way in which they support the successor is defined by past experiences, with a link between their personal identity and their guidance of the successor.

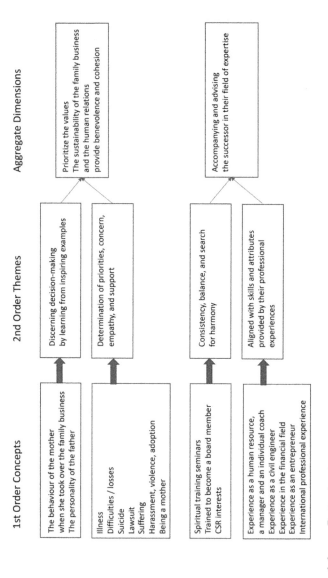

Figure 1.1   Data structure

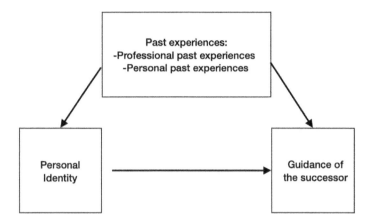

Figure 1.2   Relation between experiences and successor support

4.1   Women Directors' Identities are Past-Experience Dependent

The women's stories and experiences were safeguarded in their memories. When narrating them, they brought them to life and added information regarding how those experiences had influenced their present selves. Women, whether or not family members, describe actions aligned with their personal identity (who they are) and undertake actions consistent with their personal and professional experiences.

Further to our data, it is worth mentioning that women directors have been influenced by people around them. In Case 2, the mother took over the FF in the middle of a difficult period. She inspires the decision-making of her daughter, who is a board member in the FF. Mary stated: "It was my mother who took over the company. It was a difficult period for seven or eight years, let's say, the time it took to turn the company around, and I think that influenced my decisions' when I make decisions now I think of her very often." In Case 3, the father is viewed by the daughter as an inspiring example. Vicky says: "His personality is visionary, he sees very far, that's exceptional, he listens and decides quickly, he has charisma. He's very rigorous. He gets to the bottom of his files when he takes something in hand. When he sets himself a goal, nothing will stop him before he reaches the goal, no matter how difficult the path."

These inspiring persons shared their experiences and wisdom, providing other perspectives. Their long careers give them the advantage of having experienced several business cycles. They use their previous experiences to share points of view and provide expertise to help the FF address certain challenges more effectively and more wisely.

It should further be noted that women's past experiences have two dimensions: personal experience and professional experience.

4.1.1   Personal past experiences

There is a common thread between the women directors whom we interviewed: the six women directors in the four cases are mothers. Motherhood is a singular experience with a major impact on the personality and temperament. It can teach a person to be less self-centered, more giving, empathic, and attentive to the good of others.

In Case 2, Mary explained: "When we disagree, we say so. We engage with the others, we take a step back to find the right balance and the best solution. We listen to each other. No animosity." In Case 4, talking about empathy, Ana confirmed: "if I feel that someone isn't doing well in the company, that worries me. The wellbeing of everyone is important for me." These comments suggest that the behavior of these women directors was influenced by motherhood. They want to maintain peace and harmony in the family and in the firm by mediating, removing fear, and avoiding conflicts. They are concerned about the welfare of both the family and the firm.

Even if past personal experiences were sad or negative, they did not represent barriers for further personal development. Women directors benefit, grow, and even thrive when they have faced some form of shock, volatility, randomness, and disorder. These events allowed them to shift to a personal transformation approach. They realized that after these experiences, a shift was required in their attitude or behavior.

In Case 3, Vicky stated: "During the illness of my father, I became deputy director with delegated powers that allowed me to protect the company and that's when I started to involve the other shareholders, who are my sisters, in the decisions. His illness is an example of how to reorientate the meaning of the company's sustainability, and how we built it."

In Case 1, Steven stated: "Victoria has been a psychotherapist and she continues to accompany managers; she herself has had a life path where she has suffered a lot, so she is a very strong human and has psychological density." In Case 1, Victoria confirmed what she had experienced in her previous professional experience: "I experienced a suicide in a team, this is clearly something that I lived through with great difficulty in this case [...] it has nourished in me, in addition to what is part of my personal life, the idea that the workplace cannot be a place of suffering, it is not possible!"

These past experiences have guided the women directors, or motivate their attitudes or actions. They help them to determine their priorities. They provide the general guidelines for conduct. These past events influence their behavior through their decision-making.

4.1.2   Professional past experiences

Professional past experiences are also represented by women directors. These experiences have taught them several fundamental things in their daily lives, such as prudence and the need to repeat certain actions or methods that have proven to be effective over time. These contributions have influenced their behavior and supported alignment with their professional experiences. In Case 4, CSR specialist Lena stated: "in my CSR approach we work on the vision of the market, we work on what our business is, we're going to integrate the elements of societal trends, what our business is, how to make it evolve, what our culture is, what we want to keep, what we want to change, what our values are, what the rules of the game are to work better together, what our positioning is and then we do the work to make it." In Case 1, Victoria, who is a specialist in human resources, confirmed: "what is important is the human relationship, being able to relate to people, listening to them, working coherently, taking responsibility for one's words." In Case 4, Charles stated that Vicky worked as a civil engineer before joining the FF. He considers her to be a good listener: "she lets people talk before she starts talking" and "there are employees who would rather see my daughter than me."

In addition to the ability to take the FF out of its inner circle to adopt an outside view, the women directors are expected to have the power to calm down debates or to steer them in a direction that is favorable to decision-making. They provide a new dynamic based not only on their specific expertise and on their experiences (professional and personal) but also on a different and complementary personality.

Women directors' personal identity is a self-definition elaborated by them. It constitutes the formulation and the interpretation of their past experiences. It is also conceived in an active way according to projects and projections of oneself toward the future, which can be in continuity or in rupture with past constructions.

4.2   Women Directors' Support for the Successor is Defined by Past Experiences

Aligning the powers of their past experiences, women directors have produced clarity and talent with the potential to benefit in the guidance of the successor. Previous experiences are likely the incentive for the guidance they provide to the successor. They are linked in some way to the key factors driving the women directors, and are consistent with their priorities and their fields of expertise.

4.2.1   Priorities

Women directors' past experiences allowed us to shed light on their vision, priorities, and values. Thus, these previous events influence their behavior and actions, particularly when it comes to learning from previous experiences and determining priorities.

In Case 1, Steven stated: "Victoria is an important resource person for me". Victoria confirmed her priorities:

> It's true that my job is to question a lot and especially to question the blind spots. For me, it's very important to help Anthony today, to make sure that he has the widest angle of vision with regard to the choice he has to make. [...] It's really to make sure that, in relation to the meaning he wants to give to the decision he is about to make, [...] in a position to clearly discern the decision he is going to make. [...] For me, the question of professional discernment is the expression of our freedom, how for each decision I have to make, I act as a free human being.

In Case 4, Richard emphasized that "Ana, who is Richard's sister, was very concerned about his freedom to decide whether to stay or go. There was something about the fraternal bond that was like a fraternal protection, both to protect me, to allow me to hold this position comfortably, etc., in relation to the family, and also so that I wouldn't feel obliged to carry this responsibility if I no longer wanted to." In Case 3, Vicky wanted "to build something by saying it's for a very long time and to be part of the decision to integrate grandchildren into the family business." In Case 4, Lena confirmed: "The future successor must have experience outside. There is training. It's essential to work on your skills, your knowledge, your experiences before taking over. Otherwise it's too much like you took the job because you're the son of the chairman [...] which develops injustice."

Helen and Ana decided to undertake training before joining the board, in order to acquire the necessary skills. They wanted to play an effective role in the governance of the FF. They did not want merely to sit on the board. They saw the quality of governance as a primary condition for the firm's sustainability.

Ana stated:

> I did a training course for directors [...] to try to fulfil my mission as a family director as well as possible [...] and it's true that this enabled me to really understand what the expectations of directors in general and family directors in particular were. I did not feel ready to join and then [...] my brother told me that we need women and that we need an outside view [...] we need a fresh eye. [...] The training for administrators gave me a bit of confidence in myself and I learned a lot of things. [...] I learnt a lot in terms of how to behave in a board meeting, how to listen to the questions, [and that] no question is [...] useless, all questions are important in a council. Since I did the training, it has enabled me to integrate into the group and

to understand how it works and not to be afraid to ask questions and not to be afraid to challenge the management. [...] The fact that I had done this training made me feel more legitimate and seeing that I have affinities with the other administrators, there's a very good understanding. And I managed to make my place on this board, and I'm delighted to be part of it now.

4.2.2 Their field of expertise

The success of an FF depends on the quality and effectiveness of the dialogue between the successor and the board of directors. This link is an essential lever for improving the FF's performance and ensuring its sustainability.

In Cases 1 and 4, women were not candidates because they were not interested; they had other projects. Still, they wanted to engage with the managerial transition and prepare for the arrival of the successor. They played a benevolent role toward the chosen successor. They participated in the definition of the role and responsibilities of the successor and wished to ensure the FF's long-term survival. In Case 3, the woman was the successor, and will lead the FF into the future. In Case 4, the women were important contributors to the succession planning process. They had the ability to influence the decision of the chairman (a family member).

When talking about Helen in Case 1, Marc explained: "She has a lot of corporate reflexes and is therefore able to question her father or her brother alone on several subjects and say to him, was it a good decision to do this? I think she has no fear and she knows that this family circle is a circle of trust." In Case 2, Mary stated: "It is necessary to appoint trustworthy and quality people. Family members working in the business must prove their qualities and qualifications. What is important is the sustainability of the company."

In Case 4, Lena remembered her professional experience in Asia, where people tended to be optimistic. However, she had seen suicides and bankruptcies. Therefore, she had explicitly asked Richard, the CEO, "to make crisis scenarios at minus 20, minus 30, minus 50% of turnover and they did it!" This enlightened the FF about their fixed expenses and allowed them to renegotiate contracts with their partners.

We identified that having a diversity of experiences on a board helps to meet the needs of the FF and help achieve its objectives of sustainability. John, in Case 2, stated: "The diverse points of view allow a rich and constructive debate." Women family board members join an FF because they want to be involved in the life of these firms and share their knowledge and experience, contributing their skills to the service of the FF. Mary, in Case 2, commented: "The choice of family directors was made on their ability to understand the strategic issues of the company."

Through their involvement in the boards, they contributed to strategic perspectives and they showed concern about social ties, firm survival, and harmony within the family and the firm when the successor is designated.

Pursuant to their past experiences, their contributions include enlightening the successor, being engaged in the succession process, highlighting risks, making sure that there is a wide range of views in relation to the choice being made, preparing for the arrival of the successor, building something and stating that it is to last for a very long time, preparing for the next generations, and ensuring the sustainability of the company.

5.   DISCUSSION

Our findings reveal that women directors' identities are dependent on past experience and that the way they support the successor is defined by their past experiences, with a link between their personal identity and the guidance provided to the successor. Our research not only advances extant theory, as discussed below, but also provides important insights for management practice and policymaking. Our findings first contribute to research on the presence of women on the board of directors in FF (Bettinelli et al., 2019; Maseda et al., 2021) by highlighting the importance of past experience, whether the women are family members or not.

In this chapter, we have explored women directors' experiences. While women's benefit to family businesses is increasingly recognized, we aim to contribute to the literature on board composition in support of gender diversity on the board, emphasizing the experiences associated with women on FF boards. We develop our knowledge on the different variables composing women directors' experiences. Women directors' personal identity and the way they support the successor in an FF have been highlighted through deepening their past personal and professional experiences.

The presence of women in the FF boardroom has been researched in previous literature. Their contributions are dependent on their knowledge, experience, skills, and expertise (Post and Byron, 2015; Kanadlı et al., 2018). Overall, research shows that women's involvement in FF boards is connected to various outcomes. Prior studies have focused on women's economic contributions on FF boards (Cruz et al., 2012; Amore et al., 2014). In addition, the effects of board gender diversity on non-economic outcomes highlighting knowledge, qualities, and capabilities have been the topic of academic inquiry (Post and Byron, 2015; Adams and Ferreira, 2009). This stream of research has established that what women in positions such as that of board member bring to the firm—their background, experience, qualifications, and connections— influences a variety of firm outcomes (Maseda et al., 2021).

However, our study goes beyond the information found on a resume. It delves into the interviewees' personal and professional experiences and reveals that their behavior is correlated to past experience. We show that it comes from within but is also shaped by situations they have faced in the past and are facing in the present. Their behavior is derived from what they have lived through, from their interpretation of those events, and from remembering past events when taking a decision regarding the future. By highlighting women directors' past experiences, we observe that their behavior is influenced by what they are. This is also in line with our work grounded on the micro-foundation approach, in the sense that a psychology-based understanding of the actions and interactions of individuals is used to explain their contributions in the boardroom (Picone et al., 2021).

Moreover, our chapter is one of the first studies to explore the effect of women's past experiences through the lens of neuroscience, particularly mental time travel theory (Ernst, 2019). It aims to identify how women directors' past experiences affect the succession process. In fact, neuroscience helps us understand how the brain works. This may all sound a bit too abstract and we may wonder what it has to do with business, but the brain is the fundamental basis for everything we do as humans, employees, and leaders. Knowing how our brains work gives us a better understanding of human behavior, which is obviously very relevant to the business field. Hence, when women directors recall their past experiences, they imagine possible future events (Schacter and Addis, 2007). Inspired by previous events, they settle the route to self-definition and identity. The interpretation of the precise memories recounted favors the probability of future action. For the woman director, autobiographical memory, through the mobilization of vivid and detailed recollections, supports the successor (Suddendorf et al., 2009; Schacter et al., 2012; Addis, 2018). In this way, past experiences mold the role the women play in the succession process. They prepare the future of the FF by accompanying and guiding the designated successor according to their field of competence. They contribute to reinforcing the sustainability of the FF.

By using this theory, we deepen our knowledge of the incentives of women's behavior. Hence, we contribute to the discussion about the relevance of interdisciplinary approaches (Nelson and Constantinidis, 2017; Nordqvist and Gartner, 2020; Maseda et al., 2021) by focusing on the suitability of the field of neuroscience, and in particular mental time travel, to understand women directors' decisions and actions.

Succession is an important challenge faced by family firms (Daspit et al., 2016). Our findings confirm the existing literature on women's contribution to the succession process (Barrett and Moores, 2009; Faraudello et al., 2017). However, this chapter tries to establish a link between women's past experiences before joining the board of directors and the guidance of the successor.

Interviewees had a wealth of experience, which allows us to understand their personality characteristics and behavior and make sense of their decisions on the boards and, in particular, the way they guide successors. Their experience and competencies arm women directors with broad perspectives and skills (Maseda et al., 2021), enabling them to identify strengths and areas in which the successor needs coaching and advice. By helping family members become effective business leaders, women directors can facilitate the transfer of leadership and ownership of an FF from one generation to the next.

In application to micro-foundational thinking (De Massis and Foss, 2018), our research focuses on the individuals, and particularly women in FF boards. They are modulated and constructed by the diversity of their experiences (Minialai, 2016). These aspects constitute their personal identity (Mequio, 2008). They "include (but are not limited to) traits, abilities, bodily self-perception, other perceived unique personal characteristics, and personality" (Hitlin, 2003, p.122).

We value gender diversity to affirm the existence of differences that reflect a variety of individuals who are recognized in their uniqueness. We have argued that every women director is unique. Her identity is the result of a successive addition of events and experiences and a progressive construction throughout life (Marc, 2016). We aim to understand and appreciate their characteristics and experiences that are different which include the way of being and the way of knowing. We have included in our study several types of experience—personal and professional—and observed their outcomes in the behavior of women on the board of directors of FF. Their thoughts intertwine the past, present, and future, which leads the women directors in the present, to remember their past and to anticipate their future (Tulving, 2001).

This chapter is grounded on the importance and the richness of the persons, and particularly women, on the board of FFs. We consider that these women are a valuable resource to the FF whether they are family members or not. Thus, the objective of the chapter was to ascertain who the women directors in the boardroom are, and to observe whether their identity, which is the product of successive experiences, events, and memories, influences the succession process and in particular the guidance of the successor. Our findings develop a detailed analysis of the women's past experiences and call for more consideration of past experiences (personal and professional) to better understand the reasons for their actions. We suggest that their decisions and priorities appear to be related to prior career or personal events, including feelings of frustration and suffering, that have shaped the course of their lives.

To summarize, our results contribute to the emerging literature on women in FF boards' influence on succession, offering an original contribution to the theory and practice on women's contribution to FF sustainability. The originality of this work is twofold. On the one hand, its value is represented by the focus on women directors' past experiences to determine how they influence the guidance of the successor. To the best of our knowledge, previous studies analyzed the outcomes of women's presence on FF boards without highlighting that lived experience influences the way they support the successor. Our results show that women directors, through the richness of their experiences, can make valuable contributions to the FF.

On the other hand, this chapter investigates the role of women in FF boards from an original perspective that has previously not been dealt with in the literature. Notably, it mobilizes the notion of mental time travel borrowed from neuroscience to enrich our understanding of the mechanisms of the memory of women directors and analyze how their past experiences influence their identity and their actions, providing an interdisciplinary viewpoint by offering research ideas in other subjects such as psychology and neuroscience.

6. LIMITATIONS OF THIS RESEARCH AND CONCLUSION

Some limitations emerge from our study. The case study method provides an in-depth analysis of the phenomena in context (Yin, 2003) and is appropriate for capturing the specific complexity and dynamics unique to family businesses. However, this method provides a limited number of informants and thereby obstructs the generalization of results. To obtain more general results, future research should include a comparison of the analyzed cases with other cases that are homogeneous in terms of the requested criteria.

While our results concern French cases, we consider that they are of broad international interest and application because they refer to a general context of women in FF boards and the past experiences of these women are not referable to a local context only.

The purpose of this chapter was to examine the influence of women's presence on FF boards (Campopiano et al., 2017). Researchers have found that women often play a crucial role (especially in succession processes) in an FF (Barrett and Moores, 2009).

In terms of theoretical implications, the chapter contributes to the discussion about the relevance of interdisciplinary approaches by focusing on the suitability of the field of neuroscience, and in particular mental time travel, to understand directors' decisions. There have been several recent calls for family business scholars to provide new empirical evidence on interdisciplinary approaches in the field of family business research in order to deepen our understanding (Nordqvist and Gartner, 2020). In fact, most research on FF is based on management and economics approaches (Evert et al., 2018; Neubaum, 2018). "[W]hile founding our perspectives on established literature is a good practice, we also need to broaden our perspectives to seek out new ways of 'seeing' and theorizing'" (Holt et al., 2018, p.173).

Furthermore, from a managerial perspective, this study has two important implications for practitioners. The first relates to the appointment of female directors to the boards of FFs. This study reveals that introducing female directors, whether family or non-family members, may provide diverse perspectives and contributions. The second implication relates to women's identity, which gives meaning to their behavior and actions and contributes to the sustainability of the FF.

This study is in line with policymaking. In fact, business and government[1] leaders have supported regulations to increase the number of women on boards. With women comprising more than half of the world's population, the involvement of women in the life of FFs will continue to grow in the future.

NOTE

1.   For example, in 2011 France introduced a law requiring publicly traded companies or firms exceeding certain thresholds to appoint women to their boards.

REFERENCES

Adams, R.B., and Ferreira, D. (2009). Women in the boardroom and their impact on governance and performance. *Journal of Financial Economics*, *94*(2), 291–309.

Addis, D.R. (2018). Are episodic memories special? On the sameness of remembered and imagined event simulation. *J. R. Soc. N. Z.*, *48*, 64–88.

Addis, D.R., Wong, A.T., and Schacter, D.L. (2007). Remembering the past and imagining the future: common and distinct neural substrates during event construction and elaboration. *Neuropsychologia*, *45*, 1363–77.

Aguinis, H., Boyd, B.K., Pierce, C.A., and Short, J.C. (2011). Walking new avenues in management research methods and theories: bridging micro and macro domains. *Journal of Management*, *37*(2), 395–403.

Al-Dajani, H., Bika, Z., Collins, L., and Swail, J. (2014). Gender and family business: new theoretical directions. *International Journal of Gender and Entrepreneurship*, *6*(3), 218–30.

Ali, M., Ng, Y.L., and Kulik, C.T. (2014). Board age and gender diversity: a test of competing linear and curvilinear predictions. *Journal of Business Ethics*, *125*(3), 497–512.

Amore, M.D., Garofalo, O., and Minichilli, A. (2014). Gender interactions within the family firm. *Management Science*, *60*(5), 1083–97.

Angelidis, J., and Ibrahim, N.A. (2011). The impact of emotional intelligence on the ethical judgment of managers. *Journal of Business Ethics*, *99*(1), 111–19.

Astrachan, J., Keyt, A., Kormann, H., and Binz Astrachan, C. (2020, 9 April). Covid-19: understanding the board's key role during a crisis. *Entrepreneurship & Innovation Exchange*.

Avenier, M.J. (2011). Les paradigmes épistémologiquesconstructivistes: post-modernisme ou pragmatisme? *Management Avenir*, *3*, 372–91.

Barrett, M., and Moores, K. (2009). Fostering women's entrepreneurial leadership in family firms: ten lessons. *Management Online REview (MORE)*, Online 1–11.

Bear, S., Rahman, N., and Post, C. (2010). The impact of board diversity and gender composition on corporate social responsibility and firm reputation. *Journal of Business Ethics*, *97*(2), 207–21.

Berthoz, A. (2012). Bases neurales de la décision. Une approche de neurosciences cognitives. *Annales Médico-psychologiques, revue psychiatrique*, *170*(2), 115–19.

Bettinelli, C., Del Bosco, B., and Giachino, C. (2019). Women on boards in family firms: what we know and what we need to know. In *The Palgrave Handbook of Heterogeneity among Family Firms* (pp.201–28). Palgrave Macmillan.

Burgess, Z., and Tharenou, P. (2002). Women board directors: characteristics of the few. *Journal of Business Ethics*, *37*(1), 39–49.

Campopiano, G., De Massis, A., Rinaldi, F.R., and Sciascia, S. (2017). Women's involvement in family firms: progress and challenges for future research. *Journal of Family Business Strategy*, *8*(4), 200–212.

Charness, G., and Gneezy, U. (2012). Strong evidence for gender differences in risk taking. *Journal of Economic Behavior and Organization*, *83*(1), 50–58.

Cherkaoui, A., and Haouata, S. (2017). Éléments de réflexion sur les positionnements épistémologiques et méthodologiques en sciences de gestion. *Revue interdisciplinaire*, *1*(2), 1–20.

Cohen, A., and Sharma, P. (2016). *Entrepreneurs in Every Generation: How Successful Family Businesses Develop Their Next Leaders*. Berrett-Koehler Publishers.

Cohen, G., and Conway, M.A. (2007). *Memory in the Real World*. Psychology Press.

Conway, M.A., and Pleydell-Pearce, C.W. (2000). The construction of autobiographical memories in the self-memory system. *Psychological Review*, *107*(2), 261.

Croson, R., and Gneezy, U. (2009). Gender differences in preferences. *Journal of Economic Literature*, *47*(2), 448–74.

Cruz, C., Justo, R., and De Castro, J.O. (2012). Does family employment enhance MSEs performance? Integrating socioemotional wealth and family embeddedness perspectives. *Journal of Business Venturing*, *27*(1), 62–76.

Daspit, J.J., Holt, D.T., Chrisman, J.J., and Long, R.G. (2016). Examining family firm succession from a social exchange perspective: a multiphase, multistakeholder review. *Family Business Review*, *29*(1), 44–64.

De Massis, A., and Foss, N.J. (2018). Advancing family business research: the promise of micrcofoundations. *Family Business Review*, *31*(4), 386–96.

De Massis, A., and Kammerlander, N. (eds). (2020). *Handbook of Qualitative Research Methods for Family Business*. Edward Elgar Publishing.

Eisenhardt, K.M. (1989). Building theories from case study research. *Academy of Management Review*, *14*(4), 532–50.

Elmagrhi, M.H., Ntim, C.G., Elamer, A.A., and Zhang, Q. (2019). A study of environmental policies and regulations, governance structures, and environmental performance: the role of female directors. *Business Strategy and the Environment*, *28*(1), 206–20.

Ernst, A. (2019). Le voyage mental dans le temps à la lumière des neurosciences cognitives et de la neuropsychologie clinique. *PSN*, *17*, 41–55.

Evert, R.E., Sears, J.B., Martin, J.A., and Payne, G.T. (2018). Family ownership and family involvement as antecedents of strategic action: a longitudinal study of initial international entry. *Journal of Business Research*, *84*, 301–11.

Faraudello, A., Songini, L., Pellegrini, M., and Gnan, L. (2017). The role of women as entrepreneurs in family business: a literature review. In Vanessa Ratten, Leo-Paul

Dana, and Veland Ramadani (eds), *Women Entrepreneurship in Family Business* (pp.72–100). Routledge.

Flyvbjerg, Bent (2011). Case study. In Norman K. Denzin and Yvonna S. Lincoln (eds), *The Sage Handbook of Qualitative Research* (4th ed., pp.301–16). Sage.

Gabrielsson, J., and Huse, M. (2005). Outside directors in SME boards: a call for theoretical reflections. *Corporate Board: Role, Duties and Composition, 1*(1), 28–37.

Galbreath, J. (2011). Are there gender-related influences on corporate sustainability? A study of women on boards of directors. *Journal of Management and Organization, 17*(1), 17–38.

Gersick, K.E., Lansberg, I., and Davis, J.A. (1990). The impact of family dynamics on structure and process in family foundations. *Family Business Review, 3*(4), 357–74.

Gioia, D.A., Corley, K.G., and Hamilton, A.L. (2013). Seeking qualitative rigor in inductive research: notes on the Gioia methodology. *Organizational Research Methods, 16*(1), 15–31.

Haberman, H., and Danes, S.M. (2007). Father–daughter and father–son family business management transfer comparison: family FIRO model application. *Family Business Review, 20*(2), 163–84.

Hambrick, D.C. (2007). Upper echelons theory: an update. *Academy of Management Review, 32*(2), 334–43.

Hitlin, S. (2003). Values as the core of personal identity: drawing links between two theories of self. *Social Psychology Quarterly*, 118–37.

Holt, D.T., Pearson, A.W., Payne, G.T., and Sharma, P. (2018). Family business research as a boundary-spanning platform. *Family Business Review, 31*(1), 14–31.

Huberman, A.M., and Miles, M.B. (1991). *Analyse des données qualitatives: recueil de nouvelles méthodes*. Éditions du Renouveau pédagogique; De Boeck.

Kammerlander, N., Dessi, C., Bird, M., Floris, M., and Murru, A. (2015). The impact of shared stories on family firm innovation: a multicase study. *Family Business Review, 28*(4), 332–54.

Kanadlı, S.B., Torchia, M., and Gabaldon, P. (2018). Increasing women's contribution on board decision making: the importance of chairperson leadership efficacy and board openness. *European Management Journal, 36*(1), 91–104.

Koryak, O., Lockett, A., Hayton, J., Nicolaou, N., and Mole, K. (2018). Disentangling the antecedents of ambidexterity: exploration and exploitation. *Research Policy, 47*(2), 413–27.

Kubíček, A., and Machek, O. (2019). Gender-related factors in family business succession: a systematic literature review. *Review of Managerial Science, 13*(5), 963–1002.

Lane, S., Astrachan, J., Keyt, A., and McMillan, K. (2006). Guidelines for family business boards of directors. *Family Business Review, 19*(2), 147–67.

Marc, E. (2016). La construction identitaire de l'individu. In Catherine Halpern (éd.), *Identité(s): L'individu, le groupe, la société* (pp.28–36). Éditions Sciences Humaines.

Maseda, A., Iturralde, T., Cooper, S., and Aparicio, G. (2021). Mapping women's involvement in family firms: a review based on bibliographic coupling analysis. *International Journal of Management Reviews, 24*(2), 279–305.

Mequio, S. (2008). The formation of personal identity: Environmental influences and opportunities that affect self-definition throughout adolescence (Doctoral dissertation).

Minialai, C. (2016). L'entreprise familiale: l'humain au coeur de l'aventure. *Economia, 366*(3225), 1–5.

Nelson, T., and Constantinidis, C. (2017). Sex and gender in family business succession research: a review and forward agenda from a social construction perspective. *Family Business Review, 30*(3), 219–41.

Neubaum, D.O. (2018). Family business research: roads travelled and the search for unworn paths. *Family Business Review, 31*(3), 259–70.

Neuman, W.L. (2007). *Basics of Social Research: Qualitative and Quantitative Approaches* (2nd ed.). Pearson.

Nordqvist, M., and Gartner, W.B. (2020). Literature, fiction, and the family business. *Family Business Review, 33*(2),122–9.

Nordqvist, M., Hall, A., and Melin, L. (2009). Qualitative research on family businesses: the relevance and usefulness of the interpretive approach. *Journal of Management and Organization, 15*(3), 294–308.

Picken, J. (2017). From startup to scalable enterprise: laying the foundation. *Business Horizons, 60*(5), 587–95.

Picone, P.M., De Massis, A., Tang, Y., and Piccolo, R.F. (2021). The psychological foundations of management in family firms: values, biases, and heuristics. *Family Business Review, 34*(1), 12–32.

Pillemer, D.B. (2001). Momentous events and the life story. *Review of General Psychology, 5*(2), 123–34.

Post, C., and Byron, K. (2015). Women on boards and firm financial performance: a meta-analysis. *Academy of Management Journal, 58*(5), 1546–71.

Randerson, K., and Radu-Lefebvre, M. (2021). Managing ambivalent emotions in family businesses: governance mechanisms for the family, business, and ownership systems. *Entrepreneurship Research Journal, 11*(3), 159–76.

Rodríguez-Ariza, L., Cuadrado-Ballesteros, B., Martínez-Ferrero, J., and García-Sánchez, I.M. (2017). The role of female directors in promoting CSR practices: an international comparison between family and non-family businesses. *Business Ethics: A European Review, 26*(2), 162–74.

Schacter, D.L., and Addis, D.R. (2007). The cognitive neuroscience of constructive memory: remembering the past and imagining the future. *Philosophical Transactions of the Royal Society B: Biological Sciences, 362*(1481), 773–86.

Schacter, D.L., Addis, D.R., Hassabis, D., Martin, V.C., Spreng, R.N., and Szpunar, K.K. (2012). The future of memory: remembering, imagining, and the brain. *Neuron, 76*(4), 677–94.

Suddendorf, T., and Corballis, M.C. (2007). The evolution of foresight: What is mental time travel, and is it unique to humans? *Behavioral and Brain Sciences, 30*(3), 299–313.

Suddendorf, T., Addis, D.R., and Corballis, M.C. (2009). Mental time travel and the shaping of the human mind. *Philosophical Transactions of the Royal Society B: Biological Sciences, 364*(1521), 1317–24.

Tulving, E. (1985). Memory and consciousness. *Canadian Psychology/Psychologie canadienne, 26*(1), 1.

Tulving, E. (2001). Episodic memory and common sense: how far apart? *Philosophical Transactions of the Royal Society of London. Series B: Biological Sciences, 356*(1413), 1505–15.

Williams, R.J. (2003). Women on corporate boards of directors and their influence on corporate philanthropy. *Journal of Business Ethics, 42*(1), 1–10.

Yin, R.K. (2003). Designing case studies. *Qualitative Research Methods, 5*, 359–86.

Zhang, J.Q., Zhu, H., and Ding, H.B. (2013). Board composition and corporate social responsibility: An empirical investigation in the post Sarbanes-Oxley era. *Journal of Business Ethics*, *114*(3), 381–92.

2. Gender equality in family business succession: do religion and sociocultural factors matter? Evidence from Tunisia

Hedi Yezza and Didier Chabaud

1. INTRODUCTION

Succession remains one of the most widely studied topics in family business research (Daspit et al. 2016; Yezza et al., 2021a), due to the number of failed transmissions from one generation to another (Bégin et al., 2014). However, the role of gender is still neglected in the family business literature (Kubíček & Machek, 2019; Nelson & Constantinidis, 2017) and, regarding succession, women remain largely "invisible successors" (Dumas, 1989).

Family business research in emerging economies is also still limited compared to that conducted in developed countries (Khavul et al., 2009; Krueger et al., 2021; Ramadani et al., 2017). Recent literature recognizes the importance of contextual diversity (Soleimanof et al., 2018; Wright et al., 2014), and the authors call for further conceptual and empirical analysis to advance dialog and research in the area of family business. The economic, institutional, and cultural context can influence family businesses' behavior and performance (Jaskiewicz et al., 2016; Randerson et al., 2020; Stough et al., 2015), and also longevity across multiple generations. Scholars have found that religion affects individual values (Ramadani et al., 2017; Rietveld & Van Burg, 2014) and family business behavior (Abdelgawad & Zahra, 2019; Astrachan et al., 2020). Recent studies have highlighted the importance of the institutional and legal context in family business research (Barrédy, 2016; Sharma & Chua, 2013; Wright et al., 2014; Zellweger et al., 2019). Regarding family succession, Carney et al. (2014) show that succession laws and legal regimes have an impact on the longevity and survival of family firms. Given the differences in laws and legal texts related to succession in each country, it would be valuable to explore new contexts that are still neglected by the literature, such as Arabic countries and the Islamic religion.

Therefore, this chapter aims to examine the role of gender in family business, and how religion and sociocultural factors affect family members' behavior and more broadly the evolution of the succession process. We start by delving into the religious and sociocultural influences in Arab Muslim countries in the context of family succession. After presenting our case study, we discuss the role of gender in such a cultural context to shed light on the peculiarities of the situation for female successors in Arab Muslim countries. Finally, we consider the scope and limitations of our approach.

2.   LITERATURE REVIEW

2.1   The Influence of Religion on Family Businesses

Despite increasing research on the impact of values, spirituality, and religion[1] on family businesses, little attention has been given to the interrelationship between religion and gender equality (Koburtay et al., 2020; Tlaiss, 2015), more precisely in the family succession context. Researchers have found that religion is an important source of values in family businesses (Barbera et al., 2020), and these values influence the business, individual decisions, attitudes (Astrachan et al., 2020; Barbera et al., 2020; Kellermanns, 2013), and strategic renewal (Abdelgawad & Zahra, 2020). Religion provides a meaningful system that guides the commercial choices of family businesses (Jarzabkowski et al., 2019). The Islamic religion is the second largest religion in the world (Ramadani et al., 2017). The Koran, the sacred book of Muslims, contains the principles, traditions, and rules of the Islamic religion. Family firms are managed through families, religion, and community (Fathallah et al., 2020; Soleimanof et al., 2018). Based on research featuring 13 Lebanese firms run by individuals of mixed Muslim and Christian faith, Fathallah et al. (2020) argue that religious values can be interpreted differently, and specifically that Muslim family firms respect a rule-based approach and Christian family firms prefer a principle-based approach. Therefore, it is relevant to understand how religion can affect family businesses and, more specifically, the role of women during the succession process.

2.2   Succession and Family Structure

Recent research proposes to examine how family structure (Sharma & Manikutty, 2005) and sociocultural contexts can affect the succession process (Bah et al., 2017, Ramadani et al., 2017) in Mediterranean and African regions (Dinh & Calabrò, 2019), and more precisely in Arab Muslim countries such as Tunisia (Yezza et al., 2021a). We mobilize the studies conducted by Todd (1985; 2011) to characterize family structures and better understand the nature of the relationship between individuals within the same family. The family structure in Tunisia is different from other family structures around the world. Todd (2011) differentiates four types of family structure: the absolute nuclear family; the egalitarian nuclear family; the authoritarian (stump) family; and the community family. This approach takes two dimensions into consideration. First, the authority–freedom dimension is strongly present in the succession process, since the father and his descendant are to share power. The behavior of family members and the nature of the relationship between parents and their children are regulated by the shared norms and values of the family system. Second, the equality–inequality dimension explains the presence or absence of common rules for the inheritance of property.

Tunisia was not directly addressed in the study conducted by Todd (2011), which analyzed 15 Arab countries, but we mobilized other research conducted by scholars in the Tunisian context (Benmostefa, 2015; Touzani et al., 2015; Yezza, 2019). These studies indicate that the Tunisian family can be considered a modern community type (patriarchal in character) given the strong involvement of women in society, with an endogamous tendency (the tendency of the family group to be closed on itself with a high rate of marriage between members of the same group, entourage, region, and family) ensuring equality among children, although supported by religion. The literature highlights another important dimension related to the nature of the relationships between individuals. Arab culture imposes respect for elders (Fahed-Sreih, 2017), which can affect behavior among siblings: in the case of a takeover by several members of the same family, sibling successors—depending on their age and/or gender—will find it difficult to clearly express their expectations and needs. Primogeniture defines the nature of the relationship between brothers and sisters. For example, Koburtay et al. (2020) explain gender inequality through patriarchal interpretations that restrict Jordan women's employment and progression.

Succession processes largely depend on the cultural and economic environment in which family firms are embedded, but also on the institutional context and rules (Carney et al., 2014; Soleimanof et al., 2018). Indeed, the legislative and institutional context is another factor that explains the heterogeneity of family firms (Barrédy, 2016; Soleimanof et al., 2018). Institutional theory (North, 1990; Scott, 1995) provides a framework to explain how institutional contexts influence firm activities. Formal institutions such as national laws and regulations explain the diversity of family businesses (Barrédy, 2016; Ge et al., 2019) and affect succession processes (Carney et al., 2014). Given the diversity of laws in each country, it is important to understand the extent to which the institutional context impacts equality between men and women in family succession. Are there inheritance laws or legal texts that favor men to the detriment of women in Arab Muslim countries?

3.   METHODOLOGY

As we aimed at inductive theory building (Reay & Whetten, 2011) and to reach "methodological fit" (Edmondson & McManus, 2007), we conducted a longitudinal interpretive case study over a period of five years (Leppäaho et al., 2016) and used grounded theory to analyze the data (Corley & Gioia, 2004; Gioia et al., 2013). We selected a purposeful sample (Hamilton, 2006) of Tunisian family businesses and mobilized "revealing" cases, in the sense of Yin (2009) and Gioia et al. (2013), which have strong potential to clarify a phenomenon and fill a theoretical gap (Langley & Abdallah, 2011). This choice is also justified by the opportunity to access family businesses that are open to sharing (private) information relative to sensitive issues and "unusual research questions" (De Massis & Kotlar, 2014, p.17). The Tunisian context is interesting because studies on the question of gender during family successions are rare, especially in the context of Arab Muslim countries. Recent research indicates the need to conduct more studies in different regions and contexts to better understand the heterogeneity of family firms and then advance family business science (Krueger et al., 2021).

Respondents agreed to share their thoughts and experience with the research team. From 2016 to 2020, we conducted semistructured interviews (Discua Cruz et al., 2013; Nordqvist et al., 2009) with successor CEOs, other family members, and nonfamily members, to understand family members' behaviors. We collected 11 semistructured interviews that we position as self-narratives (Fletcher et al., 2016). Following previous research in the family business field, we also collected additional data from nonparticipant observations (Kotlar and De Massis, 2013; Jaskiewicz et al., 2015). After obtaining the manager's agreement, one of the authors observed working meetings, interactions between individuals, and the roles of each in the organization. We witnessed high-tension discussions between family members involved in the business and took notes to help us with the data analysis. We recorded and transcribed all of the interviews.

The company was founded in 1984 as a commercial nail-clamping and manufacturing business. The founder developed a distribution network and launched a production unit (it became its own supplier at points of sale). Then, he launched a business in the real estate sector. In 2009 the founder delegated certain responsibilities to his children (two sons and two daughters), while ensuring control and monitoring. The father always supported his children, and the eldest girl and the eldest boy went to France to finish their studies. The father was very open-minded, and he made sure to be fair with his children. In 2013, following his death, his children took over the management of the company. Several professional and family conflicts developed among the siblings. They stopped communicating with each other, no longer shared company information and finally pursued their own interests to the detriment of the company and the family. This had a strong impact on the financial stability of the company and the family atmosphere.

Responders' statements were treated using "Gioia methods" (Corley & Gioia, 2004; Gioia et al., 2013) to understand the roles of specific elements and factors related to the religious and sociocultural contexts. We asked open questions related to the family sphere (for example, relationships between family members, difference between feminine and masculine behavior) and the business sphere (for example, management, leadership) to obtain raw data that respected a first-order coding that was close to the respondents' verbatim quotations. We coded a second level that allows a rise in abstraction by realizing several round trips between theory and field (Figure 2.1).

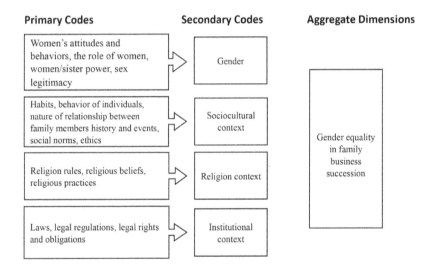

Figure 2.1   Data structure

4.   FINDINGS

4.1   Succession under the Pressure of the Law

The Tunisian constitutional and legal system are strongly inspired by French practice in matters of decrees and laws (Jaidane, 2002). Some aspects differ from the French model, particularly the inheritance regime, which is mainly derived from the Muslim religion. In fact, inheritance law in Islam is based on several passages from the Koran. Succession procedures favor the male gender by applying the double-share rule for men, to the detriment of women.[2] Therefore, the women inherit half of the men's share: article 103 of the Tunisian Code of Personal Statute thus states that "the male heir has a share double that attributed to a female heir." This measure discriminates against women and can create conflicts within the family. However, it is important to emphasize that there is a "testamentary freedom" that allows the owner to share the inheritance equally between his children (men and women) before his death. In our case the data analysis shows that the founder transferred part of the ownership of the company to his children before his death, in particular to circumvent the rule of double shares for sons and half for daughters, which was confirmed by the younger sister. However, the analysis of the results shows that favoritism remained in the mind of the founder: "It's true my father shared the heritage before his death to be fair with his children; on the other hand, there is always favoritism because he gives each of us a house, for example, but the value of the houses is not necessarily the same. The boys have properties better placed than us" (eldest female successor). This perception is also conveyed by one of their brothers: "My children will bear the name of the family. I must be more privileged compared to my sister. Her children will be part of her husband's father's family" (successor brother). This perception is reinforced in Arab countries due to the patriarchal dimension sustained by society. This was confirmed by the previous interviewee's sister: "My brother has very old cultural values (he is stupid). It seems like we are in the Fifties. He didn't accept that we have the same rights and obligations."

4.2   When an "Equal" Succession Is Challenged

The choice of potential successor is determined by primogeniture, age, gender, and skills. In the context of this research, sex was not a determining factor in the choice of successors because the founder decided to pass the business on to all the siblings (brothers and sisters). The eldest daughter was already involved in the business. There were no stereotypes associated with a more "masculine" industry. This was confirmed by the eldest successor: "Fortunately, my father accompanied me during my integration into the company, so I can talk openly with the employees. I go between the different units every day."

However, we have to notice that this formal posture is challenged due to the organization of the inheritance. The "double-share" rule for men offers a certain legitimacy in decision-making since they are the majority sharehold-ers. This is seen as a source of conflict, as siblings do not agree on all decisions. Legally, the women do not have enough power to contradict the decisions of their brothers. This facilitates factions in family businesses and opportunistic behavior by some successors. The pursuit of personal interests to the detriment of collective interests affects the longevity of family firms. This was confirmed by a younger female successor: "My brothers don't accept my position in the company. They can't decide alone, He is obligated to receive our validation. Now we form clans, girls against boys. We have several companies. So, sometimes when we own the majority of the business shares, we blackmail our brothers: if they don't accept our decisions in company A, we don't accept their decisions in company B." The analysis of the results shows that one of the female successors is less involved and less present in the company than her sister. This was confirmed by the eldest sister: "My sister is married. She has two children. She cannot be present every day, so I replace her."

The analysis of the results shows that the women encounter difficulties with their brothers on two levels. The first concerns leadership style and decision-making. The men are more rational in making decisions, according to the eldest brother: "Personally, I only look for the financial benefits and the profitability of the activities. I am not too interested in anything else." On the other hand, one of the sisters said she is more oriented toward noneconomic objectives: "When I make a decision, I take our family needs into considera- tion. Sometimes I make concessions with my brothers just to maintain cohesion and family solidarity. My brothers, on the other hand, are rather selfish." The second concern is management style. The women say they seek consensus, collaboration, and the participation of all stakeholders. This was confirmed by the older sister: "Our brothers make important decisions without informing us. They always want to show us that they are independent from us, and they don't need our opinions. On the other hand, we share all the information with them. We are frustrated because it is only going one way. It's not balanced."

In this way, we observe that the "equal" succession chosen by the father is put under pressure, as the brother uses all the elements at his disposal— shareholders, religion, and culture—in order to justify his decisions.

5. DISCUSSION

This manuscript highlights the importance of taking into account the role of religion and sociocultural factors in order to better understand the succession process in family firms. This study offers a new perspective to better under- stand the role of women in family businesses and how religion and sociocul- tural and institutional factors can explain inequalities between men and women (Ahrens et al., 2015; Kubíček & Machek, 2019). It is specifically interesting to observe that religion appears to be both a contextual element and a tool that can be used in order to negotiate the decision power.

5.1   Tunisia: A Changing Context…

The case of Tunisia, an Arab Muslim country, confirms the importance of conducting research in several countries to better understand the heterogeneity of
family businesses around the world (Daspit et al. 2021; Neubaum et al., 2019;
Rau et al., 2019). Since 1956, the official signing of the "personal status code"
has ensured that Tunisian women enjoy the same rights and obligations as their
male counterparts, in all areas. For example, the law has abolished polygamy,
prohibited forced marriage, legalized abortion, and allowed divorce. Tunisia is
a pioneer in the Muslim world in terms of equality between women and men.
These conditions give Tunisian women an unprecedented place in society
compared to other Arab countries. The achievements of Tunisian women
are numerous and are the subject of international recognition, as evidenced
by the award for "Best Businesswoman in the Arab World" in 2013, the
"Oslo Business for Peace Award" in 2014 and finally the Nobel Peace prize
awarded in 2015 to the quartet sponsoring the national dialog in Tunisia—led
by a woman, who is president of the Tunisian union of industry, commerce,
and crafts. Fahed-Sreih (2017) confirms this position of growing equality by
pointing out that women occupy key positions in the country, such as judges,
politicians, and government officials. In 2021 Tunisia appointed a woman to
serve as prime minister (the first woman to head a government in the Arab
world). Todd (2011) also returns to the signs of modernity and the birth of
democracy after the Tunisian revolution in 2011. The modernity of Tunisian
society was confirmed in 2018 by the proposal of a bill that reformed the laws
of succession to allow women equality in matters of inheritance. The proposal
is still in progress and has created great controversy in Tunisian society, given
the disagreement between citizens who support and those who oppose it.
Tunisia shows itself to be a modern country given the emancipation of women,
which dates back a number of years, but remains attached to tradition with
respect to religious practices. In Tunisia, despite the proclaimed secularism,
society is still influenced by religion (Younes et al., 2016), which is considered
a source of moral values that govern social relations between individuals and,
more broadly, values to be respected within the community (Bentebbaa, 2017).
Recent research has examined the role of religion and cultural variations in
the expression of emotions and conflicts between family members during the
succession process (Yezza et al., 2021b).

5.2   … Facing Both Cultural and Individual Resistance

Although the role of women is strongly supported by laws and legal texts
(Yezza, 2019), women's authority is not yet accepted. This can be explained
by previous religious and sociocultural beliefs. For example, the style of

leadership—oriented toward collaboration and the participation of all actors—adopted by women (Remery et al., 2014; Sonfield & Lussier, 2012) can be interpreted as a source of weakness by the brothers in the case of a sibling succession, but also by employees and other stakeholders. The results of our study show that men still struggle to accept women's decision-making power. These stereotypes are still present in the Tunisian context, which also explains the sometimes "hostile" behavior of men toward women. Regarding the choice of potential successors, we note that primogeniture is much more important than gender. Finally, we can qualify Tunisian society as being masculine with very strong feminine involvement. However, given family responsibilities and their primary role in the education of children, women are likely to be less involved in family businesses, especially where several successors take over the business. These results add to the debate on the role of women in family businesses (Elam et al., 2019; Nikina et al., 2015; Shelton, 2006) and how they balance family and professional commitments.

However, the situation seems quite different in our case study, as the father arranged largely equal decision-making power among the siblings (even having involved the elder daughter). Here, the situation was influenced not by religion or the elder brother's strong beliefs, but by personal interest. The brother wanted to maintain authority over the whole firm, and uses religion as a way to impose his own views. In the same way, it is interesting to observe that his sisters try to discuss decisions and negotiate.

5.3   The Need for a Research Program

While we have examined the relations between religion, family structure, sociocultural factors, and institutional dimensions, this single-case study only allows a partial vision because our empirical observation comes from one town, in a tourist region in Tunisia. It would be useful to complete the study with cases from rural areas. It is also of interest to consider the influence of religion and sociocultural aspects on succession in the context of community families, and our results are different from those of studies conducted in the Western context, which is more marked by nuclear families. A comparative research program is needed to complement this knowledge and better identify other contextual factors. A comparative study between several Muslim and non-Muslim countries would be interesting to refine the analysis of religion and sociocultural particularities as determinants of gender inequality and its influence on the family succession process.

6.   CONCLUSION

More than 20 years ago, Dumas (1989) noted women as "invisible successors" in family business. We emphasize here the difficulty for such women to become visible in the context of a Muslim country. The results indicate that religion can be considered a source of individual values that affects family members' behavior, institutional rules, and inheritance laws in family businesses in Arab Muslim countries. Moreover, we observe that even in a changing context—in which the formal place for women has changed—it is difficult to change minds, especially when religion can be used to preserve individual interest.

NOTES

1.   Among others a recent special issue of *Journal of Business Ethics* (2020).
2.   Tunisian law prohibits the disinheritance of children.

REFERENCES

Abdelgawad, S.G., & Zahra, S.A. (2020). Family firms' religious identity and strategic renewal. *Journal of Business Ethics, 163*(4), 775–87.
Ahrens, J.-P., Landmann, A., & Woywode, M. (2015). Gender preferences in the CEO successions of family firms: family characteristics and human capital of the successor. *Journal of Family Business Strategy, 6*(2), 86–103.
Astrachan, J.H., Binz Astrachan, C., Campopiano, G., & Baù, M. (2020). Values, spirituality and religion: family business and the roots of sustainable ethical behavior. *Journal of Business Ethics, 163*(4), 637–45.
Bah, T., Boussaguet, S., de Freyman, J., & Ndione, L. (2017). La transmission des entreprises familiales au Sénégal: quelles spécificités culturelles? *Revue internationale P.M.E., 30*(3–4), 127–61.
Barbera, F., Shi, H.X., Agarwal, A., & Edwards, M. (2020). The family that prays together stays together: toward a process model of religious value transmission in family firms. *Journal of Business Ethics, 163*(4), 661–73.
Barrédy, C. (2016). In search of future alternatives for family business: family law contributions through civil and common law comparison. *Futures, 75*, 44–53.
Bégin, L., Bonnafous-Boucher, M., Chabaud, D., & Fayolle, A. (2014). La longévité des entreprises familiales en question. *Revue de l'Entrepreneuriat, 13*, 11–23.
Benmostefa, F. (2015). La transmission des entreprises familiales en Tunisie, Thèse de Doctorat, Université de Bordeaux.
Bentebbaa, S. (2017). Moroccan family businesses: specific attributes, logics of action and organizational learning dynamics, in *Family Businesses in the Arab World: Governance, Strategy, and Financing*, Sami Basly ed., Springer International Publishing.
Carney, M., Gedajlovic, E., & Strike, V.M. (2014). Dead money: inheritance law and the longevity of family firms. *Entrepreneurship Theory and Practice, 38*(6), 1261–83.

Corley, K.G., & Gioia, D.A. (2004). Identity ambiguity and change in the wake of a corporate spin-off. *Administrative Science Quarterly, 49*(2), 173–208.

Daspit, J.J., Chrisman, J.J., Ashton, T., & Evangelopoulos, N. (2021). Family firm heterogeneity: a definition, common themes, scholarly progress, and directions forward. *Family Business Review, 34*(3), 296–322.

Daspit, J.J., Holt, D.T., Chrisman, J.J., & Long, R.G. (2016). Examining family firm succession from a social exchange perspective: a multiphase, multistakeholder review. *Family Business Review, 29*(1), 44–64.

De Massis, A., & Kotlar, J. (2014). The case study method in family business research: guidelines for qualitative scholarship. *Journal of Family Business Strategy, 5*(1), 15–29.

Dinh, T.Q., & Calabrò, A. (2019). Asian family firms through corporate governance and institutions: a systematic review of the literature and agenda for future research. *International Journal of Management Reviews, 21*(1), 50–75.

Discua Cruz, A., Howorth, C., & Hamilton, E. (2013). Intrafamily entrepreneurship: the formation and membership of family entrepreneurial teams. *Entrepreneurship Theory and Practice, 37*(1), 17–46.

Dumas, C. (1989). Understanding of father–daughter and father–son dyads in family-owned businesses. *Family Business Review, 2*(1), 31–46.

Edmondson, A.C., & McManus, S.E. (2007). Methodological fit in management field research. *Academy of Management Review, 32*(4), 1246–64.

Elam, A., Brush, C., Greene, P., Baumer, B., Dean, M., & Heavlow, R. (2019). Global Entrepreneurship Monitor: 2018/2019 *Women's Entrepreneurship Report.* Wellesley, MA: Babson College.

Fahed-Sreih, J. (2017). Founder legacy in Arab dynastic entrepreneurship, in *Family Businesses in the Arab World: Governance, Strategy, and Financing*, Sami Basly ed., Springer International Publishing.

Fathallah, R., Sidani, Y., & Khalil, S. (2020). How religion shapes family business ethical behaviors: an institutional logics perspective. *Journal of Business Ethics, 163*(4), 647–59.

Fletcher, D., Massis, A.D., & Nordqvist, M. (2016). Qualitative research practices and family business scholarship: a review and future research agenda. *Journal of Family Business Strategy, 7*(1), 8–25.

Ge, J., Carney, M., & Kellermanns, F. (2019). Who fills institutional voids? Entrepreneurs' utilization of political and family ties in emerging markets. *Entrepreneurship Theory and Practice, 43*(6), 1124–47.

Gioia, D.A., Corley, K.G., & Hamilton, A.L. (2013). Seeking qualitative rigor in inductive research: notes on the Gioia methodology. *Organizational Research Methods, 16*(1), 15–31.

Hamilton, E. (2006). Whose story is it anyway? Narrative accounts of the role of women in founding and establishing family businesses. *International Small Business Journal, 24*(3), 253–71.

Jaidane, R. (2002). L'influence du droit français sur le droit tunisien des concentrations économiques. *Revue internationale de droit economique, 4*(4), 655–78.

Jarzabkowski, P., Kavas, M., & Krull, E. (2021). It's practice. But is it strategy? Reinvigorating strategy-as-practice by rethinking consequentiality. *Organization Theory, 2*(3), 26317877211029664.

Jaskiewicz, P., Combs, J.G., & Rau, S.B. (2015). Entrepreneurial legacy: toward a theory of how some family firms nurture transgenerational entrepreneurship. *Journal of Business Venturing, 30*(1), 29–49.

Jaskiewicz, P., Heinrichs, K., Rau, S.B., & Reay, T. (2016). To be or not to be: how family firms manage family and commercial logics in succession. *Entrepreneurship Theory and Practice*, *40*(4), 781–813.

Kellermanns, F.W. (2013). Spirituality and religion in family firms. *Journal of Management, Spirituality & Religion*, *10*(2), 112–15.

Khavul, S., Bruton, G.D., & Wood, E. (2009). Informal family business in Africa. *Entrepreneurship Theory and Practice*, *33*(6), 1219–1238.

Koburtay, T., Syed, J., & Haloub, R. (2020). Implications of religion, culture, and legislation for gender equality at work: qualitative insights from Jordan. *Journal of Business Ethics*, *164*(3), 421–36.

Kotlar, J., & De Massis, A. (2013). Goal setting in family firms: goal diversity, social interactions, and collective commitment to family-centered goals. *Entrepreneurship Theory and Practice*, *37*(6), 1263–88.

Krueger, N., Bogers, M.L.A.M., Labaki, R., & Basco, R. (2021). Advancing family business science through context theorizing: the case of the Arab world. *Journal of Family Business Strategy*, *12*(1), 100377.

Kubíček, A., & Machek, O. (2019). Gender-related factors in family business succession: a systematic literature review. *Review of Managerial Science*, *13*(5), 963–1002.

Langley, A., & Abdallah, C. (2011). Templates and turns in qualitative studies of strategy and management, in *Research Methodology in Strategy and Management*, D.D. Bergh & D.J. Ketchen eds, Emerald Publishing.

Leppäaho, T., Plakoyiannaki, E., & Dimitratos, P. (2016). The case study in family business: an analysis of current research practices and recommendations. *Family Business Review*, *29*(2), 159–173.

Nelson, T., & Constantinidis, C. (2017). Sex and gender in family business succession research: a review and forward agenda from a social construction perspective. *Family Business Review*, *30*(3), 219–241.

Neubaum, D.O., Kammerlander, N., & Brigham, K.H. (2019). Capturing family firm heterogeneity: how taxonomies and typologies can help the field move forward. *Family Business Review*, *32*(2), 106–130.

Nikina, A., Shelton, L.M., & LeLoarne, S. (2015). An examination of how husbands, as key stakeholders, impact the success of women entrepreneurs. *Journal of Small Business and Enterprise Development*, *22*(1), 38–62.

Nordqvist, M., Hall, A., & Melin, L. (2009). Qualitative research on family businesses: the relevance and usefulness of the interpretive approach. *Journal of Management & Organization*, *15*(3), 294–308.

North, D.C. (1990). *Institutions, Institutional Change and Economic Performance*. Cambridge University Press.

Ramadani, V., Dana, L.-P., Gërguri-Rashiti, S. and Ratten, V. (2017). *Entrepreneurship and Management in an Islamic Context*. Springer.

Randerson, K., Seaman, C., Daspit, J.J., & Barredy, C. (2020). Institutional influences on entrepreneurial behaviours in the family entrepreneurship context: towards an integrative framework. *International Journal of Entrepreneurial Behavior & Research*, *26*(1), 1–13.

Rau, S.B., Schneider-Siebke, V., & Günther, C. (2019). Family firm values explaining family firm heterogeneity. *Family Business Review*, *32*(2), 195–215.

Reay, T., & Whetten, D.A. (2011). What constitutes a theoretical contribution in family business? *Family Business Review*, *24*(2), 105–110.

Remery, C., Matser, I., & Hans Flören, R. (2014). Successors in Dutch family businesses: gender differences. *Journal of Family Business Management*, *4*(1), 79–91.

Rietveld, C.A., & van Burg, E. (2014). Religious beliefs and entrepreneurship among Dutch Protestants. *International Journal of Entrepreneurship and Small Business, 23*(3), 279–95.

Scott, W.R. (1995). *Organizations and Institutions (Foundations for Organizational Science)*. Sage.

Sharma, P., & Chua, J.H. (2013). Asian family enterprises and family business research. *Asia Pacific Journal of Management, 30*(3), 641–56.

Sharma, P., & Manikutty, S. (2005). Strategic divestments in family firms: role of family structure and community culture. *Entrepreneurship Theory and Practice, 29*(3), 293–311.

Shelton, L.M. (2006). Female entrepreneurs, work–family conflict, and venture performance: new insights into the work–family interface. *Journal of Small Business Management, 44*(2), 285–97.

Soleimanof, S., Rutherford, M.W., & Webb, J.W. (2018). The intersection of family firms and institutional contexts: a review and agenda for future research. *Family Business Review, 31*(1), 32–53.

Sonfield, M.C., & Lussier, R.N. (2012). Gender in family business management: a multinational analysis. *Journal of Family Business Management, 2*(2), 110–29.

Stough, R., Welter, F., Block, J., Wennberg, K., & Basco, R. (2015). Family business and regional science: "bridging the gap." *Journal of Family Business Strategy, 6*(4), 208–18.

Tlaiss, H.A. (2015). How Islamic business ethics impact women entrepreneurs: insights from four Arab Middle Eastern countries. *Journal of Business Ethics, 129*(4), 859–77.

Touzani, M., Jlassi, F., Maalaoui, A., & Bel Haj Hassine, R. (2015). Contextual and cultural determinants of entrepreneurship in pre- and post-revolutionary Tunisia: analysing the discourse of young potential and actual entrepreneurs. *Journal of Small Business and Enterprise Development, 22*(1), 160–79.

Todd, E. (1985). *The Explanation of Ideology, Family Structures and Social Systems*. Basil Blackwell.

Todd, E. (2011). *Les origines des systèmes familiaux*. Gallimard.

Wright, M., Chrisman, J.J., Chua, J.H., & Steier, L.P. (2014). Family enterprise and context. *Entrepreneurship Theory and Practice, 38*(6), 1247–60.

Yezza (2019). La succession dans les entreprises familiales: Le rôle de compétences sociales du successeur (Thèse de doctorat), IAE de Paris, Sorbonne Business School, Université Paris 1—Panthéon Sorbonne, France.

Yezza, H., Chabaud, D., & Calabrò, A. (2021a). Dynamics of conflicts in family firms: towards a non-linear approach to the succession process. *Journal of Enterprising Culture, 29*(2), 79–107.

Yezza, H., Chabaud, D., & Calabrò, A. (2021b). Conflict dynamics and emotional dissonance during the family business succession process: evidence from the Tunisian context. *Entrepreneurship Research Journal, 11*(3), 219–44.

Yin, R.K. (2009). *Case Study Research: Design and Methods*. Thousand Oaks: Sage.

Younes, M., Salah, L.H., & Touzani, M. (2016). Gouvernance participative et nouvelles pratiques managériales dans un contexte postrévolutionnaire: cas des entreprises sociales tunisiennes. *Management Avenir, 90*(8), 175–94.

Zellweger, T.M., Chrisman, J.J., Chua, J.H., & Steier, L.P. (2019). Social structures, social relationships, and family firms. *Entrepreneurship Theory and Practice, 43*(2), 207–23.

PART II

Women's autonomy and distance from the family

3. Women's access to debt finance for small businesses in Bangladesh: the role of family members (excluding husbands)

Jasmine Jaim[1]

1. INTRODUCTION

While women's entrepreneurship scholarship mostly concentrates on Western developed nations (Brush and Cooper, 2012), it has been established that studies in underexplored areas of the world can yield insightful findings (Welter, 2019). While the family is intrinsically associated with the life of women (Walby, 1990), studies on Western developed nations, seeking to explore the role of family in women's entrepreneurship, have concentrated almost exclusively on the impact of domestic responsibilities and childcare activities on their businesses (Ahl, 2004; McGowan et al., 2012). Work–family conflicts concerning the familial responsibilities of women entrepreneurs have been revealed (Shelton, 2006; Welter, 2004). Thus, studies on developed nations mostly focused on nuclear families by considering domestic chores, while the involvement of family members in women's sole-proprietorship activities has been overlooked (Jaim, 2022a). Nevertheless, the limited literature (Alexandre and Kharabsheh, 2019; Jaim, 2021a; Roomi et al., 2018; Williams and Gurtoo, 2011; Xheneti et al., 2019) considering under-researched areas, such as developing nations, has already generated valuable insights by unveiling positive and negative roles played by relatives, including extended family members, in women's entrepreneurship.

As accessing financial capital is challenging for women entrepreneurs (Coleman et al., 2019), this particular field deserves attention when exploring the roles of family members in developing nations. While the extremely limited literature addresses the influences of menfolk of the family in women entrepreneurs' access to debt finance in this context (Ahmad, 2011; Constantinidis et al., 2019; Jaim, 2021a, 2022a), the detailed discussion focuses on the patronising and patriarchal roles of husbands (Jaim, 2021a,

2022a); the roles of other family members, including distant relatives, have largely been overlooked. Whilst assistance of certain close relatives other than husbands in meeting the guarantor obligation of a loan has been mentioned in the literature (Ahmad and Naimat, 2011; Constantinidis et al., 2019), whether and how other family members support women regarding different activities in the debt-financing process is yet to be known. Further, the literature reveals negative effects of religious restrictions on women's mobility for their business operation (Ahmad and Naimat, 2011; Lindvert et al., 2017), but little is known regarding whether there exists any specific religious binding concerning accessing loans through which family members might adversely affect women's firms. As entrepreneurship is considered an effective way to positively change the socio-economic conditions of developing regions (Rindova et al. 2009), diversified roles of relatives in women's ventures are worthy of investigation, particularly for those developing nations where the government is taking financial initiatives to support women's businesses.

The research aim is to explore the role of family members (excluding husbands) regarding women's access to debt finance for their small businesses in a patriarchal developing nation. To respond to the aim, the first objective is to investigate the positive roles of the relatives concerning the debt-financing process of women business-owners. The second objective is to explore the negative influences of the family members with regard to women's access to bank loans for their sole proprietorship. The study is conducted in a South Asian developing country, Bangladesh, where women are subject to highly patriarchal practices (Khatun, 2020), and, where a growing number of women are acquiring bank loans for their small firms (Hasan, 2019).

To address the research aim, the chapter is structured as follows. A literature review sets the background for the study. Methods of data generation and analysis used are then explained. After presenting the empirical findings, a discussion and policy recommendations are provided. The chapter concludes by highlighting the major contributions of the research.

2.   THEORETICAL FOUNDATION

Women's entrepreneurship scholarship is criticised on the ground that it is mostly concentrated on Western developed nations (Brush and Cooper, 2012). Other regions of the world, such as developing nations, are underexplored (Fielden and Davidson, 2005). Entrepreneurship is intrinsically associated with social aspects (Steyaert and Katz, 2004) and it has been established that studies on entrepreneurship in under-researched areas of the world can yield insightful findings (Jaim and Islam, 2018; Welter, 2019). The notion of the family can illustrate the issue. Whereas the traditional family considers only the household and parent–child relationships, the extended family comprises affines, who are related by marriage, along with kins, which include relatives at different distances (Nordqvist and Melin, 2010). Western societies generally consider the traditional nuclear family and family-related issues concerning women's entrepreneurship mostly revolve around the negative impacts of domestic responsibilities and childcare for women's businesses (Ahl, 2004; McGowan et al., 2012). As such, considering the family as the primary responsibility of women, work–family conflicts of women entrepreneurs in developed nations have been discussed (Shelton, 2006; Welter, 2004). Studies in developing nations further bring to the fore the influences of various relatives with regard to the entrepreneurial efforts of women (Al-Dajani and Marlow; 2010, Alexandre and Kharabsheh, 2019; Constantinidis et al., 2019; Xheneti, 2019). In considering the notion of the family, the experiences of women entrepreneurs of developing nations are substantially different from that of developed nations (Jaim, 2021b).

More specifically, different family members play strong positive and negative roles in women's sole proprietorship in developing nations, which is not the case in Western developed nations (Alexandre and Kharabsheh, 2019; Roomi et al., 2018; Williams and Gurtoo, 2011; Xheneti, 2019). Women in developing nations not only depend on their close female relatives – for instance, mothers-in-law – for managing responsibilities in the domestic sphere, but also rely on different family members in activities in the business domain (Alexandre and Kharabsheh, 2019; Roomi et al., 2018; Williams and Gurtoo, 2011; Xheneti, 2019). For example, women receive financial support and labour from family members (Roomi, 2013; Williams and Gurtoo; 2011, Xheneti, 2019). They also depend on their relatives in building networks in the masculine framework-based business arena in countries such as Bangladesh, Bahrain, and Pakistan (Constantinidis et al., 2019; Jaim, 2021c; Lindvert et al., 2017). Moreover, in certain developing nations, for instance Saudi Arabia, legal restrictions mean close male relatives must be involved in the women's ventures; international travel without a close male relative is restricted for women (Danish and Smith, 2012) and this condition eventually leads women to depend on menfolk of the family for their businesses. Women entrepreneurs further face challenges from the extended family in developing nations (Roomi et al., 2018; Xheneti, 2019). For example, in Pakistan, women seeking to initiate a business need permission from the natal family before their marriage and the in-law family after their marriage (Roomi et al., 2018). This decision is associated with the shame of the family, which is shaped by the socio-cultural norm 'izzat' (ibid.).

While the literature unveils insightful findings on different family members concerning women's firms, family members' influences on debt financing for small firms owned by women are yet to be explored. In general, financing businesses is important for women entrepreneurs (Coleman et al., 2019); the issue is particularly significant for women in developing nations, where entrepreneurship is regarded as a means to positively change the socio-economic status of people (Rindova et al., 2009). There is a proliferation of studies on microcredit programmes in developing nations (Jaim, 2019) and the interference of male family members in women's businesses has been highlighted (Aslanbeigui et al., 2010; Isaga, 2019; Schuler et al., 1998). For example, after receiving loans from microfinance institutions, many women feel obliged to give the funds to the menfolk of the family for guaranteed food supply or security at home (Goetz and Gupta, 1996; Lindvert et al., 2017). While studies on micro-level firms consider poor, almost illiterate women of developing nations, middle-class, educated women in small businesses are largely underexplored (Jaim, 2019). Hence, exploring the roles of family members in debt financing for small firms of women in developing nations is a useful line of enquiry.

As far as debt financing of women's ventures is concerned, it is worth noting that studies on developed nations have almost exclusively focused on bank officers' discrimination towards women entrepreneurs, overlooking any role of the family (Jaim, 2021a). Nonetheless, the extremely limited literature on developing nations (Ahmad, 2011; Constantinidis et al., 2019; Jaim, 2021a, 2022a) highlights the significant impact of family members on women entrepreneurs' access to bank loans. The assisting and constraining roles of husbands regarding the debt financing process are evident from the extant literature (ibid.). For example, the dominance of husbands in women's decision-making process with regard to accessing loans has been uncovered (Ahmad, 2011; Jaim, 2022a). Nevertheless, little is known regarding influences of other family members concerning this particular aspect of women's small businesses.

The existing literature (Alexandre and Kharabsheh, 2019; Jaim, 2021a; Roomi et al., 2018; Williams and Gurtoo, 2011; Xheneti et al., 2019) demonstrates diversified impacts of family members on women's businesses. Investigation of the roles of family members, excluding husbands, in the debt-financing process for women entrepreneurs in developing nations can provide insightful findings. For example, while it has already been established that women are dependent on husbands in dealing with stereotypical or other gendered problems in the public sphere in accessing bank loans (Jaim, 2021a), whether other family members can help women in the case of a husband's patriarchal practices bear examination. Such exploration is important because the literature makes evident severe patriarchal problems on the part of husbands concerning women's access to bank loans in developing nations (Jaim, 2022a). Besides, while husbands are found to be the guarantors of loans in some developing nations (Constantinidis et al., 2019; Jaim et al., 2015), it is not yet clear whether other relatives are also engaged in this crucial purpose.

It is worth noting that in some countries, such as Tanzania, business networks are kinship-based due to cultural restrictions on relationships with the opposite sex (Rutashobya et al., 2009). The involvement of male relatives in developing effective networks is also evident in Pakistan (Roomi, 2009). Given the restricted networks of women, investigating the roles of other relatives as guarantors is a rich line of enquiry.

Furthermore, questions can be raised regarding the negative intervention of family members other than husbands in the debt-financing process. Certain religious value-based restrictions on managing businesses of women have been addressed in the literature on developing countries (Jaim, 2019). It has been established that the religious obligation of the veil ('Purdah') restricts the potentiality of women's entrepreneurial endeavours in developing countries, such as Pakistan (Lindvert et al., 2017). This leads us to enquire whether there exists any other religious restriction imposed by family members regarding the specific issue of women's business loans in developing nations.

Therefore, this study explores the positive and negative roles of family members, excluding husbands, regarding women's access to bank loans for their small firms in a highly patriarchal developing nation. In so doing, this study is based on the feminist standpoint theory and the stance considers that the lives of women are substantially different from those of men (Harding, 2004). It also offers the opportunity to women to articulate social realities based on their own experiences in order to unveil gender subordination (Bowden and Mummery, 2009). Accordingly, this stance facilitates this study to bring to light women's experiences of gender subordination concerning access to bank loans for small businesses in both the private and public spheres, which they address with the support of their relatives. Simultaneously, it unveils how family members impose gendered barriers on women in their businesses' debt-financing processes. Moreover, women are oppressed in dissimilar ways in different parts of the world, resulting in distinct insights (Harding, 2004). As the feminist standpoint is based on the voice of women concerning their interpretation of social relations (Bowden and Mummery, 2009), it is an appropriate choice to explore underexplored areas, such as developing nations, to unveil gendered experiences within the context of the family.

This study is conducted on a developing nation, Bangladesh. In this highly patriarchal country, many women are subjected to private patriarchal issues, such as domestic violence, by different male relatives (Johnson and Das, 2009; Naved et al., 2011). Women are considered as dependent on their family members (Chowdhury, 2009) and this is not limited to domestic affairs. They depend on their relatives in order to avoid public patriarchal issues (Zaman, 1999). To empower women in this highly patriarchal context, microcredit is offered to poor women to initiate businesses, but deep-rooted patriarchal practices of family members concerning this issue are evident (Aslanbeigui et al., 2010; Schuler et al., 1998). Nonetheless, the microcredit programme has seen large-scale effectiveness and the government has initiated special package loans for middle-class women who are engaged in small businesses in Bangladesh (Bangladesh Bank, 2014). The loan is offered to women without collateral, with a low interest rate and with other such relaxed conditions. Accordingly, a significant number of women access loans for their small ventures through this scheme (Bangladesh Bank, 2016). The patronising and patriarchal roles of husbands concerning women's access to this particular loan package for small firms have already been revealed (Jaim, 2021a, 2022a). This feminist research explores how other family members positively or negatively influence the process of access to bank loans for women business-owners in the highly patriarchal developing nation of Bangladesh.

3.   METHODOLOGY

This feminist study uses the qualitative method. Qualitative research considers that the social world is inextricably related to individuals (Lincoln and Guba, 1985). In a qualitative study, it is important to recognise the social context of people in order to understand their accounts (Golafshani, 2003; Hammersley and Atkinson, 1995). This emphasis on social relationships means qualitative research is considered useful for this study that explores the impact of family members on the debt-financing experiences of women business-owners. Moreover, as feminist study is concerned with presenting the voices of women in order to generate knowledge (Frisby et al., 2009), the qualitative method is deemed an appropriate way of revealing women's experiences (Depner, 1981). In this study, the qualitative method supports exploring the roles of relatives through the voices of women in this underexplored context.

Selection of the respondents was driven by the research aim, which links women business-owners, family members and debt finance in the highly patriarchal developing country of Bangladesh. Purposive sampling was applied in the study to ensure certain characteristics of the research participants (Lincoln and Guba, 1985). The first criterion was that all the women were sole proprietors and founders of their small businesses. The issue of ownership is crucial as it ascertains that there was no formal involvement of other family members while exploring their influences on these ventures. The second condition is that the businesses were at the growth stage as, by that time, the women were supposed to have established their entrepreneurial potentiality and gained experience in that field. At the initial stage of a venture, women might be more dependent on their family members. The third issue was related to the debt-financing experiences. For consistency of experience among the participants, the study considered those women business-owners who had accessed bank loans not more than two years before data generation for this study. Finally, all women were married and were living with either a joint or unit family.

A list of clients accessing loans from the special loan scheme of IBDS Bank[2] was used to identify women business-owners. This bank was purposively chosen as it operates extensively in this particular loan sector. To ensure a good understanding of the debt-financing issue, this study also considered three women who acquired loans from the conventional loan scheme, which offers comparatively large loans (more than Tk. 25,00,000) with conditions applied irrespective of gender, such as loans at a higher interest rate, with collateral, and so forth. In total, 21 women business-owners were selected for this study. Table 3.1 below presents the information regarding the women and their businesses.

Data generation took place through face-to-face semi-structured interviews. This kind of interview offers interviewees flexibility to raise new concepts that are important for them (Musson, 2004). Simultaneously, semi-structured interviews facilitate interviewers to raise probing questions and to request detailed explanations (King, 2004). As the study is conducted in an underexplored context, and the influence of family members in women's businesses is an under-researched field, semi-structured interviews were deemed appropriate for exploring novel issues of this study. At the initial phase of the interviews, business and family-related issues were enquired into in order to ensure a good background against which to investigate in-depth aspects at the later stage. The interviews were generally conducted at the place of business or the home of the respondents, based on their convenience.

The interviews were conducted in Bangla, the mother tongue of the interviewer and the respondents, to enable effective communication. The voice-recorded data were transcribed verbatim, and then the interviews were translated into a form of English which made sense in that spoken language (Pilnick and Zayts, 2016). Some words were added in square brackets in the interviews to clarify the respondents' comments (Bryman, 2016). It is worth noting that translations were checked with the back-translation process (Brislin, 1980) and necessary consultations were made with linguistic experts to ensure the accuracy of the translation (Nes et al., 2010).

Thematic analysis has been applied to the data following the guidelines of Braun and Clarke (2006). The first step is to gain familiarity with the data (ibid.). I had a good understanding of the data due to the transcribing and translating activities. Codes were generated based on data-driven codes (Kvale and Brinkmann, 2009). In so doing, some recommendations of Ryan and Bernard (2003) were followed, such as emphasising similarities and dissimilarities of data. After reviewing and refining the codes, two themes were developed. The first theme, 'Positive Roles of Relatives', responds to the first research objec-

Table 3.1   Women's business-related and demographic information

SI No.	Name of woman business-owner	Type of business	Demographic characteristics		
			Age of woman	Educational background	Family type
1	Zarah	Boutique and Tailoring	50–55	Masters	Joint Family
2	Meera	Boutique and Tailoring	40–45	Masters	Joint Family
3	Zainab	Boutique and Tailoring	50–55	SSC	Unit Family
4	Mayesha	Boutique and Tailoring	35–40	MBA (Ongoing)	Unit Family
5	Fahliza	Boutique and Tailoring	50–55	Masters	Unit Family
6	Rasheda	Boutique and Tailoring	35–40	SSC	Unit Family
7	Nourin	Boutique and Tailoring	30–35	Undergraduate	Unit Family
8	Lara	Boutique and Tailoring	30–35	SSC	Joint Family
9	Faria	Boutique and Tailoring	30–35	Masters	Unit Family
10	Aleema	Boutique and Tailoring	60–65	SSC	Joint Family
11	Shyama	Boutique and Tailoring (Embroidery Factory)	40–45	Grade 7	Unit Family
12	Shabana	Dress and Handicrafts (Manufacturing and selling in the outlet)	50–55	HSC	Unit Family
13	Monika	Trading (Retailing curtains, bed-covers etc.)	25–30	SSC	Joint Family
14	Binita	Trading (Retailing curtains, bed-covers etc.)	50–55	Grade 10	Joint Family
15	Sumaiya	Trading (Retailing dress, toiletries, accessories etc.)	35–40	SSC	Unit Family
16	Nazneen	Trading (Retailing accessories, henna etc.)	35–40	SSC	Joint Family
17	Lucy	Trading (Retailing shoes)	35–40	Grade 8	Unit Family
18	Rubina	Beauty parlour	25–30	SSC	Joint Family
19	Pakiza	Beauty parlour	45–50	HSC	Joint Family
20	Neera	Grocery shop	25–30	Diploma	Unit Family
21	Runa	Manufacturing ground spice	45–50	Grade 8	Unit Family

Note: For confidentiality, pseudonyms are used. In Bangladesh, SSC (Secondary School Certificate) is the qualification achieved after Grade 10 and HSC (Higher Secondary Certificate) is the qualification to be eligible for university admission.

tive; the second, 'Negative Roles of Relatives', addresses the second research objective.

4.   FINDINGS

The interviews with women business-owners demonstrate that different relatives were involved in their experiences of debt financing in diversified ways. The empirical evidence unveils that the roles of the relatives were so strongly tied to women's debt-financing process that some of them even applied for bank loans as a result of their gendered experiences with family members in this highly patriarchal country. For instance, Mayesha illustrated that her reason for approaching banks for funds was based on her bitter experiences with her brothers in seeking informal loans. She brought to light how the patriarchal approach of male family members places women in a disadvantageous position in accessing informal funds:

> They [the brothers] know that I am doing much better compared to them. They know everything, but that [financial] help – nobody wants to do it. It has been found that one brother has incurred loss; still another brother is helping him. But, the sister is shining – they will not give [money] to that sister. (Mayesha)

Mayesha's comments reveal her brothers' discriminatory attitude towards her. Given the patriarchal norms of the country, lending decisions are made on the basis of gender of the sibling instead of their potentiality as a businessperson. It is further disclosed that, in a society where gender subordination is deeply rooted in the family, the brothers could not accept their sister's success because of her gender. The gender subordination of women in society in accessing funds from the family is clearly articulated in the quotes. Mayesha explained that it would be convenient for her to access a loan before the peak season of her boutique business to have a good return during the specified period. She preferred informal loans from her brothers, considering the debt-financing process as a complicated and lengthy one. While informal loans generally charge little or no interest, Mayesha offered a high amount of interest if she was supported. Nevertheless, her brothers did not agree to lend her anything. Mayesha shared her experiences:

> For example, now I need money for my business. My [peak] season is coming. My brother owns a lot of money. If I ask him, he can give me Tk. 100,000 for three months. Still, I am not getting it – even I have given such an offer that I shall give the double amount of FDR [Fixed Deposit Receipt] monthly – but I didn't get money. For that reason, I approached the bank. (Mayesha)

Mayesha's example brings to light why some women are compelled to go through the complicated debt-financing process even though the funds might not be received in time to meet their business needs. While the reason for accessing debt finance is inherently linked to the gendered experiences of some women within their family, the study uncovers diversified influences of family members concerning this process. A range of positive and negative roles of different relatives are articulated in the experiences of women business-owners in the highly patriarchal developing country that is Bangladesh. Table 3.2 below maps the issues.

4.1   Positive Roles of Relatives

The empirical evidence reveals diversified positive roles of family members concerning women's debt-financing experiences. Relatives were found to support women in dealing with patriarchal obstacles put in place by other family members in the private sphere and to help women meet different requirements of the banks in the public arena. Some women also sought assistance from their relatives for other loan-related issues, such as accessing information concerning specific debt-finance schemes. While the literature (Jaim, 2021a) has already disclosed that many women have a strong sense of dependence on their husbands regarding accessing bank loans in Bangladesh, this research brings to light the patronising roles of different other family members concerning this issue.

4.1.1   Dealing with husbands' patriarchal problems
While patriarchal practices of husbands regarding accessing bank loans in Bangladesh have already been addressed in the literature (Jaim, 2022a), a few women business-owners in this research narrated how they dealt with the husband's problems related to guarantors, with the support of their children. Study respondents mentioned that the bank demanded the husband to be the first guarantor of a loan to a woman business-owner. If the husband did not want to support access to loans, the woman was faced with problems in applying for the debt finance. The issue was explained in the words of Shabana: 'My husband was never my guarantor indeed. He does not like it. [In his view:] "Doing business! On top of that, taking loans!" He does not like that I would take a loan. [...] but without him, I could not take a loan. It's a problem.'

From Shabana's comments it is evident that the husband was considering the business in a negative way and had a strong dismissive approach concerning accessing business loans. The patriarchal approach of the husband was clearly reflected in his teasing tone, as noted by Shabana. Consequently, Shabana could not meet the guarantor requirement of the bank in applying for the loan. She further explained her previous experiences regarding a loan application to a non-bank financial institution. The officer did not provide her with a loan due to the negative attitude of her husband. The lack of financial aid eventually had an adverse impact on her business. A few years later, she said to that officer: 'If you [had given] me the loan at that time, I would do much better, but you didn't provide [me any loan].' The quotes demonstrate the loss of opportunity for the progress of the business with external funds. The disadvantaged business position was manifested in the patriarchal practices of the husband. Shabana expressed her deep grievances concerning this issue during the interview. Finally, a bank considered the condition of Shabana and asked her to provide a bank officer as her guarantor: 'bring a bank officer.' Shabana's daughter, who was a bank officer, became the guarantor: 'My daughter just joined [the bank]. So, if she becomes the guarantor, the loan will be provided. My daughter became [the guarantor].' Nevertheless, in this highly patriarchal context, a female guarantor was not deemed sufficient. When Shabana's son became another guarantor, along with his sister, the loan was sanctioned. The guarantor requirement of the husband was fulfilled by the children with the particular condition of a professional qualification. Runa's case echoes these findings. The son was a bank officer who became a guarantor as Runa's husband was not interested in the business. These examples bring to the fore how women overcome the gendered barriers of certain close relatives, particularly husbands, through the support of other close family members in accessing debt finance in this highly patriarchal context.

4.1.2   Relatives as guarantors of loans

Whereas it has already been established that meeting the guarantor requirement is a potential problem for women business-owners in Bangladesh (Chowdhury et al., 2018), this research reveals the strong support of the family members in seeking to address this problem. While the extant literature (Constantinidis et al., 2019; Jaim et al., 2015) simply mentions the close male family member as the guarantor of loans to women business-owners in developing countries, this study precisely unfolds how various relatives were involved in addressing the guarantor requirement of the bank. This research unveils the roles of different relatives concerning the issues of first guarantors as well as other guarantors. As far as the first guarantor is concerned, the bank stipulated that this was required to be the husband, but that condition could not be applied to Aleema and Zarah. As Aleema was a widow, there was no scope to consider her husband. In the case of Zarah, her husband's age meant he could not sign any contract. In both women's cases, their sons were the first guarantor, as a close male relative. The absence or inability of the husband to meet the formal obligation of the women business-owner's loan application was addressed by the son. Thus, the study brings to light the conditions and circumstances that involve different family members as the guarantor of women's business loans. The only exceptional case was Fahliza. Her sister was the first guarantor despite the eligibility of the husband.

Furthermore, the bank required additional guarantors for loans to women's small firms. Generally, the bank considered those as appropriate guarantors who were businessmen or government job-holders or house-owners or officers of a private bank. A large number of women (13) reported that various relatives became the additional guarantors for bank loans. For instance, when Binita was asked about her second guarantor, she briefly responded: 'My son-in-law was there.' From the narrative accounts of the women, it is revealed that the relatives included their father, brother, son, husband's nephew, father-in-law, brother-in-law, and so on. While the literature (Constantinidis et al., 2019; Jaim et al., 2015) mentions husbands, fathers and brothers as guarantors for women's business loans in developing nations, it is evident from this study that a large number of other family members are involved in the debt-financing process in this highly patriarchal country.

4.1.3   Family property in addressing the collateral issue

While the literature has already demonstrated the constraining roles of family members regarding collateral issues for women business-owners, some women in this study drew attention to the assisting role of relatives concerning this aspect. It is widely recognised that women in Bangladesh face problems of inheritance and many do not possess property (Kabeer, 1999; Kibria, 1995). In considering this issue, Nourin highlighted that many women business-owners do not operate their businesses on their own property. The requirement for a rented business place brings complications for the bank loan process. Nourin's opinion is also supported by the empirical evidence of a previous study in Bangladesh (Chowdhury et al., 2018). By raising this issue, Nourin illustrated with examples the advantageous position of some other women in relation to their relatives' property:

> [The officer asks:] 'Where is your shop?' [The response is] 'Rented'. They [officers] will call the landlord of the shop and they will talk to him – whether you [woman business-owners] are paying the rent or not. They will ask others around [neighbouring businesspersons]. That process is a comparatively lengthy one. It is very difficult to get a loan for women – not easy. But for us – it's easy. [The officer says:] 'Ok. All right. You are a permanent resident here. You have a house. Oh! You have your father's house. You have your father-in-law's house in here. We don't have any question.' (Nourin)

By elucidating the problems of women business-owners in general, Nourin explained how some women business-owners like her could acquire loans for the property of their close relatives. When a woman's father and father-in-law own houses in that city, the bank officers prefer that woman to sanction a loan.

It is worth noting that the special loan package is offered to women without collateral. Nevertheless, Nourin's comments indicate that the property of the close family members provides a sense of security to the bank in considering the woman as a potential loan applicant.

Moreover, Nazneen described how bank officers went to her father-in-law's house to inspect it, though she lived separately at another house. She submitted the necessary documents to provide evidence of the father-in-law's ownership and possession of the house, as she asserted: 'I had to give the electricity bill of my father-in-law's house – then I had to give the papers of the property tax. Then duplicate [of the deed] of my father-in-law's house. These [papers] were all I had to show to them.' This reflects the strong support of the father-in-law, who provided all these important documents for Nazneen's bank loan application. It can be concluded that while the collateral constraint for bank loans is a well-recognised issue for women business-owners (Marlow and Patton, 2005), these women's examples indicate that some women business-owners were in a privileged position through their support from close male relatives in this developing country.

4.1.4   Other assistance

Different family members were found to assist women in some other ways. Whereas strong interference of some husbands in deciding upon access to bank loans in Bangladesh is revealed in the literature (Jaim, 2021a), this study brings to light that a few women discussed their loan decisions with their children. For instance, Runa stated: 'I discussed with my son. I didn't discuss it with my husband because he is out of reach. I said to my son. He said – take it [the loan].' It is worth noting that Runa's husband never showed interest in her business. She involved her son in the decision-making process of the loan.

Furthermore, while a lack of information regarding bank loan schemes is an issue for many women business-owners in Bangladesh (Ahmed, 2014), Faria noted that she came to know about the special loan package through her brother-in-law, who was a bank officer. A study in the same context (Jaim, 2021c) also reveals that some women access information regarding the special debt-financing facility from bank officers from their informal community. Faria further received constructive suggestions regarding choosing a bank from a relative who supported her with his banking industry experience. She described the instance:

> When I said to my brother-in-law, he told me: 'You can take [the loan] from that bank [IBDS Bank]. That bank disburses a large amount of loan.' At first, I thought that I would take [the loan] from his bank. Then he said: 'Century Bank doesn't provide good facilities. Compared to this one, IBDS Bank is better.' (Faria)

Table 3.2   Positive and negative roles of family members in women's access to debt finance

	Involved relatives	Specific bank loan issues	Explanation
Positive roles			
Dealing with husband's patriarchal problems	Children	Guarantor	Children's support in meeting bank requirements when husbands exerted patriarchal practices by negative approach to acting as guarantors
Relatives as guarantors of loans	Father, brother, son, sister, daughter, father-in-law, brother-in-law, son-in-law, husband's nephew, and so on	Guarantor	Different relatives' patronage concerning guarantor requirement of loans
Family property in addressing the collateral issue	Father, father-in-law	Collateral	Certain relatives' ownership of house in the city addressed the collateral issue
Other assistance	Son, brother-in-law, etc.	Diversified issues	Relatives' assistance in accessing loan information, deciding upon loan acquisition, accomplishing loan application tasks
Negative roles			
Religious restrictions on taking loans	Father-in-law, mother-in-law	Interest on loans	In-laws' reservations against taking loans for religious reasons negatively influenced women's experiences
Inheritance problem regarding collateral issue	Brother	Collateral	Brothers' deprivation of the property of father led to collateral crisis
Other problems	Son-in-law and others	Loan repayment and other issues	Sons-in-laws' probable patriarchal practices towards daughters adversely shaped the loan repayment issue

While it is evident that many women seek help from their husbands to deal with different problems related to accessing loans in Bangladesh (Jaim, 2021a), a few women in this study mentioned their sons supporting them in the bank loan application process. When Shyama was asked about approaching a bank for a loan or preparing or collecting documents for the loan application, she explained her son's assistance concerning these tasks: 'I did these [activities] with the help of my son.'

4.2   Negative Roles of Relatives

The narrative accounts of some women disclose the negative influences of some relatives in women's experiences of accessing bank loans in this highly patriarchal country. The problems emerged from the in-laws as well as the natal family. There is also evidence of concern regarding patriarchal issues on the part of sons-in-law. While the literature has already established the strong negative roles played by husbands of many women in their access to bank loans (Jaim, 2022a), this study brings to the fore how other family members can also adversely affect the process.

4.2.1   Religious restrictions on taking loans

The interviews with a few women unveiled the negative interference of in-laws concerning the debt-financing process based on their religious values. While Islam supports profit sharing on an investment, it does not allow taking interest on loans (Rasyid, 2020). Given this religious restriction, some elderly family members did not like loaning to women for their businesses. For instance, the negative approach of her in-laws concerning accessing loans was depicted in comments from Meera:

> My father-in-law, mother-in-law never took loans. They built houses, did many things but they didn't take any loan. They don't like it. If they will take loans, they will have to pay the interest. From the Islamic rules, the interest is not good. It is Haram.[3] It is not good to do that. That's it! They don't like taking loans at all. In fact, as many times as we [my husband and I] took loans for my business, even when we took the loan for the third time, we did not inform them. We actually did it by hiding it from them. (Meera)

It is evident that despite the in-laws' negative attitude concerning formal loans, Meera accessed debt finance. Although the in-laws did not directly set barriers to Meera accessing bank loans, she tried to avoid any unwanted situation by concealing this issue from them. In other words, she needed to hide the instance from her in-laws because of the patriarchal norms in the society. The scenario implies that religion played a role in restricting the access to loans due to the interest payment issue while the in-laws indirectly influenced Meera's debt-financing process due to their religious concern, executed based on their patriarchal position in the family.

In the case of Lara, the mother-in-law was aware of the bank loans for her business, and, she considered the issue negatively. Her negative approach was articulated in the quotes of Lara: 'She [the mother-in-law] also says that interest is "haram". My mother-in-law says – I do the business with the money on which I pay interest.' The mother-in-law was so annoyed with the issue that she consistently reminded Lara about the loan. The teasing approach of the mother-in-law was reflected in the statement of Lara: 'She [the mother-in-law] always says – I live on loans. I live on borrowing money from others.' Whereas the literature (Ahmad, 2011; Ahmad and Naimat, 2011; Lindvert et al., 2017) addresses religious concerns regarding the influence of restricted mobility or the veil on the businesses of women, this example more precisely uncovers in-laws' negative approaches regarding the specific debt-financing issue for women's businesses.

4.2.2   Inheritance problem regarding collateral issue

While collateral for bank loans is a problematic issue for many women in Bangladesh (Chowdhury et al., 2018), a few women in this study raised the issue of patriarchal experiences in their personal lives. They mentioned the negative role of the natal family concerning property inheritance, which is related to the constraint of utilising the asset as collateral. Zarah put in plain words the inheritance law for Muslim women in Bangladesh:

> They [women] have less property. […] The person who has not got the property from the inheritance, cannot provide it as collateral. According to the rule, the woman should get the property. If the father is alive, she can't get it. She gets it in the absence of the father. A woman – a Muslim woman will have to get half of the property of her brother. But in reality, they don't get the property in our country. Brothers don't let them to get it. (Zarah)

Zarah's comments demonstrate that, after the death of their father, Muslim women are officially allowed to have a share of the property; nonetheless, brothers do not permit women to have property in this highly patriarchal society. It has already been established that, although Muslim women are entitled to inherit property in Bangladesh, generally women cannot acquire it or are forced to waive it in favour of their brothers (Kabeer, 1999; Kibria, 1995). According to Zarah, as women have less property, they have a lack of assets to offer as collateral when applying for a large loan. Aspirational and growth-oriented women business-owners cannot apply for loans due to the prevailing gendered norms that permeate their personal lives. Zarah's comments reinforce the findings of another study (Jaim, 2022a) that reveals the oppressive roles of the natal family in depriving women of their legal right to property, resulting in problems when seeking collateral for business loans.

4.2.3 Other problems

There were some miscellaneous problems mentioned by a few women business-owners. The case of Aleema can be cited here. After the death of her husband, Aleema initiated her business to support her family. Her son played an important role both in her business and her access to debt finance. Nonetheless, Aleema highlighted that she intentionally had little involvement from her married daughters and her sons-in-law regarding the bank loans process. She particularly highlighted the financial difficulties of her business during a period of political unrest in the country. During that time she was facing difficulty in repaying loans, as was the case for many women business-owners in Bangladesh (Jaim, 2022b). However, she would not think of seeking financial aid from her sons-in-law. Aleema poignantly expressed her position:

> Now, where will you [I] go? To the sons-in-law? If you [I] go to the sons-in-law, they will say tomorrow – 'What's that, Mother?' […] [They will say to the daughters:] 'Your mother came to me to ask for money!' They may not insult my daughters. Again they may do it. I am not like that type of woman. (Aleema)

Aleema's comments demonstrate that she worried her sons-in-law might insult her daughters due to their financial contribution to the business. She did not want to involve her sons-in-law during this critical financial period due to the probable patriarchal practices concerning her daughters. Her quote 'I am not like that type of woman' indicates that she did not place her daughters in a 'disgraceful' position due to her problems with the bank loan repayment. The limited literature (Ahmad, 2011; Constantinidis et al., 2019; Jaim, 2021a, 2022a) on debt financing of women business-owners in developing nations that seeks to explore gender subordination is limited to issues related to women owners themselves, but this example extends the understanding to the probable patriarchal problems of their daughters and illustrates how the concern to protect daughters from patriarchal issues can shape women's loan-accessing process.

5.   DISCUSSION

This feminist study substantially advances understandings of women's entrepreneurship with reference to the family. Research regarding women's entrepreneurship is mostly concentrated on developed nations (Brush and Cooper, 2012), where the body of literature pivots on the nuclear family with regard to familial aspects. This research substantially extends the understanding by revealing the roles of different relatives, particularly extended family members, in women's attempts to access bank loans for their sole proprietorship. The literature (Ahl, 2004; McGowan et al., 2012; Shelton, 2006; Welter, 2004) on women's entrepreneurship in Western developed nations that seeks to discuss the role of the family concerning businesses is mostly concentrated on women's domestic responsibilities and child-rearing activities in terms of the negative impact of these issues on their firm operation or work–family conflict. The current research potentially enriches the body of knowledge on women's businesses by revealing different roles of the relatives, beyond the issue of homebound responsibilities. While the Western nations-based literature tends to focus on the indirect influences of husbands or such close male relatives on women's businesses by concentrating mostly on the domestic activities of women (Jaim, 2022a), this study extends the view by bringing to the fore how different family members are actively involved in the ventures of women in a developing country. Within the specific context of debt financing, whereas the studies on Western developed nations have almost exclusively focused on issues regarding bank officers and women entrepreneurs (Jaim, 2021a), this study establishes the significance of the family in this process by demonstrating positive and negative roles of different family members.

This research brings to light novel insights on patronising roles of different family members in women's debt-financing processes in a developing country context. For example, studies (Ahmad, 2011; Constantinidis et al., 2019; Jaim, 2021a, 2022a) in developing nations reveal the assistance of family members by overlooking their roles in overcoming the patriarchal practices of menfolk of the family, and this research sheds further light on this issue. Husbands are found to play significant negative roles in women's debt-financing processes in developing nations (Jaim, 2022a) and it is important to explore whether their adverse effects on the firms can be mitigated. This research addresses the auspicious gap of understanding by revealing ways in which close relatives can support women in accessing loans, against the patriarchal practices of the husbands. While assisting roles of family members concerning women's debt financing in developing nations have elsewhere been discussed in terms of dealing with public patriarchal issues (Jaim, 2021a), this feminist research advances the understanding by critically examining the interplay of the relatives in addressing patriarchal problems in the private sphere.

The study also generates valuable insights into the negative interference of relatives of women seeking to access bank loans. While their religion, Islam, is a recurring issue in influencing women's entrepreneurship, imposing various restrictions in developing countries (Jaim, 2019), this research potentially extends the understanding within the particular context of debt financing for small firms by disclosing the religious restriction on taking loans with interest. Moreover, in the extant literature (Constantinidis et al., 2019; Jaim, 2021a, 2022a) the discussion on the involvement of family members in the debt-financing process is limited to only the gendered experiences of women entrepreneurs, whereas this feminist research potentially advances the under-standing by considering interwoven relationships of family members with the debt-financing process. It generates novel insights into how the bank loan process may result in patriarchal problems of close relatives of women, and how this concern shapes women's experiences of debt financing. Thus, this feminist research enriches the existing knowledge by critically scrutinising the debt-financing process within the familial context, unveiling gendered experi-ences of women entrepreneurs and their relatives in a comprehensive manner.

This research yields unique insights by unveiling the influences of various relatives in the debt-financing process in a developing nation. The body of literature (Alexandre and Kharabsheh, 2019; Constantinidis et al., 2019; Jaim, 2021c; Jaim, 2022a; Roomi et al., 2018; Williams and Gurtoo, 2011) on developing countries generally mentions certain blood-related relatives (father, brother) and other relatives by marriage (husband, mother-in-law, father-in-law) in relation to women's businesses. More specifically, the limited literature (Constantinidis et al., 2019; Jaim, 2021a, 2022a) on debt financing in this context only recognises the requirement of husband, father or brother. This research substantially extends the view by providing examples of a range of family members that include the relatives of the next generation of women, for instance, children or sons-in-law, and distant relatives such as a husband's nephew or brother-in-law. While the existing literature remains silent about the direct involvement of female relatives in women's business activities concern-ing external organisations, this study brings to light that, in a highly patriarchal country, female relatives – for instance, a sister or daughter – can also play important roles by acting as guarantors of bank loans for women in business.

The research advances the understanding on this topic by disclosing that in such a context, the assistance of many relatives is required when women seek to access bank loans for their small firms. In so doing, this research reinforces the findings of previous studies (Jaim, 2021c; Roomi, 2009; Rutashobya et al., 2009; Xheneti, 2019) which have established that women entrepre-neurs depend on their networks of relatives in highly patriarchal developing nations. It further extends the understanding by unveiling unique insights into the diversified ways in which different family members assist women in the process of accessing bank loans. Simultaneously, the study enhances the current knowledge by demonstrating that familial relationships in such countries of this country let different family members negatively influence the debt-financing experiences of women.

6.   POLICY IMPLICATIONS

The study has significant policy implications. The experiences of women business-owners in Bangladesh demonstrate that they generally require the assistance of different family members in accessing bank loans. This scenario implies that there might be some potential women business-owners who cannot apply for loans because of a lack of support from family members. While the government has expressed concern about women's access to bank loans (Bangladesh Bank, 2014), it should pay further attention to the debt-financing process to consider the ways of extending support to other potential women. For example, this study unveils that many women asked a number of relatives to become guarantors. Banks might relax the condition of the second guarantor to facilitate women. In sum, by critically considering the findings of the research, policies can be designed and implemented to effectively support women in gaining easy access to loans for small firms.

7.   CONCLUSION

This feminist research potentially extends the developed nations-based women's entrepreneurship scholarship by unveiling the roles played by different family members in relation to the businesses of women in developing nations. Whereas the family issues of women business-owners in developed nations are mostly discussed in terms of the impact of homebound responsibilities on their businesses (Ahl, 2004; Jaim, 2022a), this research brings to light diversified roles of family members regarding women's firms. This study contributes to the prevailing knowledge within the specific context of debt financing, whereas the developed nations-centric literature overlooks the role of the family concerning this process (Jaim et al., 2015). Further, while the limited literature (Alexandre and Kharabsheh, 2019; Roomi et al., 2018; Williams and Gurtoo, 2011; Xheneti, 2019) on developing nations reveals the influences of a few close relatives in women's ventures, this study significantly extends the understanding by unveiling diversified positive and negative roles of a range of family members in women's businesses. Considering the entwined relationship of the family and women in developing nations (Jaim, 2021b), it is time for future researchers to put the spotlight squarely on the roles of family members in different aspects of women's businesses to reveal their gendered experiences. Now it is essential to move beyond the nuclear family perspective which is imbued with the Western developed societal norms and extend consideration to family issues in developing nations in order to critically advance the understanding of women's entrepreneurship scholarship.

NOTES

1.   The study was a part of a larger project and was principally funded by the University of Nottingham, UK. The author acknowledges the financial support of the university in conducting this research. The author is also grateful to the

respondents who allowed her to delve into their personal and family lives; this research would not be possible without their support.
2. Pseudonyms were used for all the banks mentioned in this study.
3. 'Haram' indicates something is forbidden by Islamic law (Halal Certifications Services, 2016).

REFERENCES

Ahl, H. (2004), *The Scientific Reproduction of Gender Inequality: A Discourse Analysis of Research Texts on Women's Entrepreneurship*, Stockholm: Liber.

Ahmad, H.M. and Naimat, S. (2011), 'Networking and Women Entrepreneurs: Beyond Patriarchal Traditions', *African Journal of Business Management*, 5, 5784–91.

Ahmad, S.Z. (2011), 'Evidence of the Characteristics of Women Entrepreneurs in the Kingdom of Saudi Arabia', *International Journal of Gender and Entrepreneurship*, 3(2), 123–43.

Al-Dajani, H. and Marlow, S. (2010), 'Impact of Women's Home-Based Enterprise on Family Dynamics: Evidence from Jordan', *International Small Business Journal*, 28(5), 470–86.

Alexandre, L. and Kharabsheh, R. (2019), 'The evolution of female entrepreneurship in the Gulf Cooperation Council, the case of Bahrain', *International Journal of Gender and Entrepreneurship*, 11(4), 390–407.

Aslanbeigui, N., Oakes, G. and Uddin, N. (2010), 'Assessing Microcredit in Bangladesh: A Critique of the Concept of Empowerment', *Review of Political Economy*, 22, 181–204.

Bangladesh Bank (2014), 'SME financing in small and women entrepreneur sector is in increasing trend', accessed 1 September 2014 at www.bangladeshbank .org/aboutus/dept/sme/recentactivities.php.

Bangladesh Bank (2016), 'Annual Report 2016–17', accessed 6 August 2016 at www .bb.org.bd/openpdf.php.

Bowden, P. and Mummery, J. (2009), *Understanding Feminism*, New York: Acumen Press.

Braun, V. and Clarke, V. (2006), 'Using Thematic Analysis in Psychology', *Qualitative Research in Psychology*, 3, 77–101.

Brislin, R.W. (1980), 'Translation and Content Analysis of Oral and Written Materials', in: Triandis, H.C. and Berry, J.W. (eds), *Handbook of Cross-Cultural Psychology*, Boston: Allyn and Bacon.

Brush, C.G. and Cooper, S.Y. (2012), 'Female Entrepreneurship and Economic Development: An International Perspective', *Entrepreneurship & Regional Development*, 24(1–2), 1–6.

Bryman, A. (2016), *Social Research Methods*, Oxford: Oxford University Press.

Chowdhury, F.D. (2009), 'Theorising Patriarchy: The Bangladesh Context', *Asian Journal of Social Science*, 37, 599–622.

Chowdhury, T.Y., Yeasmin, A. and Ahmed, Z. (2018), 'Perception of Women Entrepreneurs to Accessing Bank Credit', *Journal of Global Entrepreneurship Research*, 8, 1–18.

Coleman, S.C., Orser, H.B., Foss, L. and Welter, F. (2019), 'Policy Support for Women Entrepreneurs' Access to Financial Capital: Evidence from Canada, Germany, Ireland, Norway, and the United States', *Journal of Small Business Management*, 57, 296–322.

Constantinidis, C., Lebègue, T., El Abboubi, M. and Salman, N. (2019), 'How Families Shape Women's Entrepreneurial Success in Morocco: An Intersectional Study', *International Journal of Entrepreneurial Behavior and Research*, 25(8), 1786–808.

Danish, A.Y. and Smith, H.L. (2012), 'Female Entrepreneurship in Saudi Arabia: Opportunities and Challenges', *International Journal of Gender and Entrepreneurship*, 4(3), 216–35.

Depner, C. (1981), 'Towards the Further Development of Feminist Psychology', *The Mid-Winter Conference of the Association for Women in Psychology*. Boston.

Fielden, S. and Davidson, M. (2005), *International Handbook of Women and Small Business Entrepreneurship*, Cheltenham: Edward Elgar Publishing.

Frisby, W., Maguire, P. and Reid, C. (2009), 'The "F" Word Has Everything to Do with It: How Feminist Theories Inform Action Research', *Action Research*, 7, 13–29.

Goetz, A.M. and Gupta, R.S. (1996), 'Who Takes the Credit? Gender, Power, and Control Over Loan Use in Rural Credit Programs in Bangladesh', *World Development*, 24, 45–63.

Golafshani, N. (2003), 'Understanding Reliability and Validity in Qualitative Research', *The Qualitative Report*, 8(4), 597–607.

Hammersley, M. and Atkinson, P. (1995), *Ethnography: Principles in Practice*, London, Routledge.

Harding, S. (2004), 'Introduction: Standpoint Theory as a Site of Political, Philosophic, and Scientific Debate', in: Harding, S. (ed.), *The Feminist Standpoint Theory Reader: Intellectual & Political Controversies*, London: Routledge.

Hasan, M. (2019), 'Women Entrepreneurs Seek More Bank Loans', accessed 3 June 2019 at www.dhakatribune.com/ business/2019/03/10/women-entrepreneurs-seek-more-bank-loans.

Isaga, N. (2019), 'Start-up Motives and Challenges Facing Female Entrepreneurs in Tanzania', *International Journal of Gender and Entrepreneurship*, 11(2), 102–19.

Jaim, J. (2019), 'Patriarchal Practices of Male Family Members: Women Business-owners in Bangladesh', Nottingham Business School, Nottingham, UK.

Jaim, J. (2021a), 'Bank Loans Access for Women Business-owners in Bangladesh: Obstacles and Dependence on Husbands', *Journal of Small Business Management*, 59(S1), S16–S41.

Jaim, J. (2021b), 'Women's Entrepreneurship in Developing Countries from a Family Perspective: Past and Future', *Global Business and Organizational Excellence*, 41(1), 31–45.

Jaim, J. (2021c), 'Does Network Work? Women Business-owners' Access to Information Regarding Financial Support from Development Programme in Bangladesh', *Business Strategy & Development*, 4(2), 148–58.

Jaim, J. (2022a), 'All About Patriarchal Segregation of Work Regarding Family? Women Business-owners in Bangladesh', *Journal of Business Ethics*, 175(2), 231–45.

Jaim, J. (2022b), 'Problems of Political Unrest: Women in Small Businesses in Bangladesh', *New England Journal of Entrepreneurship*, ahead-of-print.

Jaim, J. and Islam, M.N. (2018), 'Context Specificities in Entrepreneurship Research', *Journal of Entrepreneurship, Business and Economics*, 6(1), 59–77.

Jaim, J., Martin, L. and Swail, J. (2015), 'Does Family Matter? Debt Finance and Women Business-owners in Bangladesh', *British Academy of Management*. Portsmouth, UK.

Johnson, K.B. and Das, M.B. (2009), 'Spousal Violence in Bangladesh as Reported by Men: Prevalence and Risk Factors', *Journal of Interpersonal Violence*, 24, 977–95.

Kabeer, N. (1999), *The Conditions and Consequences of Choice: Reflections on the Measurement of Women's Empowerment*, UNRISD.

Khatun, S. (2020), 'How We Combated Violence against Women in 2019', accessed 4 January 2021 at www.thedailystar.net/opinion/news/how-we-combated-violence -against-women-2019-1846438.

Kibria, N. (1995), 'Culture, Social Class, and Income Control in the Lives of Women Garment Workers in Bangladesh', *Gender and Society*, 9(3), 289–309.

King, N. (2004), 'Using Interviews in Qualitative Research', in: Cassell, C. and Symon, G. (eds), *Essential Guide to Qualitative Methods in Organizational Research.* London: Sage.

Kvale, S. and Brinkmann, S. (2009), *Interviews: Learning the Craft of Qualitative Research Interviewing*, London, Sage.

Lincoln, Y.S. and Guba, E.G. (1985), *Naturalistic Inquiry*, Beverly Hills, CA: Sage.

Lindvert, M., Patel, P.C. and Wincent, J. (2017), 'Struggling with Social Capital: Pakistani Women Micro Entrepreneurs' Challenges in Acquiring Resources', *Entrepreneurship & Regional Development*, 29(7–8), 759–90.

Marlow, S. and Patton, D. (2005), 'All Credit to Men? Entrepreneurship, Finance, and Gender', *Entrepreneurship, Theory and Practice*, 29(6), 717–35.

McGowan, P., Lewis, C., Cooper, S. and Greenan, K. (2012), 'Female Entrepreneurship and the Management of Business and Domestic Roles; Motivations, Expectations and Realities', *Entrepreneurship and Regional Development*, 24(1–2), 53–72.

Musson, G. (2004), 'Life: Histories', *in:* Cassell, C. and Symon, G. (eds), *Essential Guide to Qualitative Methods in Organizational Research*, London: Sage.

Naved, R.T., Huque, H., Farah, S. and Shuvra, M.M.R. (2011), *Men's Attitude and Practices regarding Gender and Violence against Women in Bangladesh*, Dhaka: UNFPA.

Nes, F.V., Abma, T., Jonsson, H. and Deeg, D. (2010), 'Language Differences in Qualitative Research: Is Meaning Lost in Translation?' *European Journal of Ageing*, 7, 313–16.

Nordqvist, M. and Melin, L. (2010), 'Entrepreneurial Families and Family Firms', *Entrepreneurship & Regional Development*, 22(3–4), 211–39.

Pilnick, A. and Zayts, O. (2016), 'Advice, Authority and Autonomy in Shared Decision-Making in Antenatal Screening: The Importance of Context', *Sociology of Health and Illness*, 38, 343–59.

Rasyid, D. (2020), 'Interest Loan in the Perspective of Islamic Jurisprudence (Comparative Studies)', *Jurnal Sosial & Budaya Syar-i*, 7.

Rindova, V., Barry, D. and Ketchen Jr, D.K. (2009), 'Introduction to Special Topic Forum: Entrepreneuring as Emancipation', *Academy of Management Review*, 34, 477–91.

Roomi, M.A. (2009), 'Impact of Socio-cultural Values and Traditions on the Growth of Women-owned Enterprises in Pakistan', *Frontiers of Entrepreneurship Research*, 29, 473–95.

Roomi, M.A. (2013), 'Entrepreneurial Capital, Social Values and Cultural Traditions: Exploring the Growth of Women-owned Enterprises in Pakistan', *International Small Business Journal*, 31(2), 175–91.

Roomi, M.A., Rehman, S. and Henry, C. (2018), 'Exploring the Normative Context for Women's Entrepreneurship in Pakistan: A Critical Analysis', *International Journal of Gender and Entrepreneurship*, 10(2), 158–80.

Rutashobya, L.K., Allan, I.S. and Nilsson, K. (2009), 'Gender, Social Networks, and Entrepreneurial Outcomes in Tanzania', *Journal of African Business*, 10, 67–83.

Ryan, G.W. and Bernard, H.R. (2003), 'Techniques to Identify Themes', *Field Methods*, 15, 85–109.

Schuler, S.R., Hashemi, S.M. and Badal, S.H. (1998), 'Men's Violence against Women in Rural Bangladesh: Undermined or Exacerbated by Microcredit Programmes?', *Development in Practice*, 8, 148–57.

Shelton, L.M. (2006), 'Female Entrepreneurs, Work–Family Conflict, and Venture Performance: New Insights into the Work–Family Interface', *Journal of Small Business Management*, 44(2), 285–97.

Steyaert, C. and Katz, J. (2004), 'Reclaiming the Space of Entrepreneurship in Society: Geographical, Discursive and Social Dimensions', *Entrepreneurship & Regional Development*, 16(3), 179–96.

Walby, S. (1990), *Theorizing Patriarchy*, Oxford: Basil Blackwell.

Welter, F. (2004), 'The Environment for Female Entrepreneurship in Germany', *Journal of Small Business and Enterprise Development*, 11(2), 212–21.

Welter, F. (2019), 'Introduction', in: Welter, F. (ed.), *Entrepreneurship and Context*, Cheltenham: Edward Elgar Publishing.

Williams, C.C. and Gurtoo, A. (2011), 'Women Entrepreneurs in the Indian Informal Sector', *International Journal of Gender and Entrepreneurship*, 3(1), 6–22.

Xheneti, M., Karki, S.T. and Madden, A. (2019), 'Negotiating Business and Family Demands within a Patriarchal Society: The Case of Women Entrepreneurs in the Nepalese Context', *Entrepreneurship & Regional Development*, 31(3–4), 259–78.

Zaman, H. (1999), 'Violence against Women in Bangladesh: Issues and Responses', *Women's Studies International Forum*, 22, 37–48.

4. The role of spousal support in the emancipation of refugee women entrepreneurs in practice: the case of Syrian women entrepreneurship in Lebanon

Rola El Ali and Séverine Le Loarne – Lemaire

1. INTRODUCTION

This chapter seeks to contribute to the literature on women's entrepreneurship while focusing on one specific context: refugee entrepreneurship in deprived economic zones of the Middle East. Moreover, it aims at contributing to this same literature by addressing questions such as: to what extent does entrepreneurship act as a means of helping refugee women entrepreneurs become emancipated? What is the role of spousal support in such an emancipation process?

Traditional western literature idealizes entrepreneurship as having the ability to bring prosperity and wealth to everybody, and to emancipate marginalized people (e.g., Ahl & Marlow, 2012; Al-Dajani & Marlow, 2013; Al-Dajani et al., 2015; Hughes & Jennings, 2012; Rindova et al., 2009). It implies that women are emancipated when they are able to explore their options, choose between different alternatives, and assume responsibility and control over their personal and business matters. Consequently, the use of the concepts of emancipation and empowerment has grown into a significant construct favorable to studying and analyzing women's entrepreneurship, and researchers have been encouraged to focus on the emancipatory power of entrepreneurship (Al-Dajani & Marlow, 2010, 2013; Rindova et al., 2009).

In their quest for self-emancipation, women—like men—are not alone: they receive support from formal and informal networks, friends, and family members. Among these various types of support, women consider spousal support (Chasserio et al., 2014; Nikina et al., 2015) to be a determinant of the success of their entrepreneurial activity. However, as these last authors mention, support differs across two key variables: the perception women have of their place in society—traditional or equalitarian—and the perception their spouses have of women's place in society.

Most studies on spousal support have implied that the spousal role and its influence on the woman's entrepreneurial activity is a global phenomenon. They continue to overlook the limitations set by various contextual factors and pay very little attention to the dynamics that shape and affect entrepreneurial actions and behaviors (Gaddefors & Anderson, 2017; Newth, 2018). In response, there has been an increase in calls for researchers to conduct more contextualized studies (Rindova et al., 2009; Welter, 2011) on entrepreneurship as an everyday heterogeneous practice (Welter et al., 2017) in diverse nontraditional, situated contexts (Rindova et al., 2009; Zahra & Wright, 2011) using different non-classical research approaches and techniques (Welter & Gartner, 2016; Welter et al., 2017) in order to develop a more accurate depiction of female entrepreneurship. The effect of context seems specifically applicable to the refugee situation, the circumstances of which differ significantly from those studied in western research as they function under disadvantageous socio-cultural and economic conditions and where gender roles are extremely traditional. Women in less developed areas try to search for sources of income to help in their family survival and emancipation. Their foremost focus is the support they can provide to their families (Doss, 2013; Duflo, 2011), rather than personal emancipation or goals of socio-economic self-fulfillment.

This research investigates the emancipatory potential of entrepreneurship, by looking into the practices of refugee women entrepreneurs in Beirut, Lebanon. It attempts to understand the role of spousal support in the emancipation of these women and explores how women in entrepreneuring navigate the complex relationships with their husbands and culture. The literature review, which takes in the literature on women's emancipation through entrepreneurship and the literature on spousal support, provides a typology of four cases that refers to the nature of emancipation based on spousal collaboration. Following an ethnographic approach, we had the opportunity to follow four women refugee entrepreneurs who do entrepreneurship. Our findings reveal that in the refugee context, women's entrepreneurship can be perceived as a sign of family emancipation but not necessarily as a sign of women's emancipation. Thus, in observing entrepreneurial practices, our investigations show that women are controlled by their spouses during their entrepreneuring activities. This practice of "control" has a major impact on the woman entrepreneur's sense of independence and emancipation.

Our conclusion complements previous research suggesting that the potential for emancipation for women entrepreneurs is inextricably linked to broader contextual restrictions. It is based on the idea of entrepreneurship-as-emancipation as a double-edged phenomenon that includes both emancipation and oppression; it can help emancipate the family but can also contribute to the entrepreneur's oppression and increase her responsibilities.

This chapter is structured as follows. First is the literature review, which leads to the enunciation of our typology of spousal support for women's emancipation. Second, we explain our research design. Findings are then introduced and discussed on two main levels: first on a theoretical level, where we talk about spousal support or spousal control; second, on a practical level for western and occidental institutions that seek to promote the emancipation of women refugee while entrepreneuring. We conclude with limitations, contributions, and potential for further research.

2.   LITERATURE REVIEW

2.1   The Emancipatory Potential of Entrepreneurship for Women

The notion of emancipation and empowerment has become an important construct appealing to the investigation and analysis of female entrepreneurship. As a result, scholars have called for study of the emancipatory potential of entrepreneurship (Rindova et al., 2009) and to shift the focus from considering "entrepreneurship as an economic activity with possible social change outcomes to entrepreneurship as a social change activity with a variety of possible outcomes" (Calás et al., 2009, p.553). Research studying women's empowerment and emancipation through entrepreneurship has shown that women entrepreneurs do acquire economic and personal rewards as a result of their entrepreneuring (Al-Dajani & Marlow, 2013; Al-Dajani et al., 2015; Goss et al., 2011). Extant literature provides examples that demonstrate how entrepreneurship allows women in developing countries (Datta & Gailey, 2012; McElwee & Al-Riyami, 2003; Sadi & Al-Ghazali, 2010) to free themselves from extreme poverty, subordination, and patriarchy as well as to partially liberate themselves from prejudiced behaviors and labor market discrimination. Moreover, it sometimes allows them to escape horrifying and frequent family violence (e.g., Al-Dajani & Marlow, 2013; Datta & Gailey, 2012; Scott et al., 2012). In this sense, entrepreneurship shifts from a force that leads to economic growth to becoming a force that enables social transformation and change; this transforms entrepreneurship into a power that can liberate individuals from various limitations and unleash their potential and strengths.

Recently, doubts about the potentiality of entrepreneurship to emancipate or empower women from oppressive and patriarchal systems in different institutional contexts have been increasing. Some studies have shown that research often understates the unpleasant side of entrepreneurship, which can obstruct emancipation (Verduijn et al., 2014). Verduijn and Essers (2013) claim that entrepreneurship is sometimes idealized and conceptualized as the ultimate objective of emancipation and development. They presume that women's endeavors can conserve their subjugation within the pervasive patriarchal and authoritative system (Verduijn & Essers, 2013; Verduijn et al., 2014). Al-Dajani and Marlow (2013) suggest that though entrepreneuring does have the ability to empower subjugated or dominated women within traditional patriarchal environments, such empowerment remains limited, as it does not challenge the prevalent patriarchal hierarchy. Gill and Ganesh (2007) explain it as empowerment which is bounded, and which gives us different and mixed viewpoints on the empowering potential of entrepreneurship and how empowerment is constructed. Jennings et al. (2016), who attempted to study the conflict between the repressive and emancipatory potential of women entrepreneurship within different contexts, questioned the belief in the emancipatory aspects of entrepreneurship within a developed economic setting and claimed that women's entrepreneurial venturing does not necessarily help in improving the existing state of affairs for women (Jennings et al., 2016). They stated that, because "entrepreneurship itself is institutionally embedded axiomatically, most entrepreneurial endeavors will reproduce constraints rather than offer liberation from them" (Jennings et al., 2016, p.21).

Diverse views and outcomes are presented concerning the potentiality of women to be "empowered" or "emancipated" from repression, patriarchal domination, and authority through entrepreneurship. Study of these arguments about the positive and negative sides of women's entrepreneurship requires a separate investigation into the two-sided phenomenon of emancipation and empowerment while taking power and contextual factors into consideration (Alkhaled & Berglund, 2018).

This research avoids studying entrepreneurship as a favorable economic process but rather focuses on the social change process that takes place under authoritative patriarchal domination.

2.2   Refugee Women's Entrepreneurship and Emancipation

Occidental research on entrepreneurship has traditionally considered financial affluence as the main purpose of entrepreneurship (Welter et al., 2017). It has romanticized entrepreneurship as having the power to create riches for everybody as well as to emancipate and elevate the livelihoods of marginalized people (e.g., Ahl & Marlow, 2012; Al-Dajani & Marlow, 2013; Al-Dajani et al., 2015; Hughes & Jennings, 2012; Rindova et al., 2009), thus emancipating them from repression and patriarchal domination within the context of developing countries (McElwee & Al-Riyami, 2003; Sadi & Al-Ghazali, 2010).

In a refugee context, the development of entrepreneurial activities is seen as vital for increasing refugee self-dependence, nurturing "social and economic interdependence" in their environments, and recreating social networks

(Jacobsen, 2002). This inclination for entrepreneurship for female refugees is caused by a multitude of factors. In many cases, entrepreneurship can be survival-oriented (Berner et al., 2012) and is driven by necessity rather than by ambition or aspiration for personal growth.

There is still a deficit in entrepreneurship research regarding individuals in indigenous, negated, and silenced communities, such as refugees in developing countries in general (Alrawadieh et al., 2018; Refai et al., 2018; Wauters & Lambrecht, 2006) and women refugees in particular (Al-Dajani & Marlow, 2013; Bastian et al., 2018; De Vita et al., 2014). The literature has shown minor interest in the contextual elements that affect entrepreneurial behavior and practices (Gaddefors & Anderson, 2017; Newth, 2018) and often overlooks the interdependency between the social and economic areas of the daily life of the entrepreneur. However, researchers such as Welter et al. (2019) embrace the importance of contextualizing entrepreneurship and encourage researchers to adopt contextualized perspectives to study entrepreneurship. Contextualizing entrepreneurship can help researchers study the variations within entrepreneurship and acknowledge differences among entrepreneurs. It can broaden our understanding of entrepreneurship; of how, why, and when it occurs; and of who takes part in the process (Welter, 2011; Welter & Baker, 2020; Zahra & Wright, 2011). It can assist in discovering and analyzing the overlooked richness of entrepreneurship that is often neglected (Welter et al. 2019) and help look beyond the mere traditional and preoccupied economic view.

In fact, in the area of research explaining life roles in work–life studies in general, there is a dearth of studies that investigate the work–life experiences and practices of refugee women entrepreneurs in the refugee context. Additional insight is vital to enhance our understanding of marginalized women's entrepreneurial activities and practices (Al-Dajani & Marlow, 2013; Bastian et al., 2018; De Vita et al., 2014), and to allow a slightly diverse consideration of the emancipatory effect of entrepreneurship. This is central not only for augmenting refugee self-reliance but also for fostering "social and economic interdependence" in local communities (Jacobsen, 2002).

2.3   Spousal Influence and Family-related Dimension of Emancipation in Practice

Studies on female entrepreneurship recognize the necessity to incorporate the dynamics of the household and family when investigating female entrepreneurs, since life and work are interwoven and significantly influence each other (Aldrich & Cliff, 2003; Brush et al., 2009; Jennings & McDougald, 2007). Some women may start a business endeavor because they assume the social responsibility of taking care of their family members (Baker & Welter,

2017), and to meet a certain model of motherhood (Foley et al., 2018). Their top priority is not growing their business or securing self-emancipation; instead, their main purpose is to secure an income to sustain the livelihood of their family members and help them out of poverty and need (Baker & Welter, 2017). In this case, entrepreneurship offers a viable option and a practical career path that helps these women to secure an income while still carrying out familial obligations (Lewis et al., 2015). However, at certain times these women may be negotiating their entrepreneurial activities while simultaneously falling victim to patriarchal domination, with partners who obligate them to stay home, dominate them, and colonize the work to manage the business on their own terms. From this standpoint, these women can be looked upon as creating distinguished entrepreneurial activities by basically starting their own business endeavors and, at the same time, negotiating and arguing their role in both the household and society (Baker & Welter, 2017). Accordingly, studying these women entrepreneurs can draw a deeper and different picture of women entrepreneurship.

However, a woman entrepreneur's household and family responsibilities vary depending on the context and environment, as gender roles differ in distinctive societies and countries. As such, this case may be more prevalent for female entrepreneurs in underdeveloped areas where women must carry out basic domestic tasks, undertake childcare responsibilities, and manage their businesses simultaneously.

It is important to note that women may not receive the same level of support from their husbands as men do from their wives (Prentice & Carranza, 2002). Conversely, women might face manipulation, oppression, or domination. In their research, Nikina et al. (2015, p.55) noted that investigating a "married female entrepreneur is incomplete without the consideration of her husband," and that spousal support is more important than any other form of support (Nikina et al., 2015). A supportive spouse could be an important factor in creating a stimulating and cooperative environment that can contribute to the woman's entrepreneurial success. He can ease work–life conflicts by helping with domestic and childcare responsibilities, providing advice or ideas, supporting and encouraging his spouse in tough times, and helping out with monetary resources. At the same time, a husband can hinder the entrepreneurial activity (Davidsson & Honig, 2003; Nikina et al., 2012) of his partner by loading her with household tasks or intervening in her business. For instance, he might dominate her business decisions or draw on her financial business resources. Problems caused by an unsupportive spouse can negatively impact a woman's entrepreneurial activity, since a lack of support from family members usually affects women more than it does men (Shinnar et al., 2012). Women usually give more attention and thought to their relationships with other individuals in their decisions (Kirkwood, 2009). Their way of managing their business is strongly affected by their relationships and is influenced by management strategies that are based on relationships (Farr-Wharton & Brunetto, 2009). A woman does not usually create a business without the consent and support of her husband (Kirkwood & Tootell, 2008); she usually consults her spouse before taking any action or decision related to her entrepreneurial endeavor (Kirkwood, 2009).

Conversely, spouses might fear that their wives' successful entrepreneurial activity might jeopardize their identity as breadwinners and may pose a serious threat to their status as the main source of income (Amine & Staub, 2009). To offset these concerns, reinforce their self-identity, and recover control over their surroundings, spouses may exert greater control over their partners (Stets & Burke, 2005) and opt to intervene in their business affairs. This interference might provide them with a sense of control, allowing them to cope with the entrepreneurial endeavors of their wife. Considering the difficult refugee situation and the challenges that come with the patriarchal refugee environment, spouses may try to impose control by interfering in their wife's entrepreneurial activity and reinforcing normative gender roles, hence contributing to the entrepreneur's oppression rather than emancipation.

In their literature review, Wolf and Frese (2018) proposed that spouses can act as resources where they can support their partner's work or as constraints where they hinder their partner's work. They recognized six distinct kinds of spousal impact that appeared in previous studies: (1) financial support; (2) emotional support; (3) practical support; (4) sharing networks, advice, and ideas; (5) overloading entrepreneurs with household and family tasks; and finally, (6) interference in the business. Wolf and Frese (2018) encouraged scholars to study the influence of the spouse on the woman's work and to investigate the conditions that turn this asset into a liability, and vice versa.

To study the different types of refugee women entrepreneurs' businesses and to understand the dynamics and impact of the spousal role and support behavior, they ought to be put into a context that enables them to be studied per type of business and support role of the spouse. Thus, this research attempts to develop a typology that classifies them according to specific characteristics and differences (e.g., Ezzedeen & Ritchey, 2008). It employs a typology that is based on two possible forms of entrepreneurial business models and spousal support/no-support modes. This typology can be useful in studying the types of support that such women receive and in assessing their relative impact on the women's businesses, their emancipation, and their family's emancipation. It can help to illuminate the emancipatory potential of entrepreneurship.

Table 4.1   *Typology of the spousal support*

	Solo entrepreneur	Copreneurs
Supportive spouse	Spousal support for the women entrepreneur can lead to the husband demanding decision-making power to cope with the wife's entrepreneurial activity Spousal support for the female entrepreneur is not intended to emancipate women or empower them	Spousal support for women entrepreneurs is a collective family strategy to improve the household income without jeopardizing the man's role as the head of the family Spousal support for refugee women entrepreneurs does not impose gender role-sharing on the couple
Non-supportive spouse	A non-supportive spouse can obstruct the wife's entrepreneurial activity out of fear that their position and role as breadwinner and leader will be jeopardized Women's entrepreneurship can be an individualistic strategy to help their families rather than emancipate themselves	A non-supportive spouse can add to the woman's responsibilities to support the family A non-supportive spouse can lead women to be trapped by a gender-based division of responsibilities and authority

3.   RESEARCH DESIGN

This work draws on empirical accounts generated by means of life-story narratives and participant observations of four Syrian refugee women entrepreneurs and their spouses, friends, and family members in Beirut, Lebanon. These particular women were chosen because each of them represented an archetypal pathway that best matched our typology.

3.1   Participant Selection Logic: Research Sample

In the beginning, women entrepreneurs were identified through local NGOs that offer support programs to fund and supervise the start-up business activities of refugee women in Beirut, and also through network connections with other refugee women entrepreneurs. The initial purpose of the study was to analyze the entrepreneurial practices of these women and explain how they were managing to create their start-up venture day by day. This helped us identify women entrepreneurs who had independently created their businesses and others who had co-founded the venture with their spouses. We conducted individual first interviews with each of the identified women entrepreneurs. The length of each interview was two hours and they resulted in a rich and extensive body of data. These interviews helped in distinguishing women who were receiving support from their spouses from those who were not. Finally, as a result, 4 out of a group of 11 cases of women entrepreneurs were randomly selected based on their consent to participate in an ethnographic study.

These four cases of Syrian refugee women entrepreneurs exemplify the four types of entrepreneurs matching the typology. These women entrepreneurs have created ventures in different sectors (retail, tailoring, food packing, and a flower shop). They were visited and observed in their business locations (either in their homes or at their shops) and long periods of time were spent with them to better understand their entrepreneurial activities and the role of the spouse in their entrepreneuring process.

3.2   Data Collection

For the data collection process, we focused on observing the refugee women entrepreneurs and studying their entrepreneuring practices, actions, behaviors, and specific events and stories that are related to their relationships and interactions with their spouses and family. For that, one of the researchers visited each of the women over a duration of eight months between 2020 and 2021. This started before the first Covid-19 lockdown and ran during the lockdown and for four months after that. Participants agreed to involve the researcher in their day-to-day interactions and allowed her to be part of their daily lives and experiences. The author stayed with each participant and her family for a minimum duration of one full day every month in addition to weekly random visits to her work location. Also, an interview with each woman was conducted every month for a duration that extended up to one hour. Last, during the time of the study, the author conducted and transcribed interviews with the friends and family members of each woman, including the spouse, children, or other relatives who happened to be present at the time of the observations, such as a sister-in-law and her spouse. All interviews were conducted in Arabic, the native language of the female entrepreneurs; they were recorded and translated into English. All observations and notes extracted from these interviews were transcribed and coded and were subject to thematic analysis using Atlas.ti qualitative software.

Open-ended questions were asked, to help us gain a deeper insight into the respondents' experiences as entrepreneurs and to encourage the participants to freely tell their stories. Discussions were then guided to address the entrepreneurial activities and practices of the women entrepreneurs, their relationship with their spouse, and its influence on their businesses and life. The questions primarily focused on the role of the spouse; the type of support received from the spouse, friends, or family members; the enactment of entrepreneuring to achieve the desired outcome of the entrepreneur; and her family's emancipation. Broadly, this explored the work–life interface experiences of the female entrepreneurs. Questions also consisted of background data of each entrepreneurial venture, including the type of business, the age of the business, the resources required to start and manage the business, the ownership

Table 4.2   Data sources: participants in the ethnographic study

Name	Solo entrepreneur/ Copreneurs	Spousal support	Job	Husband's job	Age	Number of children	Previous work	Reason for starting a business
Nofa	Solo entrepreneur	Non-supportive spouse	Tailor/works from home	Husband always between jobs	38	4	No	Family support
Falak	Copreneurial couple	Non-supportive spouse	Retail shop	Husband and wife work together	42	3	No	Family support
Nada	Copreneurial couple	Supportive spouse	Flower shop	Husband and wife work together	32	2	No	Family support
Embashar	Solo entrepreneur	Supportive spouse	Preparing and cooking food	Husband unemployed	41	4	Yes	Family support

format (copreneurs or solo entrepreneurs), and the type of work–life roles/ responsibilities.

3.3   Data Analysis

In this research we followed an ethnographic methodological approach, namely eight months of participant observation at the workplace of the participant female entrepreneurs.

Initially, a master coding framework was developed using a representative number of transcripts (27 transcripts). It was discussed and refined as the study progressed. This involved constant comparison to systematically link and develop key themes and detect patterns, differences, and connections. We shifted back and forth between inductive and deductive reasoning while conforming to quality measures that meet the essential standards of qualitative research (Gioia et al., 2013).

In accordance with the above, our data collection, data coding, and data analysis were carried out in conjunction (Charmaz, 2011; Gioia et al., 2013) and in cycles of coding, displaying, dissecting, and analyzing in order to assess findings and obtain conclusions.

3.4   Reasoning for Studying Control Practices

After witnessing the participants' daily practices and activities, listening to their experiences and interpretations, and comparing their entrepreneurial experiences, we were able to identify different practices and ideas that were extrapolated from the data. Noticeable and prominent throughout the initial phase of analysis was the "control" practice that the spouses imposed on their wives during the entrepreneuring process. Interestingly, spouses often appeared to intentionally "impose control" (64 observations) on their wives and obstruct their business activities and emancipation; alternatively, some husbands supported their wives and allowed them to have a degree of control over the business and family affairs, "conveying control" (30 observations). The wives appeared to use different methods to "navigate through the spousal control" (35 observations) without confronting the spouse. Accordingly, we tried to build on this idea and on our understanding of the entrepreneuring phenomenon. We started to closely investigate the control practices of the spouses, the events that shaped the spouses' controlling behavior, what "control" meant for them, how they imposed control on their wives and their businesses, the wives' navigation techniques, and the emotional and reflective elements of the entrepreneurs' journeys.

4.   FINDINGS: SPOUSAL SUPPORT— EMANCIPATING OR CONTROLLING WOMEN ENTREPRENEURS?

Findings showed that the role of the spouse can take the form of support (a theme supported by literature) for the female entrepreneur in her entrepreneuring process, as well as the form of control (a theme generated from the data) that the spouse exerts over his wife and her entrepreneuring activities. Consequently, we honed in on two key practices related to spousal roles enacted during the entrepreneurial process: "imposing control practices" (where there are stories of dominance and supremacy and where the husband tries to impose control over the business, wife, and family) and "the interplay between support and control practices" (where there are stories of empowerment and support and where the husband allows his wife to assume a certain degree of freedom and exercise a level of control, though limited, over some business matters). In addition, generated data showed that the control practices imposed by the spouse led to a practice enacted by the wives to navigate through these control practices; accordingly, we investigated a key entrepreneuring practice that the wives used to navigate the control practices of their spouses: "strategizing to overcome control practice" (where the wife develops strategies to overcome spousal constraints). We studied how these practices become intertwined and what ideas emerged.

4.1   Signs of Control Depending on the Type of Collaboration with the Spouse

"Imposing control" was found to be one of the most frequently encountered practices in the dataset. Our findings show that husbands can impose control over the business affairs, financial resources, income, decision-making process, and autonomy of their wives, the female entrepreneurs, to ensure that she remains in a subsidiary position in relation to his position as the head of the family. One of the primary ways through which husbands assert control over their wives and the business is through controlling financial resources and income. Findings show that husbands can control their wife's income by indirectly persuading her to give it to him willingly or by making sure she spends it all on household expenses.

Controlling decision-making and autonomy were found to be other means by which the spouse imposes control over his wife and her business affairs. Our finding revealed that husbands set boundaries on their wives' autonomy. Women did not have the luxury to make their own decisions or to manage their businesses freely. Quite the contrary: approval of the husband has to be sought at all levels of the entrepreneurial activity. Their entrepreneuring journey is subject to and is linked to their husband's approval as they undertake different entrepreneurial practices.

The practice of imposing control was strongly evident in the cases of Nofa and Falak, whose non-supportive husbands impose control, both directly and indirectly, over their business affairs. With attention and focus on the specific entrepreneurial activities of Nofa and her husband, we examine how he imposes control over her financial resources, income, and autonomy while maintaining his dominant position as the head of the household. During our fieldwork, we witnessed multiple incidents that demonstrate how Nofa's husband imposes control, both directly and indirectly, over her business affairs.

The following vignette, which took place during one of our sessions at Nofa's workshop, is illustrative of such practice. One day, Nofa, who operates her solo entrepreneurial activity from her workshop at home, and who was busy sewing a dress for one of her clients, received an angry call from a supplier to whom her husband had previously introduced her. The supplier threatened to stop working with her as she had not settled the invoice for the fabric supplied earlier through her husband. Nofa listened with as much calmness as she could gather, perplexed as she had already sent the money with her husband to settle the due payment. She finished the call with a bewildered look on her face; Nofa had asked this customer to give her one day and she explained she would come back to him. Looking at me, Nofa clarified that the supplier was a "very decent person" who helped her business, and she did not want him to be disappointed or angry.

Nofa: I will have to wait until my husband comes back from work. I gave him the money two days ago; I wonder why he has not given it to the supplier yet. I am worried that he might have taken the money for himself, as this is not the first time that he has taken my money.

Nofa continued her day absent-minded and anxious, apprehensively waiting for her husband to return from work. Nofa's husband usually arrives home after 6:00pm. Upon arrival, he is routinely irritable, with semi-constant complaints about his unprofitable business. That particular day was no exception; he walked in with scoffs and, on cue, started venting. Nofa prepared his dinner and served it to him on the floor of her workshop. After he and the children had finished their meal, Nofa was not able to keep herself calm or hold her anger; she did not mind confronting her husband even in our presence. Nofa asked him why he did not give the money to the supplier.

Nofa: You were supposed to give the money to the supplier. What happened?

Without remorse, he answered that he had taken it for himself.

Husband: I took the money to settle some debts. I had to use the money; I had no other choice. The shop owner came to me and asked for the rental fees, I had no other choice but to give him whatever I had. I will give you back your money whenever I get paid.

Nofa attempted to maintain her composure despite her being visibly hurt and agitated, likely because we were present with them in the workshop. Her voice broke as she asked:

Nofa: And what about my debts? This money is not mine and it is neither yours. You know that I had to work day and night to save this money for the supplier's payment.

The husband stared at her with contempt and stood up and walked away without uttering a single word in response.

Nofa: He will never give me my money back; I will never forget when he took my gold and sold it. At that time, he promised that he will give me the money back, but he never did. This is not the first time he takes money from me. But the difference is that this time the money is not mine. He always says that he has to settle his debts, but honestly, I don't know where he spends all that money.

We began to note Nofa's suspicion of her husband as she doubted the truthfulness of his statement. Nofa spent all of her income on household expenses and did not have the opportunity to save any of her hard-earned money for herself.

Nofa: I sometimes feel that he wants to make sure I have no savings or backup money. Every time he sees that my business is doing well, he tries to find reasons to take the money; when I complain he says that it is my duty as a wife to help my husband through difficult times.

Nofa's above statement was confirmed by her husband when we asked him during our interview about his expectations of his wife's work.

Husband: Since my work is not always very productive, she has to help me and help her family.

We hypothesized that Nofa's husband deploys a strategy to keep Nofa in a subordinate position. He does so by implicitly ensuring she has no extra money or savings of her own. He makes sure that she spends all of her money on household expenses and cites a personal need for money whenever there is a surplus. Additionally, he forced her to sell the gold jewelry that she kept as insurance against tough times, hence keeping her financially dependent and subordinated to his will. Another incident that encapsulates the above notion is when he tacitly pressured her into covering the rental fees for their apartment. It is important to note that within the ascribed and expected gender roles, the man is supposed to pay the rental fees for their apartment. It began during another visit to Nofa's workshop; the landlord passed by and asked for the rental fees, and Nofa had no choice but to pay him his dues. She excused herself and asked him to wait a few minutes at the entrance door. She raged into her workshop while muttering to herself. She swiftly opened the drawer next to her sewing machine and took out 6,000,000 Lebanese Liras. She gave the money to the landlord, returned to sit at her sewing machine, and sighed deeply before sharing:

Nofa: Do you see how he makes sure I have no extra money with me? This is not the first time the man passes by to take the rent. I told him yesterday that he either has to give the man the fees himself or simply give me money so I can give him the fees. But he will definitely not pay as he always expects me to pay. I am tired of moving from one apartment to the other. I simply pay the fees and buy my peace of mind.

During our encounters with Nofa over the eight months of the study, we visited her in two different apartments as she had been forced to relocate twice during that relatively brief period. Another telling episode, which is significant in terms of how Nofa's husband imposes control on her and her business activities, was related to requiring his permission prior to leaving her workshop or visiting customers at their homes. Nofa's husband strictly disallows her from mobilizing without his prior knowledge and consent, even if her movement is strictly to buy groceries or accessories that she uses for her work. Nofa has one particular Lebanese customer, an old lady, who properly compensates her for her services. One day while we were at the shop, Nofa explained that she needed to visit this lady to take measurements for a dress that she wanted to be altered.

Nofa: I will tell my husband that I will go to buy groceries. Even
                   though he knows the lady very well and knows that she is a fre-
                   quent customer, he will not allow me to go to her even if I ask
                   for his permission. She is decent and pays very well, but still,
                   he does not allow me to go to her place. I usually don't tell him
                   everything, he doesn't have to know.

Nofa asked us whether we would prefer to stay at the workshop or join her visit
to the customer, and we readily chose the latter. Nofa asked her neighbor to
watch her children during her absence and we left together. Nofa swiftly took
the needed measurements and stopped to buy some groceries on our way back
to her workshop. The restraints imposed on Nofa by her husband demanded
that she mitigate the hindrances creatively to maintain her business amid her
personal challenges. The above quote suggests that Nofa was aware of the
injustice her husband was subjecting her to by controlling her income and
restricting her freedom of movement. However, she also seemed to be aware
of her realistic capacity to change the situation at hand, and instead, Nofa opted
to find ways to circumvent his domination and control.

As evidenced in these examples, the control practices imposed by the
husband contribute to constantly reaffirming the husband's control over
the wife, her income, and her entrepreneurial activity; here the husband
retains power over his wife and the wife has limited room for autonomy and
decision-making. Indeed, the wife knows that any action or resistance will
result in actions that she would not be in favor of, such as running the risk
of having to move apartment if she did not pay the rental fees. The wife has
a better chance of meeting her objective of providing a decent and stable life
for her family by taking the path of least resistance, accepting the current
dynamics as they are, and managing her husband's control practices to achieve
the greater good—which, for her, is emancipating her family.

Another case that clearly demonstrates the practice of imposing control is
that of Falak and her husband, who share a copreneurial business. For Falak's
husband, the importance of ascertaining and imposing control is drawn from
his patriarchal authority and desire for domination over his wife and family.
This case is a more subtle form of imposing control, yet it is simultaneously
more insidious and harder to overcome. It is important to mention that during
our exchange with Falak, she avoided discussing details in the presence of her
husband. Rather, Falak's demeanor was significantly more comfortable and at
ease when her husband was away from the shop. At certain times we would
plan visits to Falak for times when her husband was not present, to reflect on
previous incidents. The following vignette, which occurred at Falak's shop,
illustrates the practice of imposing control. Falak had repeatedly asked her
husband to install a shelf in the shop, only to have her request complained

about. He would dismiss it, tell her it was a bad idea, and argue there was no need. This continued over the course of many weeks and sometimes months.

Falak: He rarely helps me and when he does, he keeps on postponing it [...] though he has nothing more important to do. He goes on complaining and criticizing me and my ideas of enhancing the shop.

One afternoon, in our presence, she reminded him once again to install the shelf in the shop. Surprisingly, on that day he finally complied with her request. Her husband asked Falak to get the shelf and the screws and asked her to borrow a fire steel from the neighbors. Eagerly, Falak retrieved everything at her husband's request, worried the slightest delay would cause his momentum to waver. He started drilling into the wall and asked her to stand next to him while he worked. He first asked her to verify that the shelf was horizontal and not inclined, after which he asked her to hold the shelf while he used the fire steel to secure the shelf in place. The entire incident was punctuated with complaints, scoffs, and orders from her husband, making it clear that he did not want to be doing this work. Even while he was in the middle of installing the shelf, he criticized Falak and demanded that she justify the need for the shelf. This likely reinforced his position as stronger and more superior. Falak ignored her husband's negative comments—"I don't think there is a need for this shelf," "I am sure it will be of no use," "stand properly," "move a little to the left," "get me the screwdriver"—and immediately jumped to answer his many requests, her body language slightly stiffening before she transitioned from one task to the next. Later in private, Falak elaborated on this incident with us:

Falak: It's like he doesn't do anything if I'm not involved and constantly assisting him.

Even after the shelf was installed, when Falak went to sit down her husband called her back and demanded that she remained standing next to him, even though she had nothing left to do there. Aside from an almost imperceptible eyeroll, Falak remained obedient. Although the incident displayed a clear exertion of dominance and control through verbal battery, Falak later informed us that this was her husband practicing extreme self-restraint and acting on his best behavior because we were present. When there was a practical need for his help, he would very reluctantly do the job, all the while reminding Falak of the need to be grateful to him.

Falak: Of course, I don't say this, but he isn't even doing the tasks for me, he is doing them for the shop which he also owns. So why should he act like he's doing me a favor?

The husband's incessant need for control and his putting Falak down is compensation for his own insecurities and inadequacies. He imposed control on Falak by undermining her efforts, submitting her to constant criticism, and holding her responsible for any decision that does not match his view; in this way, her husband ensures that Falak remains in a subsidiary position in relation to his position as the head of the family. Undermining Falak's decisions and second-guessing her actions seemed to be her husband's way of diminishing her power.

During our observations, we noticed that the distribution of roles between the couple was made clear. The gender ideologies that shape their social roles and responsibilities also reinforced them. Falak took care of the shop's daily activities without any decision-making capital. Her husband was more likely to have the final say on all major business-related decisions, while Falak ended up subordinately performing the job of a paid employee. This was obvious during the observation at Falak's shop, where we noticed that the husband acts as the boss: always sitting on the chair behind the desk while Falak sits on a smaller chair on the other side, her husband continually orders Falak around as she attends to her customers' requests as well as his demands.

As such, the discovery that Falak controls the finances, not her husband, came as a surprise. Inspecting the dynamics further, we later saw that Falak only spends money on the household, and even then, she consults her husband on everything first. Put simply, Falak did all of the labor, and her spouse retained all of the control. By gaslighting her into believing that her decisions were insufficient and that he had to be the end reference for all decision-making, Falak's husband maintained his control with very little effort. He imposed control on her thoughts and her autonomy; so much so that when Falak wanted to introduce us to another participant, she paused and said she would have to ask him first.

One afternoon during our observation at Falak's shop, her husband entered yelling "What is this idiot?!" as he threw a bag of goods on the table. We were sitting in the back, unsure what was happening, as we heard stifled snickers. We looked to the left and saw his children holding back laughter. Their mother motioned sternly, asking them to keep quiet. He left as swiftly as he came in, with the room erupting in giggles as soon as he was gone. Falak joined in, gracefully smiling at her kids. We also smiled, albeit in bewilderment, as we had no idea what had just happened. Falak noticed our confusion and directly offered context. She told us that they needed forks at the shop, so she had placed an order with their trusted supplier. Yet, when her husband purchased from the supplier, he bought rolling pins instead of forks. Falak told her husband, "No, no, this is a mistake. Go and tell him he's mistaken! We need forks!"

Upon mentally replaying the incident in her head as she held the bill, Falak realized that it was she who was mistaken, not the supplier. The words "rolling pin" and "fork" in Arabic are very similar (*shawbak* and *shawkeh* respectively), and in her commotion of multi-tasking on the phone, she asked for rolling pins by mistake. To avoid her husband's anticipated fits of anger because of her mistake, she called the supplier and begged him to say that it was his mistake, not hers. Since the supplier is one they regularly work with, there was an already established relationship that allowed her to make such a request.

The above vignette is very insightful as it illustrates how Falak's husband indirectly imposes control by instilling a sense of fear that leads her to avoid challenging him or even acknowledging a simple oversight that she had accidentally made. Indeed, her husband's continuous flow of criticism of her efforts and work, in tandem with his attempts to hold her accountable for any oversight or mistake that might happen, keeps Falak alert to the need to remain within his mandate. This vignette reveals how she maneuvers around her husband's reactions and outbursts. It was evident in the observation that Falak's daughters were well aware of those dynamics, and that lying to their father was both normalized and accepted as long as the end result was deemed justified. Falak recognized her husband's anger and knew she would have been its recipient had she not called the supplier and asked him to inherit the blame; her quick thinking directed her husband's emotions at someone else and this was celebrated as a success. This explains the laughter and aura of relief after her husband angrily left the shop. The infantilizing approach the husband took to Falak was apparent, both in the language he employed when lecturing her and in how Falak subverted situations to her advantage without challenging his authority.

When her husband yells at or berates her, Falak just takes it silently. At first, we assumed this was because Falak believed that her being treated this way was the acceptable norm and that she was unaware of a different reality. However, after observing her for a while, we noticed that it was more tactical. Responding to her husband would be counterproductive and would magnify the argument both in duration and severity. So, for Falak, allowing verbal abuse is, in fact, the path of least resistance.

At several points in the exchanges with Nofa and Falak, both portrayed themselves as women who do not have control over their partners. Both women expressed that it was a priority for them that their husbands felt in power, even if they had gone behind their back on a matter. They tried to disentangle themselves from their husband's authority by strategically navigating through these control practices.

4.2   Control or Support

Our findings show that supportive spouses do allow their wives a certain degree of autonomy, as long as it is under their umbrella of control and consent. Women with supportive spouses can enjoy a certain degree of control, though very limited, over decision-making and autonomy if it does not affect the husband's power position or disturb the status quo. The husband's permission and authorization must be given at all times in order for the wife to maintain her subordinate position.

In the following examples we focus on the dynamic nature of social interactions, specifically the fluctuating balance between the degree of control and freedom that the husband allows his wife and the degree of control he imposes on his wife and the business. This introduces, in a very specific way, the role that the husband plays in sometimes maintaining the status quo and at other times prevailing over it.

The interplay between imposing control over and delegating control to the wife is revealed in the following vignette in Nada's and her husband's flower shop. While we were in the field, a customer contacted Nada's shop requesting event planning services for her wedding ceremony in a small venue. Both Nada and her husband were in the shop that day. The customer specifically asked for Nada as she had heard about the quality of her work through word of mouth when she was working for one of the most famous wedding planners in Beirut. Nada took care of the customer while her husband and Anas, a part-time employee, were managing other tasks. The layout was quickly agreed on and the customer loved Nada's suggestions. The customer was on a low budget, so she limited her order to flower and balloon centerpieces for 12 tables in the venue, a wedding Styrofoam 16-inch table base with the letters LOVE, and a few decorating items and flower arrangements for the wedding table to make the table look more attractive. They agreed to use artificial gold flowers because they are more cost-efficient and more manageable. Upon deciding on the final price, the customer asked Nada for a discount on the total invoice. Nada excused herself and went to discuss the price and the possibility of a discount with her husband. She returned with a confirmation that she could extend a 5 percent discount on the total invoice.

After the customer left, Nada discussed with her husband the deal that she closed with the customer and took his confirmation on the next steps. They agreed to sub-contract Zafer, a Styrofoam crafter, to supply her with the Styrofoam table base. Zafer had the table base ready-made, as he usually rented it out to his clients and would paint the letters in a different color if requested. As agreed, Nada informed her husband that she would call Zafer to book the table base and ask him to paint the letters in light gold as per the customer's request. A few days later, Zafer called Nada's husband to inform him that he had finished painting the four letters on the table base and that he was ready to deliver them. We visited Zafer the next day alongside Nada and her husband. Nada was shocked at the quality of the end product: the paint finishing was poor and one of the letters on the base had been broken and reglued. In frustration, Nada told Zafer: "This work is unacceptable."

Nada asked her husband to check the table base and voiced her concern that the base might not be strong enough to hold all the table decorations. Her husband was unconcerned, leaving Nada to take care of the details. A few days later, Zafer called Nada to inform her that he had finished the table base as per their requirements. Nada asked him to send her pictures of the final product as she did not have the time to inspect them in person. Nada checked the pictures, showed them to us and her husband, and stated:

Nada: He should always be reminded to do his work better. I don't understand why I should always follow up with him in order for him to deliver quality work. The table now looks much better than before. I hope he will deliver it safely to the wedding venue.

This indicates that although Nada's husband delegates a certain level of authority to her and allowed her to assume power, responsibility, and control over specific tasks, he expected her to come back to him and seek his confirmation when it came to important business-related matters. The example shows that Nada always made sure to take her husband's opinion and seek his approval at every step of the decision-making process. This was evidenced with regard to the pricing of the project when Nada requested her husband's permission to contact the supplier, and again when she sought his opinion on the quality of the table base.

Nada: I always consult him and seek his approval for all business and family-related matters [...] I still prefer if we decide on all matters jointly [...] I cannot go to the supplier's workshop or accept any project without his approval. It is better for me if he accompanies me to the workshop [...] I want to avoid any conflict.

This shows that Nada prefers to request her husband's permission to avoid any conflict that might arise should anything go wrong. In this sense, Nada's husband indirectly imposed control on Nada's decision-making and autonomy, though he allowed her to assume a minimal level of control over business-related matters that fell under his consent and approval.

Another telling episode came on the wedding day, when we joined Nada and Anas on a trip to the wedding site. With the help of her husband, Nada arranged to call a minivan that could deliver the table base, the arrangements, and the decoration material to the wedding venue. Nada's husband ensured she had all of the materials and equipment needed to decorate the venue. He insisted that she call him should anything go wrong. He stayed at the shop preparing flower arrangements for Mother's Day, which happened to be one day after the wedding. He kept calling and checking on Nada, reminding her to call him immediately in case of any emergency that might arise.

Husband: You call me immediately in case you need any help […] Don't discuss details with the venue manager, I will call him and discuss all the details with him.

We arrived at the venue five hours before the wedding. Anas and the driver carried all the decorating material and the wedding table base to the venue and arranged it in place. Nada supervised them confidently yet anxiously, screaming in panic when the wedding table accidentally bumped into one of the walls in the venue. Once everything was set, Nada immediately started working on the centerpieces and assigned other important tasks to Anas, such as inflating the balloons and preparing the flower bases for the centerpieces. Every now and then, Nada would inspect Anas' work, identifying errors and faults and asking for improvement and corrections. She would call her husband and inform him about the work progress and the time at which they expected to finish all the installations and arrangements.

This outlines the type of control Nada's husband frequently imposed on her. He kept checking on her and required her to inform him about every simple detail of the work progress. Though he did not contribute much to the project beyond his frequent calls, in this he was practicing his authority as a husband; he assured himself and Nada of his position as the primary decision-maker by showing and imposing control over all business-related activities.

Another case that demonstrates clearly how husbands can interplay between control and support is that of Embashar and her husband. Embashar's husband exerts control over decision-making practices related to his wife's business affairs while simultaneously imposing his control over her financial resources, income, and autonomy, as shown in the following vignette at Embashar's apartment and workshop.

One day while we were at Embashar's workshop, her husband arrived and started talking about a preliminary idea for a potentially very profitable business. He suggested that she could make and sell peanut butter to her customers and to mini markets in the neighborhood. He observed a high demand for this product and concluded that it would be a good business investment that could generate good revenue.

Husband: I have been going and checking in nearby minimarkets and I have noticed a high demand for peanut butter. More than one customer asked about peanut butter while I was there. I knew as well that more than one person started making peanut butter at home and selling them.

He tried to convince Embashar by showing her how rewarding this project could be and by narrating examples he encountered in and around the nearby minimarkets.

Persuading Embashar was not easy. Embashar was worried about financing the project and later asked us about our opinion of the business venture and whether it was viable. She explained her fears to us and to her husband; they mainly revolved around the funding of this project:

Embashar: Our money is barely enough for us to survive. Where do you expect us to get the money to buy a good food processor and good quality peanuts?

Her husband tried to dispel her fears and suggested she sell a piece of her gold if she was convinced about the project and interested in starting it. The idea of selling her gold made Embashar even more hesitant; her gold is deeply cherished, and she would not consider selling it unless there was a good reason. Embashar addressed her husband: "You know that I don't like to sell any of my gold, there are only a few pieces and I want to give them to my daughters when they grow up and get married."

Husband: I believe that from the money you will make from this project, you can buy back the gold that you will sell. Anyway, and as I told you earlier, it is only an idea and you can take it or leave it.

In these words, Embashar's husband allowed her the autonomy to decide whether to adopt his idea or abandon it. This illustrated how he allows her a certain degree of control over her own business-related matters. On one hand, although the business is Embashar's, it has always operated under her husband's consent. On the other, Embashar's husband does not force her to work or take on more than she can handle. He conveys control regarding small business details but also on the income that she generates. It is important to note that she willingly gives him all of her income without feeling exploited, as she trusts her income will be well spent on household expenses.

Embashar: I usually give all the money that I generate from my work to my husband since I rarely leave the house and he is the one responsible for the expenses.

He controls her autonomy and freedom to choose the type and location of her work. For example, her husband decides whether she can work outside the house or not. While we were there, a customer passed by and asked Embashar whether she could provide in-venue food catering for an event that she was arranging in her apartment. Embashar refused, stating that her husband does not allow her to leave her place and work for clients at their apartment. "I am sorry, I cannot accept any work outside my home. My husband does not allow me, no matter how good the pay is."

For Embashar, her husband's permission and approval must be sought at all times. His authorization is necessary for any business or family-related decision to be taken. He appears to be in control of both his wife and her business and Embashar does not mind or complain as she assumes this is the norm. Embashar believes her husband to be a good man who has worked a lot and has in turn earned some time to rest.

Embashar: My husband has always been a good man and husband, but now he is sick, and it is our job to take over his responsibilities as the breadwinner of the family.

We frequently visited Embashar over the eight months of the study, regularly seeing her husband during the visits. He was not bedridden, nor did he appear to be ill. One day during our field visit to Embashar, we saw him helping a neighbor move a very heavy cupboard and load it into a big truck parked in the neighborhood. This incident caused us to exchange smirks as he seemed to be a very healthy man, who looks younger than his age (52 years). After that episode, the relationship between Embashar and her husband appeared to contain a subliminal level of manipulation. Her husband did not work and spent most of his time either at home or wandering around in the neighborhood. He is listed within the UNHCR database as a refugee, and this entitled him to a 200-dollar allowance. On top of that, he took money from his sons and wife to spend on household expenses.

Despite the above, Embashar's husband provides his wife with functional and emotional support and encourages his children to work. He utilizes their efforts and hard work towards the family's collective emancipation, a legitimate reason according to all the family members. Embashar's son's quote below offers a hint that men sometimes become dependent on their wives to support the family. However, he believes that his father's case is different since he is sick and unable to work.

E's son: Many refugee men nowadays are spending their time sleeping or on Facebook while women are working to support their families. This is sad but it is the reality […] My dad is a different case. My dad has been working all the time, but unfortunately, he is sick now and had to stay at home.

Significantly, none of the family members see themselves as being utilized or exploited. They willingly give the husband their income, as they believe this to be their duty as good and obedient family members.

E's son: We are all responsible. We all participate in one way or another. We never divide our income or split our expenses. I give all my salary to my mother or father. My father got sick two years after our arrival to Beirut. He stopped working since then and it became our responsibility to support the family.

In this sense, it can be said that Embashar, her husband, and her children all share the same objective, which is their family's survival and emancipation, though some of them carry that burden and responsibility disproportionately.

4.3   Nature of Emancipation Depending on the Control

Methods of navigating the control practices imposed by the spouse were frequently encountered in the dataset. Our findings reveal that negotiating spousal control is a strategy used by women entrepreneurs to run their business activities. Wives develop tactics to work around and navigate the control that is imposed on them by their spouses. Hence, women entrepreneurs are not just passive recipients of patriarchal norms but are conscious actors who constantly subvert, strategize, and negotiate their way within the constraints of life in a patriarchal society.

In many circumstances, women would have to be diplomatic to circumvent disagreement with their spouses should they explicitly resist the control imposed on them. For example, in Nofa's case it was obvious from the vignette discussed earlier that her husband does not allow her to leave her home and attend to customers outside her workshop. His permission is a prerequisite, which he uses as a tool to control her oftentimes critical mobility. Despite Nofa's successful entrepreneurial activity and her ability to balance work and family, we found that her husband attempts to minimize his feelings of inadequacy by exerting control wherever possible over his wife's business affairs and financial resources. Nofa navigates her husband's control by hiding information from him. She attends to her customers without telling him. For her, he does not need to know the details of all her work activity.

Nofa: He does not have to know everything; a smart woman should know what information to hide and what to reveal. I make good money from my customers who cannot come to this area. Why should I lose that money just to inflate his ego as a man who has control over me?

Nofa is, of course, not without power. She carefully inspects the constraints that surround her, and she works around them. For instance, because her husband would definitely reject her keeping money for herself (he would find reasons or ways to take her money), Nofa would inconspicuously save some cash whenever possible and hide it away. Her hidden money is reserved for emergencies or for enhancing the business at a later date.

Nofa: Sometimes I don't tell him how much money I make; I try to hide this information from him. I reserve this money for emergencies.

Nofa's resolve to continue her venture by devising workarounds allowed her to confront her status as a housewife with little authority and gave her a platform to act. This enabled her to micro-emancipate herself from her husband's constraints. It is important to note that even if he finds out that she has challenged his authority, he will not be able to question her intentions or force her to stop working since she is the main breadwinner in the household.

In Nada's example, Nada seemed determined to assume a certain level of authority and display control over her business. However, despite this, she liked to give her husband the impression that his opinion was the one that mattered. Her strategy was centered on making her husband feel that he was the one in control of their family and business affairs. By doing so, she deflected and avoided conflict with him while enjoying the freedom and authority he extended to her. Her strategy was premised on her perception and belief that the husband should always feel in control and that his masculinity should remain intact: "I always consult him and seek his approval for all business and family-related matters"; "I want to avoid any conflict."

Meanwhile, Nada's husband takes the credit for his wife's success.

Husband: I encouraged her to manage my first shop and to take balloon decoration and English courses, [...] she is handling her job

> very well, but she always comes to me for advice and guidance when necessary. [...] She does all this for our family.

In saying this, Nada's husband wanted to assure us that he had helped Nada become the person she had turned out to be and that all negotiations and decisions were the result of his training and taken with his consent. He made it clear that she always comes to him for help or advice when needed, and that the level of authority he allows her is all for the sake of their family and its survival.

These strategies and practices were also evident when observing Falak and her husband. In one of the incidents, Falak pretended to show conformity with her husband's decision against expanding the business or adding different lines of products to their shop. Even though she did not show any objection to his decision at first, she slowly started blaming their low profit margin on the fact that people were spending less on unnecessary items (such as gadgets and utensils) and prioritizing food (such as oil, rice, or powder milk), which was in high demand due to the economic crisis in Lebanon. She kept repeating that the business would perform better if they added a food line to their existing products; Falak gave examples of neighboring competitors who had started to attract more customers and generate more income once they added food items to their shops. Falak's strategy was not to express any objection to her husband's decision; she did not confront him as she believed that this would lead nowhere. On the contrary, she tried to convince her husband of the need for expansion for the business to survive. During our visits to their shop, Falak brought up this expansion more than once, and kept glancing in our direction, seeking encouragement and validation of her ideas.

Falak: [to her husband] It is about time we add food items to the shop. Selling food nowadays is a good business [...] What do you think about adding an ice cream fridge as well? It is summer and there is a high demand for ice cream and cold beverages.

Her strategy involved bringing up the same topic until her husband caved and agreed to her requests. She would talk about her expansion ideas to friends and relatives (whom she knew would encourage her plans) in his presence and repeat the same argument within his earshot until he hesitantly allowed her to do "whatever she sees convenient and practical." She believed that talking about the same topic to a husband over and over—what she referred to as "Zann"—can lead most women to achieve their desired objective with their husbands. This constant repetition allows it to become familiar and more reasonable or plausible. Falak followed a traditional Arabic proverb: "slow and steady knocking on a certain object can lead to disassembling it," which can translate to "repetition makes things seem more plausible."

In the case of Falak, repeated pleas for permission accompanied by cited examples of successful business expansions, and constantly reassuring her husband that any success that might come would be for the benefit of the family, convinced him to allow her to execute her plans. Yet, his reluctant permission was manifested in his regularly negative attitude and constant criticism, which severely demotivated her. However, after her success in attracting more customers and consequently improving the business' performance and profit, Falak's husband began attributing the credit to himself—a fact that Falak did not mind as long as she was able to achieve her objective.

Falak: He does not support or encourage me with my plans, he always demotivates me and gives me the feeling that I am talking nonsense. [...] But in case I was able to execute a plan or idea and it turns out to be successful, he takes the credit for himself.

The above observations show that the women participants try to give their husbands the impression of obedience and conformity with the patriarchal practices the husbands impose on them. Women work around these practices by developing strategies to exercise their agency while navigating their husbands' control.

In the case of Embashar, her strategy to circumvent her husband's control was to indirectly reassure him that he was the head of the household. She gave him the household's income, both hers and her sons', and would go out of her way to give him the impression that he is still in control of all family affairs.

Embashar: I usually give all the money that I generate from my work to my husband since I rarely leave the house and he is the one responsible for the expenses. Even my sons give their salaries to their father. [...] I don't let him feel that my kids or I are taking over any responsibility or authority from him. I make sure I let him feel that he has the final say in everything [...] I didn't want my husband to feel weak or that he had no support.

According to Embashar, holding or exerting control over income represents holding power; accordingly, allowing her husband to be in charge of the family income allows him to feel that he is maintaining his position as the head of the household. For Embashar, her husband does not mind taking the money as he believes that this serves a greater purpose, which is, in this case, the family's well-being and emancipation. However, her husband does not acknowledge that he takes his sons' and his wife's money, as he considers them to be working to cover their own expenses.

Husband: After Embashar started the business, she was able to cover her own expenses and our daughters' personal expenses as well, and she was able to provide a very small income for the family.

Embashar was confident that her husband spent their money appropriately and that he would always put his family's needs above his personal desires. She pointed out that this arrangement had come about because of how she and her husband understood one another. She believes that this approach is due to the nature of their relationship and their understanding of each other. "My husband has always been a good man and husband, but now he is sick and it is our job to take over his responsibilities as breadwinners."

Generally, the above examples demonstrate that, although women were able to exercise limited agency, their freedom remained restricted within the dominant patriarchal system. They choose to survive within the patriarchal structure and ideology rather than challenging or confronting the existing system.

5.   DISCUSSION

The results of this study can be discussed on two main levels: first, at the level of the family dynamics; second, at the level of emancipation.

5.1   Control and Spousal Support: The Testimony of a Patriarchal Family?

Our results are somewhat surprising in comparison to what has been established in the existing literature on spousal support. The prevalent literature claims that the spouse, among others, is considered by women to be the main support for women entrepreneurs. Yet, support that is negatively perceived by the woman is often attributed to either discrepancies in the individual perceptions of each of the woman and her spouse regarding their roles in society or to a strained or unhealthy relationship. In the cases we investigated, we were not able to judge the nature of the couple relationships; in addition, we were hardly able to identify cases of spousal support to women entrepreneurship. For example, in two cases we found evidence of slight logistical support, but in other cases we could not see any sign of moral or logistical support at all. On the contrary, the woman's activities seem to be controlled by the spouse, who monitors these activities to ensure they are done as per his directions. How can we interpret such role-sharing from a scientific point of view? One interpretation relates to the context of entrepreneurship and the fact that the studied participants are refugees. Rizkalla and Segal (2019) reveal that Syrian refugees' experiences of war and escape from it cause them suffering, resulting in a loss of intimacy between the wife and her spouse. Here, we could interpret this controlling behavior as a result of the necessity for the couple to survive, on a financial level, which makes complicity and support a secondary priority.

A second interpretation could be related to a form of jealousy, or the reflection of a negative emotion expressed by the head of the family, the man, who has "lost" face and his domineering position. Results of studies conducted with Syrian immigrants refer to the deeply dominant patriarchal beliefs and culture of this country (Sözer, 2021). Being forced to escape their country and "obliged" to live on the woman's income can be perceived as disturbing to Syrian male refugees. In a sense, controlling their spouse could be interpreted as a sign of their coping strategy, seeking to keep face as the family head.

5.2   Where Is Emancipation for Women?

Our results also provoke a second level of discussion by questioning the generally acknowledged assumption that entrepreneurship can be a solution for women's emancipation across contexts. In occidental countries, women's entrepreneurship is promoted as a way to escape the glass ceiling that prohibits women from pursuing the careers that they aspire to. Entrepreneurship is also presented as a means to solve work–life balance issues that women face, considering that work prevents them from becoming emancipated. Here, our results suggest that family can also be an obstacle to the emancipation of women entrepreneurs. They also question the nature of women's emancipation as a result of entrepreneurship. In a sense, we can argue that the family as a whole is emancipated because of the entrepreneurial activity of the mother; income is simply generated to make a living and escape poverty. However, if our results can be generalized, what a price women entrepreneurs might have to pay! At least, thanks to their entrepreneurial behavior, women can be emancipated from their spouses.

6.   CONCLUSION: LIMITATIONS, CONTRIBUTION, AND FURTHER RESEARCH

The findings demonstrate that even though refugee women entrepreneurs may experience emancipation, in particular family emancipation, through entrepreneuring, their emancipation is bounded as they are still controlled and dominated by their husbands and culture. This shows a contradictory facet of entrepreneuring-as-emancipation, which is a state that cannot be totally achieved for the refugee female entrepreneur and would certainly not transform their disadvantaged position in business and society—though it can help in emancipating the family. The feminist twist employed in this analysis revealed that husbands of refugee women entrepreneurs do not play a passive role in their wives' entrepreneurial ventures, but intentionally and continuously influence their activities by keeping them under their control and supervision.

6.1   Limitations

We are aware that this study, concerning the rather under-investigated subject of the role of spousal support in the emancipation of the refugee woman entrepreneur, contains limitations.

Our particular research environment may have influenced the findings of the observed process. Considering the specific context of refugee women entrepreneurs in Beirut, who have a distinctive social and psychological profile, these results are of limited support and only enable a better understanding of women's entrepreneurship in this area.

The sample and its recruitment are further unique limitations of this study. The empirical material was generated in one city, with a small group of Syrian refugee women entrepreneurs and their husbands, family members, and friends. In that respect, the study is confined primarily to the insights provided by the sampled set of entrepreneurs. As a result, rather than offering generalizable conclusions, findings from this study may thus be limited in terms of transferability to other refugee groups or other settings or places due to its temporal and geographical limitations.

Because we conducted ethnographic research within refugee communities, the empirical data generated and the analysis did not take into consideration the broader conditions of entrepreneurship in refugee communities. We were also constrained in our knowledge of how practices that take place during our observations are affected by other practices that take place away from the action scene we observed (Nicolini, 2012).

Another limitation that affected our observations is related to our inclination to study the "dark side" of entrepreneurship. That is, we were more driven to investigate the negative features of the social and cultural phenomenon of entrepreneurship, to understand how the actions around entrepreneurship can produce exclusive meanings in terms of power relations. This implies that we may have overlooked some of the inferences that may have been made concerning the practices under consideration.

6.2   Contribution

The specific contribution of this research is to expand our understanding of society as a distinctive and historically situated construction (Bourdieu, 1984; Giddens, 1979). This study paints a thorough picture of the socio-cultural factors that influence refugee women's entrepreneurship. It focuses on under-standing social support roles, gender, and power dynamics, as well as how these factors interact to impact refugee women's entrepreneurial experi-ences. It contributes to extant entrepreneurship research by responding to calls to draw a more rounded picture of entrepreneurship (Tatli et al., 2014) and provide insight into the entrepreneuring processes of women entrepre-neurs, particularly those who are in disadvantaged positions. It employs an entrepreneurship-as-practice approach to examine how entrepreneurship is constructed and studies entrepreneurship as a processual phenomenon that considers entrepreneurship as a part of society in the context in which it occurs.

On a more theoretical level, this research contributes to a better understand-ing of the role of spousal support in women entrepreneuring within a specific context, namely that of the refugee entrepreneur. Moreover, it contributes to empirical studies examining the emancipatory potential of entrepreneurship by tending to shed light on the dark side of women entrepreneurship. Following Jennings et al. (2016), who note that women entrepreneurs are sometimes disappointed by their entrepreneurial experiences as a means of emancipation, we argue that, in our studied context, entrepreneurial experiences can become at worst a source of coercion of women, who may be trapped by their families, and at best a means of controlling women by their spouses.

The study contributes methodologically to the field of entrepreneurship by using a combination of ethnographic and narrative interview methods, hence enabling the exploration of contextually rich empirical data through studying and analyzing the practices and their enactment in their normal set-tings. Furthermore, interviews with key informants such as family members, husbands, neighbors, friends, and relatives reinforced the women's interviews and offered a distinct viewpoint that contributed to a wide grasp of the study and better triangulation between the data sources. In addition, the repeated back-and-forth movement between data collection and analysis increased the data's trustworthiness.

Further, this research may provide insights for NGOs who work on pro-viding entrepreneurship development programs for refugee women. It can aid them in taking decisions to successfully implement and assess the usefulness of entrepreneurship development programs that NGOs provide for refugee women. It can help them assess the role of the spouse in the life of a woman entrepreneur and the possibility of promoting change in societal attitudes toward women's entrepreneurship.

6.3   Further Research

Despite its limitations, the study has a number of implications for future research.

First, the growing focus on "everyday entrepreneurship" (Welter et al., 2017) emphasizes the importance of understanding places as contexts for entrepreneurship and studying diverse, typically less ideal, locations where entrepreneurship occurs (Welter & Baker, 2020). Accordingly, more contextually sensitive studies incorporating a range of empirical settings should be conducted in order to celebrate diversity and expand contributions to entrepreneurship research.

In addition, this research may indicate that we are referring to refugee people as if they were a homogenous group. We are well aware of the huge variation within the refugee environment in various regions or places that differ significantly in culture, population, religion, and history. Our study is merely a beginning point, and we urge more research that can present a more detailed picture of women entrepreneurs' circumstances in refugee settings.

Another recommendation for future study is to conduct more ethnographic studies of women's entrepreneurship in order to gain a better empirical knowledge of the influence of the role of the spouse in women's entrepreneurial activity in light of difficult business conditions. The four Syrian cases in this study represent a start, but further in-depth research in other regions is required.

Finally, our participants revealed common challenges that they experienced during their entrepreneuring process. Exposure to constraints imposed by the spouse on the female entrepreneur and her business (domination, control of income, control of mobility, control on decision-making, reliance on the wife's income) was experienced by the women after they started and managed their business and was indicative of a continuous repressive state. Future research should extend efforts to further explore the emancipatory potential of entrepreneurship for the woman entrepreneur and her family, and deepen our understanding of the spousal support role at various phases of the entrepreneuring process. This may lead to a better understanding of the emancipation/ oppression spectrum in this field.

REFERENCES

Ahl, H., & Marlow, S. (2012). Exploring the dynamics of gender, feminism and entrepreneurship: Advancing debate to escape a dead end? *Organization, 19*(5), 543–62. https://doi.org/10.1177/1350508412448695.

Al-Dajani, H., & Marlow, S. (2010). Impact of women's home-based enterprise on family dynamics: Evidence from Jordan. *International Small Business Journal: Researching Entrepreneurship, 28*(5), 470–86. doi: 10.1177/0266242610370392.

Al-Dajani, H., & Marlow, S. (2013). Empowerment and entrepreneurship: A theoretical framework. *International Journal of Entrepreneurial Behaviour & Research, 19*(5), 4.

Al-Dajani, H., Carter, S., Shaw, E., & Marlow, S. (2015). Entrepreneurship among the displaced and dispossessed: Exploring the limits of emancipatory entrepreneuring. *British Journal of Management, 26*(4), 713–30.

Aldrich, H.E., & Cliff, J.E. (2003). The pervasive effects of family on entrepreneurship: Toward a family embeddedness perspective. *Journal of Business Venturing, 18*(5), 573–96. https://doi.org/10.1016/S0883-9026(03)00011-9.

Alkhaled, S., & Berglund, K. (2018). "And now I'm free": Women's empowerment and emancipation through entrepreneurship in Saudi Arabia and Sweden. *Entrepreneurship & Regional Development, 30*(7–8), 877–900. https://doi.org/10.1080/08985626.2018.1500645.

Alrawadieh, Z., Karayilan, E., & Cetin, G. (2018). Understanding the challenges of refugee entrepreneurship in tourism and hospitality. *Service Industries Journal, 39*(9–10), 717–40. https://doi.org/10.1080/02642069.2018.1440550.

Amine, L.S., & Staub, K.M. (2009). Women entrepreneurs in sub-Saharan Africa: An institutional theory analysis from a social marketing point of view. *Entrepreneurship and Regional Development, 21*(2), 183–211. https://doi.org/10.1080/08985620802182144.

Baker, T., & Welter, F. (2017). Come on out of the ghetto, please! Building the future of entrepreneurship research. *International Journal of Entrepreneurial Behavior & Research, 23*(2), 170–84. doi: 10.1108/IJEBR-02-2016-0065.

Bastian, B.L., Sidani, Y.M., & El Amine, Y. (2018). Women entrepreneurship in the Middle East and North Africa. *Gender in Management: An International Journal, 33*(1), 14–29. doi: 10.1108/gm-07-2016-0141.

Berner, E., Gomez, G., & Knorringa, P. (2012). *Helping a large number of people become a little less poor: The logic of survival entrepreneurs.* The Hague: ISS.

Bourdieu, P. (1984). *A social critique of the judgment of taste.* Cambridge, MA: Harvard University Press.

Brush, C.G., de Bruin, A., & Welter, F. (2009). A gender-aware framework for women's entrepreneurship. *International Journal of Gender and Entrepreneurship, 1*(1), 8–24. https://doi.org/10.1108/17566260910942318.

Calás, M.B., Smircich, L., & Bourne, K.A. (2009). Extending the boundaries: Reframing "entrepreneurship as social change" through feminist perspectives. *Academy of Management Review, 34*(3), 552–69. https://doi.org/10.5465/amr.2009.40633597.

Charmaz, K. (2011). Grounded theory methods in social justice research. In N.K. Denzin & Y.S. Lincoln (eds), *The Sage Handbook of Qualitative Research.* Thousand Oaks, California: Sage Publications.

Chasserio, S., Lebègue, T., & Poroli, C. (2014). Heterogeneity of spousal support for French women entrepreneurs. In *Women's Entrepreneurship in the 21st Century.* Cheltenham: Edward Elgar Publishing.

Davidsson, P., & Honig, B. (2003). The role of human and social capital among nascent entrepreneurs. *Journal of Business Venturing, 18*(3), 301–31.

Datta, P.B., & Gailey, R. (2012). Empowering women through social entrepreneurship: Case study of a women's cooperative in India. *Entrepreneurship Theory and Practice, 36*(3), 569–87. https://doi.org/10.1111/j.1540-6520.2012.00505.x.

De Vita, L., Mari, M., & Poggesi, S. (2014). Women entrepreneurs in and from developing countries: Evidences from the literature. *European Management Journal, 32*(3), 451–60. https://doi.org/10.1016/j.emj.2013.07.009.

Doss, C. (2013). Intrahousehold bargaining and resource allocation in developing countries. *The World Bank Research Observer*, *28*(1), 52–78. https://doi.org/10 .1093/wbro/lkt001.

Duflo, E. (2011). Women's empowerment and economic development. *National Bureau of Economic Research*. https://doi.org/10.3386/w17702.

Ezzedeen, S.R., & Ritchey, K.G. (2008). The man behind the woman: A qualitative study of the spousal support received and valued by executive women. *Journal of Family Issues*, *29*(9), 1107–35. https://doi.org/10.1177/0192513X08315363.

Farr-Wharton, R., & Brunetto, Y. (2009). Female entrepreneurs as managers. *Gender in Management: An International Journal*, *24*(1), 14–31. doi: 10.1108/17542410910930725.

Foley, M., Baird, M., Cooper, R., & Williamson, S. (2018). Is independence really an opportunity? The experience of entrepreneur-mothers. *Journal of Small Business and Enterprise Development*, *25*(2), 313–29. https://doi.org/10.1108/JSBED-10 -2017-0306.

Gaddefors, J., & Anderson, A.R. (2017). Entrepreneursheep and context: When entrepreneurship is greater than entrepreneurs. *International Journal of Entrepreneurial Behavior & Research*, *23*(2), 267–78. https://doi.org/10.1108/IJEBR-01-2016-0040.

Giddens, A. (1979). *Central Problems in Social Theory: Action, Structure, and Contradiction in Social Analysis*. Berkeley: University of California Press.

Gill, R., & Ganesh, S. (2007). Empowerment, constraint, and the entrepreneurial self: A study of white women entrepreneurs. *Journal of Applied Communication Research*, *35*(3), 268–93. https://doi.org/10.1080/00909880701434265.

Gioia, D.A., Corley, K.G., & Hamilton, A.L. (2013). Seeking qualitative rigor in inductive research: Notes on the Gioia methodology. *Organizational Research Methods*, *16*(1), 15–31.

Goss, D., Jones, R., Betta, M., & Latham, J. (2011). Power as practice: A micro-sociological analysis of the dynamics of emancipatory entrepreneurship. *Organization Studies*, *32*(2): 211–29.

Hughes, K.D. & Jennings, J.E. (2012). *Global women's entrepreneurship research: Diverse settings, questions and approaches*. Cheltenham: Edward Elgar Publishing.

Jacobsen, K. (2002). Livelihoods in conflict: The pursuit of livelihoods by refugees and the impact on the human security of host communities. *International Migration*, *40*(2), 95–123.

Jennings, J.E., Jennings, P.D., & Sharifian, M. (2016). Living the dream? Assessing the "entrepreneurship as emancipation" perspective in a developed region. *Entrepreneurship Theory and Practice*, *40*(1), 81–110.

Jennings, J.E., & McDougald, M.S. (2007). Work–family interface experiences and coping strategies: Implications for entrepreneurship research and practice. *Academy of Management Review*, *32*(3), 747–60.

Kirkwood, J. (2009). Spousal roles on motivations for entrepreneurship: A qualitative study in New Zealand. *Journal of Family and Economic Issues*, *30*(4), 372–85. https://doi.org/10.1007/s10834-009-9169-4.

Kirkwood, J., & Tootell, B. (2008). Is entrepreneurship the answer to achieving work–family balance? *Journal of Management & Organization*, *14*(3), 285–302. doi: 10.5172/jmo.837.14.3.285.

Lewis, K.V., Harris, C., Morrison, R., & Ho, M. (2015). The entrepreneurship–motherhood nexus: A longitudinal investigation from a boundaryless career perspective. *Career Development International*, *20*(1), 21–37. https://doi.org/10.1108/CDI -07-2014-0090.

McElwee, G., & Al-Riyami, R. (2003). Women entrepreneurs in Oman: Some barriers to success. *Career Development International*, *8*(7), 339–46. https://doi.org/10.1108/13620430310505296.

Newth, J. (2018). "Hands-on" vs "arm's length" entrepreneurship research. *International Journal of Entrepreneurial Behavior & Research*, *24*(3), 683–96. doi: 10.1108/ijebr-09-2016-0315.

Nicolini, D. (2012). *Practice Theory, Work, and Organization: An Introduction.* Oxford: Oxford University Press.

Nikina, A., Le Loarne-Lemaire, S., & Shelton, L.M. (2012). Le rôle de la relation de couple et du soutien du conjoint dans l'entrepreneuriat féminin. *Revue de l'Entrepreneuriat*, *11*(4), 37. https://doi.org/10.3917/entre.114.0037.

Nikina, A., Shelton, L.M., & Le Loarne, S. (2015). An examination of how husbands, as key stakeholders, impact the success of women entrepreneurs. *Journal of Small Business and Enterprise Development*, *22*(1), 38–62.

Prentice, D.A., & Carranza, E. (2002). What women and men should be, shouldn't be, are allowed to be, and don't have to be: The contents of prescriptive gender stereotypes. *Psychology of Women Quarterly*, *26*(4), 269–81. https://doi.org/10.1111/1471-6402.t01-1-00066.

Refai, D., Haloub, R., & Lever, J. (2018). Contextualizing entrepreneurial identity among Syrian refugees in Jordan: The emergence of a destabilized habitus? *International Journal of Entrepreneurship and Innovation*, *19*(4), 250–60. https://doi.org/10.1177/1465750317750322.

Rindova, V., Barry, D., & Ketchen, D.J. (2009). Entrepreneuring as emancipation. *Academy of Management Review*, *34*(3), 477–91. https://doi.org/10.5465/amr.2009.40632647.

Rizkalla, N., & Segal, S.P. (2019). War can harm intimacy: Consequences for refugees who escaped Syria. *Journal of Global Health*, *9*(2). doi: 10.7189/jogh.09.020407.

Sadi, M.A., & Al-Ghazali, B.M. (2010). Doing business with impudence: A focus on women entrepreneurship in Saudi Arabia. *African Journal of Business Management*, *4*(1): 1–11.

Scott, L., Dolan, C., Johnstone-Louis, M., Sugden, K., & Wu, M. (2012). Enterprise and inequality: A study of Avon in South Africa. *Entrepreneurship Theory and Practice*, *36*(3), 543–68. https://doi.org/10.1111/j.1540-6520.2012.00507.x.

Shelton, L.M. (2006). Female entrepreneurs, work–family conflict, and venture performance: New insights into the work–family interface. *Journal of Small Business Management*, *44*(2), 285–97. https://doi.org/10.1111/j.1540-627X.2006.00168.x.

Shinnar, R.S., Giacomin, O., & Janssen, F. (2012). Entrepreneurial perceptions and intentions: The role of gender and culture. *Entrepreneurship Theory and Practice*, *36*(3), 465–93. https://doi.org/10.1111/j.1540-6520.2012.00509.x.

Stets, J.E., & Burke, P.J. (2005). Identity verification, control, and aggression in marriage. *Social Psychology Quarterly*, *68*(2), 160–78. doi: 10.1177/019027250506800204.

Sözer, H. (2021). Categories that blind us, categories that bind them: The deployment of the notion of vulnerability for Syrian refugees in Turkey. *Journal of Refugee Studies*, *34*(3), 2775803.

Tatli, A., Vassilopoulou, J., Özbilgin, M., Forson, C., & Slutskaya, N. (2014). A Bourdieuan relational perspective for entrepreneurship research. *Journal of Small Business Management*, *52*(4), 615–32.

Verduijn, K., & Essers, C. (2013). Questioning dominant entrepreneurship assumptions: The case of female ethnic minority entrepreneurs. *Entrepreneurship &*

Regional Development, 25(7–8), 612–30. https://doi.org/10.1080/08985626.2013 .814718.

Verduijn, K., Dey, P., Tedmanson, D., & Essers, C. (2014). Emancipation and/or oppression? Conceptualizing dimensions of criticality in entrepreneurship studies. *International Journal of Entrepreneurial Behavior and Research, 20*(2): 98–107.

Wauters, B., & Lambrecht, J. (2006). Refugee entrepreneurship in Belgium: Potential and practice. *International Entrepreneurship and Management Journal, 2*(4), 509–25. https://doi.org/10.1007/s11365-006-0008-x.

Welter, F. (2011). Contextualizing entrepreneurship—conceptual challenges and ways forward. *Entrepreneurship Theory and Practice, 35*(1), 165–84. https://doi.org/10 .1111/j.1540-6520.2010.00427.x.

Welter, F., & Baker, T. (2020). Moving contexts onto new roads: Clues from other disciplines. *Entrepreneurship Theory and Practice, 45*(5), 1154–75. https://doi.org/ 10.1177/1042258720930996.

Welter, F., Baker, T., & Wirsching, K. (2019). Three waves and counting: The rising tide of contextualization in entrepreneurship research. *Small Business Economics, 52*(2), 319–30. doi: 10.1007/s11187-018-0094-5.

Welter, F., Baker, T., Audretsch, D.B., & Gartner, W.B. (2017). Everyday entrepreneurship—a call for entrepreneurship research to embrace entrepreneurial diversity. *Entrepreneurship Theory and Practice, 41*(3), 311–21. https://doi.org/10.1111/ etap.12258.

Wolf, K., & Frese, M. (2018). Why husbands matter: Review of spousal influence on women entrepreneurship in sub-Saharan Africa. *Africa Journal of Management, 4*(1), 1–32. https://doi.org/10.1080/23322373.2018.1428019.

Zahra, S.A., & Wright, M. (2011). Entrepreneurship's next act. *Academy of Management Perspectives, 25*(4), 67–83. doi: 10.5465/amp.2010.0149.

5. The role of the family environment in innovative female entrepreneurship in Latin America: cases from Colombia, Peru, and Argentina

Luz Marina Ferro-Cortes, Nancy Matos and Florence Pinot de Villechenon

1. INTRODUCTION

Entrepreneurship plays a leading role in economic development worldwide, but has usually been considered as a predominantly male activity (Schumpeter and Nichol, 1934; De Vita et al., 2014). In the global context, however, there is increasing recognition that women-led businesses have made significant contributions to innovation, employment, wealth creation, and the wellbeing of people (De Bruin et al., 2007; Jennings & Brush, 2013; Henry et al., 2016).

Contemporary trends in female entrepreneurship (FE) were reported in 2019 and Latin America was reported to have the second highest rate of entrepreneurship worldwide, with a growing rate of opportunity-oriented ventures (Elam et al., 2019; Bosman et al., 2021). Thus, from the perspective of opportunity, a new phenomenon of study has emerged: namely, innovative female entrepreneurship, or IFE (Nair, 2020). IFE responds to intrinsic motivations of entrepreneurs oriented to opportunity and their creation of value beyond the economy (Bruyat & Julien, 2001; Orser et al., 2013; Hechavarria et al., 2017). This type of entrepreneurship is observed in different activity sectors: wholesale/retail, financial/consumer services, manufacturing, education, and so on (Elam et al., 2019), and with variations in family environment (Kelley et al., 2020).

The process perspective, with emphasis on value paradigms (Bruyat & Julien, 2001) and the identification, evaluation, and exploitation of opportunity (Shane & Vetakaraman, 2000), is particularly appropriate to research this phenomenon. However, it is little explored (DeTienne & Chandler, 2007; González-Álvarez & Solís-Rodríguez, 2011; Sullivan & Meek, 2012; Orser et al., 2013). Little analysis has been done on the role of the family environment in this process. However, it is known that the family values instilled in entrepreneurs (Orser et al., 2013) motivate them to launch businesses that provide social, environmental, and economic value.

The phenomenon of women entrepreneurs who follow a process of opportunity identification and value creation has been little explored (DeTienne & Chandler, 2007; González-Álvarez & Solís-Rodríguez, 2011; Sullivan & Meek, 2012; Orser et al., 2013), and even less studied is the family's role in the process of identification and exploitation of opportunities (Shane & Vetakaraman, 2000).

The early family embeddedness perspective (Aldrich & Cliff, 2003) has been reconsidered by Aldrich et al. (2021), who incorporate historical changes in the role of the family in entrepreneurship and family business research. The authors suggest new avenues of research, placing families at the core. Along this line, Jennings and Brush (2013) recommend examining the influence that the family system may have on processes of evaluating and exploiting opportunities for female entrepreneurs. In our research we focus on understanding the distinct roles that the family environment plays in the dynamics of Innovative Female Entrepreneurship (IFE) (Alsos et al., 2013; Fuentes-Fuentes et al., 2017; Chatterjee & Ramu, 2018). We seek to address the following question:

What is the role of the family environment in the dynamics of innovative female entrepreneurship in Latin America?

After this introduction, the chapter is structured into four main sections. Section 2 presents a review of the literature about innovative female entrepreneurship and the impact of family environment on entrepreneurship. We explore the family embeddedness perspective and address the dynamic using the process perspective. In section 3 we present our methodological framework of longitudinal research and case study selection, and develop the contextual framework and context of female entrepreneurship. In section 4 we present the results of the cases studied to illustrate the phenomenon and in section 5 we present the findings and constructs to be discussed. We end by presenting a synthesis of the limitations of the study and future directions for research. We integrate a model that represents the family environment role of the IFE in emerging countries. In this way, we hope to contribute to strengthening understandings of the virtuous dynamics of the family and its impact on women entrepreneurs in Latin America.

2.   THEORETICAL FRAMEWORK

Female entrepreneurs build value for society; they provide (self-)employment and family income, and create jobs and innovative market solutions (Elam et al., 2019). However, women are underrepresented in terms of power and decision-making: it was recently found that globally only 28 percent of women held managerial positions and only 18 percent of chief executive officers were women (UN, 2020), and figures for women's nascent entrepreneurships are at 5.5 percent compared to about 7.5 percent of men, although some countries (Peru and Brazil) are nearly at parity (Elam et al., 2019).

We discuss three points in this section: Innovative Female Entrepreneurship (IFE), the role of family in entrepreneurship, and the processual perspective, to establish the role of the family environment in the entrepreneurial process in developing countries.

2.1   Innovative Female Entrepreneurship

An early paradigm to understand entrepreneurship was proposed by Jean Baptiste Say (1821/1968) as new combinations of production factors creating value or as new combinations, involving products, materials, processes, organizations, and markets (Schumpeter and Nichol, 1934), known as creative destruction, and conducted by entrepreneurs who act as agents of change. In female entrepreneurship, the use of typologies that classify entrepreneurship as necessity-driven (subsistence entrepreneurship) and opportunity-driven (GEM reports) has predominated. The nuances of innovation among FE were identified in the latter group using labels of "high growth potential" (Terjesen & Lloyd, 2015) or "high impact" (in the 2019 and 2020 GEM reports), with the growth dimension standing out in them. The 2019 and 2020 GEM report shows that IFE is a growing trend in Latin America and the Caribbean. However, research on innovation-oriented women's entrepreneurship is just emerging (Nair, 2020).

The participation of women in entrepreneurship is concentrated in SMEs (ITC, 2015; Akter et al., 2019). Innovation in these organizations is considered as a decisive element for their business models and to maintain a competitive advantage, which is inherent to the entrepreneurial orientation; it is further linked to the ability to develop new products, processes, markets, materials, and organizational forms. The evolution of innovation is embodied in the Oslo Manual of Innovation (OECD/Eurostat, 2018). However, little attention has been paid to the role of gender in innovation. The focus has been mostly on the innovation capacity of organizations, which is crucial in the case of SMEs. In a recent study, Bauweraerts et al. (2022) found that female directors of family-owned SMEs exert a positive influence on the intensity of R&D according to their socio-emotional wealth preferences.

We consider innovation capacity as the potential to create novel and valuable products or knowledge (Zheng et al., 2011), and it is defined by multiple dimensions that contribute to it (Boly et al., 2014; Saunila & Ukko, 2014; Saunila, 2017). Saunila (2020) cites among these contributing factors a culture of participative leadership, development of know-how, and ideation and organizing structures (Sosa-Sacio & Matos-Reyes, 2019; Saunila, 2020), as well as others such as external knowledge utilization, competence management, and creativity of employees.

Innovation is a gendered concept with a strong male connotation due to its association with science and engineering (Alsos et al., 2013). Innovative capacity or "innovativeness" is contingent on a firm's interaction with users and customers, as well as institutions (Fuentes-Fuentes et al., 2017), and is related to the absorptive capacity (ACAP) concept proposed by Cohen & Levinthal (1990), defined as the ability to recognize value in external information. This factor depends on the managerial capability to monitor the external environment and to translate information into a viable idea. Furthermore, this skill is based on prior related knowledge (Zou et al., 2018). In the case of new ventures, these characteristics would be present in the founder. However, there tends to exist a social perception of lower innovativeness in firms owned or led by women (Fuentes-Fuentes et al., 2017). Other authors have remarked that difficulty in accessing funding inhibits women's entrepreneurial innovation (Nair, 2020).

Innovation is mandatory for firms to achieve a competitive advantage in the dynamism of a knowledge-based society (Centobelli et al., 2018); hence, the study of IFE becomes relevant to understand innovation. An approach featuring opportunity and innovation goes against traditional paradigms of female entrepreneurship, which has often been considered a response to adverse conditions or necessity, oriented to a lesser extent toward growth (Brush & Brush, 2006; Jennings & Brush, 2013).

2.2   Family Embeddedness Approach

According to Aldrich and Cliff (2003), the family embeddedness perspective includes the dynamics of the natural interrelationship between the family and business, primarily impacting the entrepreneurial process of "recognition of opportunities and the decision to create and leverage resources" (p.574). This dynamic in the entrepreneurial model is associated with changes in the formal institution of the family (marriages, children, divorces).

The family is one of the informal institutions that influence behavior in entrepreneurship and its role is even more marked in FE (Giménez & Calabrò,

2018). The family has been a growing topic of study in FE; close attention has been given to its role in developed countries such as the United States, United Kingdom, Canada, but its role in emerging countries still needs to be understood (Cardella et al., 2020). Thus, while the role of family in emerging countries has been considered in the literature in specific aspects—such as motivation, work–family balance (Eddleston & Powell, 2012), resource leverage, and moral support—some theoretical models on female entrepreneurship assert that family is crucial to motivation and provides resources to FE. Given men and women's marked gender roles in Latin America, Terjesen and Amorós (2010) argue that entrepreneurial activities led by women constitute an extension of the family and usually result from the need to complement the family income. The dynamics of IFE have been less studied.

Incorporating family as a support for entrepreneurs has received a lot of attention this century (Cardella et al., 2020; Aldrich et al., 2021), yet there is no holistic view of the dynamics of the family environment in female entrepreneurship. One group of studies finds that one of the positive effects of family is the provision of resources (Kirkwood, 2009; Zhang & Zhou, 2021); others have found that in cases where family comes first, the difficult family–work balance can generate negative effects for entrepreneurship (Boz et al., 2016). Ambiguous results suggest the possibility of considering a double effect of family as stimulating and moderating the female entrepreneurial project. For example, Welsh et al. (2018) found that in less developed economies the context favors the economic support of the family and in more developed economies it tends to be moral support. On the other hand, Aldrich et al. (2021) found that, given that members of a family have shared the same socialization process since birth, they share norms and values and therefore fit into a normative framework that guides their actions, although it is not clear if family support differs depending on gender (Lindquist et al., 2015; Muntean & Ozkazanc-Pan, 2015). Thus, although the composition of families has evolved over time, affecting the nature of resources, a family is usually willing to support its members. According to Olson (2000) and Olson et al. (2019), in studying the functionality of family, there are three dimensions to consider: cohesion (emotional ties between members), flexibility (tolerance to changes in leadership roles and relationships), and communication (enabling the interrelation between the other two dimensions). An analysis of these dimensions in the processes of the innovative female entrepreneur will help to understand the role of the family.

2.3   The Process Perspective

From a process perspective, in the field of entrepreneurship, various authors (Gartner, 1990; Kim et al., 2005; Vetstraete & Fayolle, 2005) have recognized four dimensions that are consolidated as research paradigms, namely, the creation of new organizations (Gartner, 1985; Katz & Gartner, 1988), opportunity recognition (Stevenson & Jarillo, 1990; Kirzner, 1997; Shane & Venkataraman, 2000), value creation (Jean Baptiste Say, 1821/1964; Bruyat & Julien, 2001) and the innovation process (Schumpeter and Nichol, 1934).

As explained by Bruyat & Julien (2001), the process of creating new value occurs in a dialogic exchange between the individual or entrepreneur, his or her process, and the context in which they interact. In this paradigm the authors place "the entrepreneur as the one responsible for the creation of new value," which manifests in multiple forms (innovation and/or a new organization). This new value creation forms part of a process. On the other hand, in the opportunity paradigm, different ontological positions are presented: in the first, the opportunity is an objective phenomenon that exists outside the individual, being the entrepreneur who identifies or recognizes it; several authors, most of them economists (Casson, 1982; Kirzner, 1997, 1999; Shane & Venkataraman, 2000; Casson & Wadeson, 2007), argue this ontological positioning. In this perspective, the *alertness* proposed by Kirzner as a competence of the entrepreneur is central to the process of recognizing opportunity.

A second ontological position, from a cognitive perspective, places importance on the subjective aspects of the individual such as mental structures, knowledge, and representations (Gaglio & Katz, 2001; Ardichvili et al., 2003). These subjective aspects are the ones that make it possible to recognize or create opportunities.

In a third position, the construction of an opportunity is a social interaction between the entrepreneurial actor and the context, as a process of value exchange (Low & MacMillan, 1988; Singh et al., 1999; Sarasvathy et al., 2003; Fletcher, 2006). Between these two orientations lies Weick (1995), who sees opportunity as a phenomenon enacted or constructed through a sensemaking process. Daft and Weick (1984) had earlier proposed four core activities for organizational dynamics that aid sense-making: monitoring, interpretation, integration, and learning.

In the field of female entrepreneurship, we identified only four empirical studies and a literature review of entrepreneurship, structured from a process perspective (DeTienne & Chandler, 2007; González-Álvarez & Solís-Rodríguez, 2011; Sullivan & Meek, 2012; Orser et al., 2013).

De Tienne and Chandler (2007) place themselves in a positivist paradigm, focusing on opportunity identification, comparing process trajectories of men and women in high-tech sectors. They found that women and men use different inventories of knowledge or human capital (general and specific) that affect the trajectories they follow to identify opportunities (learning–acquiring and learning–replications); no differences between men and women were found in terms of degree of innovation. In this study, the authors only mention work–family balance as a major concern of women.

González-Álvarez and Solís-Rodríguez (2011), through an empirical study, conclude that individuals who have a greater stock of human capital and those who are immersed in broad social networks will discover more opportunities for business creation. At the same time, this work shows that there are gender differences in terms of the discovery of business creation opportunities.

Sullivan and Meek (2012) organize the research into female entrepreneurship from a process perspective based on the model proposed by Baron and Henry (2011) identifying four phases: motivations, opportunity recognition, resource acquisition and entrepreneurial performance. They classify the conflicts of family/work balance as motivations for women's entrepreneurship, leading them to seek greater flexibility in their schedules to reduce conflict and stress. In the opportunity recognition phase, the authors argue that women mobilize social capital from less diversified and closer networks (family, friends). In the acquisition of resources, research suggests that there are greater obstacles faced by women in obtaining external resources, which leads them to rely on close networks of strong ties (family and friends) to a greater extent than men do. The authors propose a final proposition related to the expectation of lower financial performance in female entrepreneurship given the motivations of women entrepreneurs towards work–family balance. These theoretical propositions have not been tested by empirical research.

Orser and coworkers (2013) use an empirical study to illustrate the values of female entrepreneurship as a factor that may impact female entrepreneurship.

The effect of the family environment and the process perspective of life transitions of the FE (Fatoki, 2014; Lindquist et al., 2015; Herdjiono et al., 2017) lack coverage in the literature. However, family network and ties play a key role in the women entrepreneurship processes in emerging markets (Aldrich and Cliff, 2003; Lindvert et al., 2017), and the desire to enhance socio-economic development or improve conditions seems to be a motivation for women to create new ventures (Rosca et al., 2020). Neneh (2018) indicates that family ties can mitigate conflicts in work–family balance in developing countries. Other studies in emerging countries (see Welsh et al., 2018 and Xheneti et al., 2019) suggest that women benefit from family–business ties in diverse ways, through both financial and moral support. In line with this, the motivation for entrepreneurship appears to reconcile professional and family life (Sullivan & Meek, 2012) (following the Baron & Henry entrepreneurship model) and greater cooperation between family and work (Brush, 1992; Eddeleston & Powell, 2012), and greater harmony between the two (Orser et al., 2013) leads to greater entrepreneur satisfaction.

In the longitudinal research framework (2014–21), we understand IFE as a recent process of women-led ventures, led alone or as part of hybrid teams, characterized by the identification and pursuit of opportunities that create value beyond the financial domain, and with the family environment playing distinct roles in the process.

To understand the IFE phenomenon, we need to study the woman entrepreneur, her enterprise, and the influence of the environment (family and context) to address the question:

What is the role of the family environment in the dynamics of innovative female entrepreneurship in Latin American countries?

3.   METHODOLOGY

According to researchers in the field of female entrepreneurship, hybrid methodologies including case studies and life stories are appropriate to understand the dynamics of IFE and the role that the family plays in the entrepreneurial process (Jennings & Brush, 2013; Henry et al., 2016). We focus on the contemporary phenomenon of IFE, which is increasingly present in emerging countries but has been poorly reflected in academia. To answer our research question, we adopt a processual perspective (Langley, 1999) and an approach using longitudinal studies of embedded multiple case studies (Yin, 2003, 2018; Eisenhardt & Graebner, 2007). Embedded design denotes several units of analysis (Bourgeois & Eisenhardt, 1988).

We started our research in 2013 in Colombia, looking at the dynamics of IFE; the study evidenced distinct roles played by the family environment in the value creation process, aligning with the findings of Calás et al. (2009) and Brush and Cooper (2012). We found that IFE provides not only economic value but also social transformation.

Acknowledging that entrepreneurship is a social phenomenon imbued in a context (Bruyat & Julien, 2001; Leitch et al., 2013), in 2019 we extended our research to Argentina and Peru to compare the preliminary findings in other contexts. As of 2021 we had studied 62 cases, with a longitudinal follow-up of the entrepreneurship processes. To illustrate the IFE process in this chapter, we chose six of those cases.

We used three units of analysis in our research: (1) women entrepreneurs; (2) the family environment role; and (3) the dynamics of the IFE (entrepreneurial process). We contrasted three countries in the region (Colombia, Peru, and Argentina) in different sectors of activity to analyze different nuances of the role of family in the dynamics of innovative female entrepreneurship.

To select the units of analysis we used hybrid sampling (Patton, 2002), combining two criteria: women entrepreneurs who receive national or international recognition for their innovative activity and/or entrepreneurs who have ventures with high growth rates. Furthermore, we verified whether the organizations reflect innovation activities, incursion into new markets, development of new products or services, and/or the creation of serial ventures. We used the contrasted sampling technique according to country and sector. For the contrast between countries, we selected Colombia and Peru as similar countries and Argentina as the contrasting country due to its macroeconomic and cultural aspects and conditions that are evident in the contextual framework. We selected the technological, service, and manufacturing sectors to show nuances of the process and follow Eisenhardt (1989) for elaboration of the propositions.

Between 2014 and 2021, we conducted interviews with women entrepreneurs in Colombia; in the case of Argentina and Peru, we conducted interviews between 2019 and 2021; in all cases we also interviewed other members of the entrepreneurial team, and monitored the organizations' news and websites. At least two members of the research team conducted the interviews, ensuring an intercultural interpretation of results; during the pandemic, we interviewed via Zoom. We assigned the name of a flower to each case that emerged from the analysis to ensure the confidentiality of the information. We then coded all the interviews, and for the analysis we used Nvivo in a dialogue between theory and what emerged from the field.

The cases were organized as proposed by Aldrich and Cliff (2003), recognizing the characteristics of the family system (nuclear and extended family) in the entrepreneurial process and using the model of Daft and Weick (1984) to make sense of the entrepreneurial process of opportunity formation and exploitation (monitoring, interpretation, integration, and learning) that expresses itself in the creation and exploitation of value (Bruyat & Julien, 2001). In the life histories of women entrepreneurs, identity emerges (Orser et al., 2013) as a central dimension that reaffirms the role of the family environment in the dynamics of the entrepreneurial process. The Appendix illustrates the structure of analysis of the role of the family environment in female entrepreneurship through the case of a serial entrepreneur, Snowball flower.

Tables 5.1 and 5.2 present the six selected cases, two per country; Table 5.1 presents a profile of each venture and Table 5.2 a profile of the entrepreneurs.

We choose cases in different sectors of activity (four in service and two in manufacturing), in traditional (education, commercial services) and less traditional areas of female entrepreneurship (manufacturing and technology-based companies). Women entrepreneurs launched their ventures alone (one case) and in teams (five cases). Two of the enterprises were set up by members of the nuclear family (sisters and nieces) and three with the support of the husbands as venture partners but led by the entrepreneurs. The orientation of the six enterprises (profit and non-profit) shows that they respond to goals that go beyond the economic. All the ventures demonstrate indicators of innovation. The entrepreneurs' ages ranged from 26 to 37 years old. This finding differs from that of the extant literature, which generally finds that women tend to undertake ventures at older ages.

3.1   Entrepreneur Profiles

Table 5.2 presents the entrepreneur profile using one or more alphanumeric denominations if other actors are involved. Profiles include marital status, education, age, previous work experience, international exposure, family background and family involvement in the venture.

3.2   Contextual Framework

In their study of entrepreneurship and innovation in emerging economies, Anderson and Ronteau (2017) explicitly emphasize that context is particularly relevant and point out that the routinized behavior of individuals and time provides explanations about the entrepreneurship process. Considering that Latin America has the second highest total entrepreneurial activity (TEA) for women worldwide (17.3 percent in 2018/19), it seems appropriate to study IFE in this region. This section describes the social, political, and economic contexts of the three selected countries.

Economically, each country has a specific trajectory. The two Andean countries implemented strategies to open their economies and experienced growth in the years prior to the COVID-19 epidemic. Argentina pursued more nationalistic policies in the twenty-first century, with the exception of the period 2015–19, and experienced a deep crisis in 2001 and a recession from 2014 to the present. All three are part of regional integrations: the Andean Community of Nations and Pacific Alliance (Colombia and Peru) and Mercosur (Argentina). While efforts to integrate demonstrate unequal economic performance (less dynamism in the case of Mercosur), they reflect a tendency toward an open economy and the desire to enlarge local markets.

Colombia and Peru have similar conditions for entrepreneurship, although Colombia is slightly better off in several areas (specific regulations). Argentina offers certain aspects (Bosma & Kelley, 2019) such as regulatory support, market dynamics, and legal infrastructure.

The similarities between Colombia and Peru and the differences with Argentina are the justification for choosing these countries to compare the case studies.

In the cultural realm,[1] Argentina, with a high score (46) in Hofstede's individualism dimension (a rating to measure the degree of interdependence that a society accepts among its members), emerges as one of the most individualistic societies in Latin America. In other words, Argentinians are expected to take care of themselves and their families above others. At the opposite extreme

Table 5.1   Profile of the companies studied

Country	COLOMBIA		PERU			ARGENTINA
Case study	*Sunflower*	*Snowball flower*	*Red rose*	*Kantuta*	*Campanemia*	*Erythina Kapok flower*
Creation date	2007	Between 2011 and 2014, five ventures	1979	2013	2015	2014
Sector/niche	Agribusiness. Diversity of food products from the microalgae spirulina	Ed-Tech Serial entrepreneur	Special education. Directed at children and adolescents with special needs	Bakery products: inclusive kitchen	Tourism/welfare: boutique hotel	Outdoor accessories (bags, backpacks)
Composition of entrepreneurial team (ET)	Family business of origin. Three founding partners, two sisters and one niece. In 2019, three members of a second generation entered	Two founding entrepreneurs and two entrepreneurs	One entrepreneur	One entrepreneur at the beginning; husband joined later	Two entrepreneurs	Family business of origin. Three founding partners: three sisters
Orientation	For-profit. Multiple social and environmental impacts	For-profit and social impact	Nonprofit	For-profit and social impact	For-profit and social and environmental impact	For-profit
Direct employees (2019)	55, of whom 80% are women	53	180	30	6	20

Country	COLOMBIA		PERU		ARGENTINA	
Case study	*Sunflower*	*Snowball flower*	*Red rose*	*Kantuta*	*Campanemia*	*Erythina Kapok flower*
Sales in US$ (2019)			US$ 1.1 million	US$ 780 mil		$ 20 million
Innovation indicators	DOI: Export 10%, two regions, four countries Good manufacturing practices Green Business Certification	DOI: presence in eight countries Endeavor Impact Award (2019) IDB, WeXchange Award for Most Innovative Entrepreneur in Latin America STEM Five new ventures	60% international revenues, three regions, 16 countries Reina Sofía Award for rehabilitation and integration Esteban Campodónico Figallo Award Harris of Rotary International Alcatel Award for Innovation and *la Orden del Sol de Perú* recognition Ashoka Fellow	Founded with OIT the National Council for the disabled Humanity and Inclusion Prize (2019) Start Up Peru (2015) Innovate Peru (2017) Kunan Challenge (2018) Wiese Foundation (2019) Romero Foundation (2015)	DOI: 30% The entrepreneur has developed a new venture as a novelist	DOI: 20% in 2017

Note: DOI=Degree of Internationalization.
Source: Field data, collected by the researchers.

Table 5.2   Entrepreneur profile

| | COLOMBIA | | PERU | | ARGENTINA |
Venture	Sunflower	Snowball flower	Red Rose	Kantuta	Campanemia	Erythina Kapok flower
Entrepreneur	E1: CO E2: SO E3: AB	E1: VR E2: MB	E1: LM	E1: CR E2: CS	E1: CLM E2:	E1: SE E2: AE E3: VS
Status	E1: Married, mother (2 daughters) E2: Married E3: Married	Married, mother (2 daughter and 1son)	Divorced, mother (1 child)	Married	Married (2 children)	E1: Married (2 children) E2: Married (3 children) E3: Single
Education	E1: Bacteriology E2: Administrative Technician E3: Pharmaceutical chemistry	E1: Industrial Engineering Masters (Finance, Marketing and Management) E2: Engineering industry, economics, and MBA	Psychology PhD	Administration & MBA	E1: tourism and psychology E2: Medicine	E1: Economist E2: Administrator E3: Industrial designer
Age at which entrepreneur launched venture	E1:34 E2: E3: 30	E1: 34	26	28	E1: 37	E1: 33 E2:29 E3: 26
Years of experience before launching venture	E1:10 E2:15 E3:10	E1: 12	5	7	E1:	E1:8 in the fashion industry

Venture	COLOMBIA		PERU		ARGENTINA	
	Sunflower	*Snowball flower*	*Red Rose*	*Kantuta*	*Campanemia*	*Erythina Kapok flower*
International exposure	E1: E3: Worked in a multinational in Nicaragua. Relationship with two sisters reunited in Switzerland and Canada	USA for 10 years Works in multinational in direct positions One master Bilingual	USA for more than 10 years Bilingual	Trips to Geneva and Paris Bilingual Agreements with India and USA	Franco-Argentinian Trilingual	E3: Master's studies in Europe

	COLOMBIA		PERU		ARGENTINA	
Venture	*Sunflower*	*Snowball flower*	*Red Rose*	*Kantuta*	*Campanemia*	*Erythina Kapok flower*
Family background	Two-generation family business Household described as matriarchy (six women, influence of the mother) Five enterprising daughters	Father was an entrepreneur in technology Household of origin formed by father, mother and four daughters, described as a matriarchy	Parents in pharmaceutical sector	Entrepreneur father and mother	Parents migrated from Argentina to France for political asylum	Father and mother economists. Original household of six daughters and a son Strong mother figure (always looking to empower her daughters to gain confidence in their processes)
Members of the family participating in the company	Founders: two sisters and a niece Second generation: two daughters of E1, one son of E2 Two sisters abroad support internationalization	E1 undertakes her latest venture with her husband	Parents support the business at the beginning but not co-owned	E1 undertakes the venture and later E2 joins as a partner before they marry	E1 with her husband E2, who initially acts as an investor and partner in the company	Three sisters Brother supports with contacts, but does not participate directly

Table 5.3   *Rating of "what is important for me" (2017–20)*

Country	Family	Religion	Politics	Trust of others	Friendships
Argentina	91.7%	24.3%	7.5%	19.2%	51.9%
Colombia	80.7%	58.4%	19.1%	4.5%	38.5%
Perú	87.8%	44.6%	12.3%	4.2%	17.1%

Source: World Value Survey. www.worldvaluessurvey.org/WVSContents.jsp.

is Colombia, with one of the lowest Hofstede individualism dimension scores in the world; this is a more collectivist society that shows great loyalty to the group and therefore a propensity to align itself with the positions of the group. Peru, in this dimension, is also among the low-scoring, collectivist countries (16). In the employee–employer relationship the employee is more conformist, preferring to have more job security than autonomy.

Considering the importance of values in entrepreneurship, we used data from the World Value Survey (WWS) for the period 2017–20 and then compared the rating of five values for each country, shown in Table 5.3.

Table 5.3 provides dimensions for understanding cultural nuances by country, with Argentina assigning greater importance to family, friends, and relationships of trust, while in Colombia and Peru family is followed in importance by religion and friends. These dimensions reflect similarities and contrasts in the three countries under study.

This relationship between family and entrepreneurship has been reported in other studies (Kelley et al., 2020). Data from the GEM 2018 global report (48 economies) shows that 75 percent of entrepreneurs and 81 percent of new business owners involve the family in their startups, with Argentina having the highest rate of family involvement in the entrepreneurial process (92 percent), followed by Peru (89 percent) and Colombia (75 percent).

4.   RESULTS

We developed the cases according to the family embeddedness perspective (Aldrich & Cliff, 2003; Aldrich et al., 2021). We collected the life history of each entrepreneur and her experience with the entrepreneurial process, focusing on the formation process, exploitation of the opportunity, the creation of the venture (Shane & Venkataraman, 2000), and its value creation (Bruyat & Julien, 2001) within the context in which the entrepreneurs develop.

The analysis of the cases was structured according to a processual perspective, inspired by two models: the processual model of Baron and Henry (2011) proposed by Sullivan and Meek (2012), and the model of Daft and Weick (1984), starting from a time zero (t0) where the background of entrepreneurship is presented, considering the value system in the context of the nuclear family (parents, siblings, and grandparents) and seeking to identify the contributions of the family in the construction of identity (Bingham et al., 2011; Lewis, 2013), followed by motivation for the entrepreneurial decision (Mmbaga et al., 2020).

We deconstruct the opportunity process based on interpretation of the context in which the entrepreneur develops and their acquisition of resources in terms of human capital (formal and tacit knowledge). Daft and Weick's (1984) model considers three moments in the opportunity process: t1 for monitoring information and understanding the context; t2 for opportunity evaluation and decision making; and t3 for integration and learning in value creation. We summarize the evolution of the roles of the family environment in these four stages of the process.

For each phase we present the events that have marked the entrepreneur, the dimensions that characterize the family environment, and the evidence that supports these dimensions. The Appendix gives an example of a case synthesized according to the dimensions.

4.1   Colombia

We present the two Colombian cases under the pseudonym Sunflower for the family agribusiness venture and Snowball flower for the serial or technology-based entrepreneur in the EdTech sector (see Table 5A.1 in the Appendix).

Sunflower is a family business founded in 2007 in Cumaral-Meta by two sisters and a niece. The inspiration for entrepreneurship was born from the values of a family that can be characterized as a matriarchy (six daughters and two sons), whose parents were displaced from their territories by violence; they educate their daughters under the principles and values of independence, solidarity, tolerance, and honesty. The idea for the business arose from a trip by one of the founders (E1) to a sister in Switzerland, who introduced her to an expert in spirulina, a microalgae used as a dietary supplement in several African countries. The expert convinced her to experiment with cultivation in Colombia. E1, seduced by the nutritional benefits of the microalgae and motivated by curiosity and an enterprising spirit, persuaded one of her sisters and a niece to share their knowledge and experience in administration and chemical engineering to produce the crop.

They brought the strain from Switzerland and adapted and standardized it to produce it on their parents' farm. This was a pioneering venture in the region, which they later diversified into a wide range of products using spirulina and other Amazonian plant species to make wellness and health products. The production process incorporates local and regional suppliers, providing formal employment for women and young people in a region that has been affected by violence and that experiences a high unemployment rate; the company's products have national coverage and it has recently begun exporting, a process supported by family networks (sisters living abroad).

The family business has evolved over time and the founders have brought in a second generation of family members (E1's two daughters and a cousin), who support the growth and expansion of the company. The founders recently brought in outside investors but retain control of this family business led by women who seek to contribute to the welfare of the population and the protection of the environment in their territory.

The Snowball flower case is one of a serial entrepreneur who has set up five ventures in which she combines technological and management knowledge to respond to needs or problems identified in different sectors. The process of identifying opportunities and creating value in successive ventures is described by the entrepreneur as a "process of continuous exchange with different social actors, where one venture leads you [to] another one." The human capital of the entrepreneur is acquired through a background in engineering, with a master's degree in marketing and finance in Colombia and a master's degree in technology project management in the United States. This entrepreneur later developed professional experience leading technological innovation projects in the Colombian financial sector and in the United States (education and insurance). Her professional experiences (human capital) foster the configuration of cross-cultural teams that contribute knowledge for new developments and ventures.

The serial entrepreneur defines herself as a *mom-preneur*, recognizing in her self- description her roles as mother and entrepreneur. These roles are permanently hybridized, providing meaning to her processes, particularly accentuated in the last two ventures in the ed-tech sector, in which the entrepreneur claims to have found her life's purpose, allowing her to balance her roles of mother and entrepreneur. Through education inspiring children and young people in science and strengthening computational and design thinking skills, Snowball seeks to transform society from childhood onward.

The entrepreneurial spirit of Snowball is incubated within a nuclear family, characterized as a matriarchy, where the father and mother, both professionals, educate their four daughters under principles of independence, self-confidence, perseverance, resilience, and solidarity. Recognition of her origins, the influence of her maternal extended family (grandmother, mother, aunts, and sisters), and the technological enterprises of her father, which were "not always successful," mark E1's entrepreneurial trajectory.

Decisions in entrepreneurship, such as the moment to start a business, moving from one country to another, the focus of the business on children's education and the configuration of work teams, among others, have been consistently guided by the search for balance between being a mother and an entre-preneur: "I have three children: AM who is nine years old [...] was the one who changed me, she was the one who made me take the leap to entrepreneur-ship." Her husband, whom she defines as her partner, has actively contributed to this endeavor. He has a similar professional profile, and he considers her home country as a priority. He leverages financial resources and knowledge for the ventures and is involved as a partner in the most recent latest ventures.

4.1.1 Lessons from the Colombian cases

The cases in Colombia (agro-industrial and technological sector) demonstrate the influence of the nuclear families of women entrepreneurs, in this case characterized as matriarchal, which strengthens their values of independence, self-confidence, integrity, solidarity, and resilience. The empowerment of women entrepreneurs since childhood and the presence of entrepreneurial parents motivates their inclination towards independence, entrepreneurship, and resilience.

The case of Sunflower shows nuances in the processes of female entrepre-neurship. It is led by a family group made up of professional women, with a high degree of awareness of the needs of the territory. The family history (displaced family) is embedded in the consolidated family entrepreneurship. The family environment strengthens values, motivations, and life purposes in the enterprise as contributions to an inclusive society. In the process of identification, development, and exploitation of opportunities, the extended family participates in leveraging networking, knowledge, and resources. A cross-generation contrast can be observed in this family business: in the second generation, awareness of the balance between personal, family, and professional life is accentuated, as is coherence with the purpose of contribut-ing to social welfare and the environment in their territories.

In the Snowball case, the decisions of the serial female entrepreneurs are moderated by the search for balance between the roles of mother and entrepreneur, in a push-and-pull dynamic. Instead of opposition (push), the entrepreneur achieves harmony in the construction of her context, affirming her identity as a "mom-preneur." This personal attitude protects her against the forces of the context (push) that may oppose her process, regarding the com-patibility between being a mother of three children and continuing an innova-tive growth-oriented enterprise. The entrepreneur is explicit in recognizing the role of her husband in achieving balance and in his direct contribution to the entrepreneurship through mentoring and leveraging resources, as well as in domestic activities. The entrepreneur assumes the acceptance of entrepreneur-ial mothers as a process of change and social construction. The identification of opportunities is aligned with a search for balance, between household values and the goal of transforming society.

4.2   Peru

For the Peruvian cases, we used the codes Red Rose for the special education venture and Kantuta for the bakery venture with an inclusive kitchen. Red Rose is a non-profit venture (NGO) launched in 1979, offering a unique model of education to people with different abilities. The model is currently being used in more than ten developed and emerging countries. Kantuta is a corporate venture that developed an inclusive kitchen and operates in the bakery industry. The entrepreneurs entered a highly competitive sector, determined to show that a business employing cooks with disabilities who produce quality products and good service can compete on equal terms in this competitive industry. The company is self-sustaining, and its growth is currently supported by angel investors in the ecosystem.

Entrepreneurs from both endeavors were raised in solid nuclear families and are older sisters with professional siblings (one sister of the Kantuta venture has Down Syndrome). Both sets of parents are also entrepreneurs or self-employed professionals.

In both cases, family values and strong maternal figures have shaped their identity. Since she was a child, the entrepreneur of Red Rose was instructed by her mother to record phrases such as "fight for your dreams," "be the change you want to see," and "reach heaven through hardship." She was taught to recognize people's potential: "in my parents' pharmacy they gave me tasks according to my potential." The Kantuta entrepreneur said: "at home I was taught inclusion, equal opportunity and empathy; my sister with Down Syndrome and I did the same activities, we learned to ride bicycles and skate."

In both cases, the entrepreneurs learned the value of perseverance and advocacy for less privileged people, which is expressed in testimonies such as "a 'no' answer will not stop me. It only makes the road more interesting," "all people have abilities; we just need to find out what they are," and "I want Peru to be recognized for its contribution to special education" (Red Rose entrepreneur). Likewise, the founder of Kantuta makes it clear in her testimony how difficult it was for her to be confronted with a society that discriminated against people with disabilities as she became aware that her sister would not have the same opportunities as her.

The Red Rose entrepreneur describes how punishment for asking too many questions led her to meet P, an autistic girl with little possibilities of social integration. She took on the challenge and decided to find ways to help people find their place in society, and to be loved and respected. It led her to study psychology and to research the subject from all angles: "I read everything there was about autism, I identified experts, I attended congresses until finally I met my mentor. It was my mother who told me that I would find my mentor among one of those doctors along the way."

The Kantuta entrepreneur formulated her business model in college. As a professional, she focused on promoting the social inclusion that she had experienced at home, participating in social responsibility (SR) within the companies where she worked. Eventually she decided that this was not enough, and she launched her own venture committed to inclusive baking: "My challenge for inclusion chooses the kitchen as the place to break down the paradigm that people with disabilities cannot do what others do. So, we opened [a] business that didn't exist in the country: the inclusive kitchens." In both cases, sensitivity toward less fortunate people was shaped in the heart of the family, inciting the motivation to step up to the challenge of social change.

The social context motivates them and points to a set of factors among which education plays a relevant role. The entrepreneurs leveraged their education, work experience, and family resources to advance their ventures and took steps to link them to support ecosystems, either through international donors or a national ecosystem.

Red Rose was divorced from her husband and had a son of only a few months old when she started her entrepreneurial project at her parents' house. Her experience as a mother and the need to maintain a work–family balance led her to include the school for parents in her venture: "From the beginning, my son was connected to my project and accompanied me on all my trips; he was influenced by two cultures and inspired me to include the parenting school in our educational model."

Kantuta started her project with the economic support of her father and with an orientation toward the protection of disabled people. This evolved into a focus on their empowerment after the incorporation of a partner: "I married my partner, and we complement each other perfectly in the company."

4.2.1   Lessons from the Peruvian cases

These two cases illustrate that the family context outweighs the social context in instilling values and providing resources for entrepreneurship. It is also clear that education and work experience empower women entrepreneurs and give them the necessary tools to carry out their dreams. The social context challenges them to take action to improve society. We also observe that altering family composition (marriage or divorce) can lead to milestones in ventures, transforming or consolidating their orientation. Both enterprises focus on the inclusion of vulnerable populations; one is for-profit (Kantuta) the other is non-profit (Red Rose), and both are economically sustainable. Red Rose operates in more than ten countries around the world; Kantuta has obtained international recognition and is a founding member of the National Council for the Disabled (CONADIS), with the support of the ILO.

4.3   Argentina

The Argentinian cases are represented by Campanemia Flower (tourism sector) and Erythina Kapok (fashion design). Both ventures began around late 2014/2015. The first belongs to the niche of small and unique boutique hotels which are not replicated on a large scale. It is located on the edge of the Misiones jungle, in northeastern Argentina. It aims to offer guests total immersion in nature, mobilizing local material and human resources. Erythina Kapok distinguishes itself by manufacturing and selling accessories, backpacks, and bags made in Argentina and is associated with urban mobility by bicycle and adventure travel.

4.3.1   Campanemia

The tourism venture is the initiative of an Argentinian woman whose artist parents emigrated to Europe, seeking political asylum, in the 1970s. The entrepreneur grew up in France and, as an adult, felt a fervent desire to reconnect with her country of origin and to embark on an emotionally restorative process to recover from the divorce and exile of her parents. After studying tourism and psychology, she returned to Argentina.

She combined a taste for detail and quality service from her childhood in France with a passion for the conservation of nature. The entrepreneur capitalized on her training in tourism and psychology and, with her husband, seized the opportunity to invest in a piece of land located in a wilderness threatened by deforestation. She positioned her enterprise at the edge of the Misiones jungle with a single objective: for each guest to find peace and tranquility in the jungle environment. Her husband contributed to the project from the beginning, through investment and by participating in design, decoration, and personnel training. The management of the project was entirely in her hands, by mutual consent. However, the entrepreneur's tendency to perfectionism and extreme dedication ends up having an impact on her family life. "There came a time when the hotel had become too much a part of our lives, sometimes it generated conflicts, it generated fights [...] and that was the part that was a little negative and that made me react [...] it was beginning to ruin family life." The struggles of her project helped her to re-define herself as a woman capable of managing a balance between family and her profession, leading her to a new occupation: writer. Throughout the process, the entrepreneur managed to overcome the push–pull dynamic of the family–entrepreneurship relationship and find a new balance by handing over management to another person. She remains engaged in the region, developing a new project: writing a series of novels set in the same area, which has welcomed European immigrants of diverse origin. Her husband supported her in this second venture as a reader and critic of the creative process.

4.3.2   Erythina Kapok

In this case three sisters, aware of their complementarities, decided to work together, to stay connected, and to support each other after one settled thousands of kilometers from Buenos Aires, in the north of Argentina. They come from a large nuclear family (five sisters and a brother), whose mother instilled in her daughters' values of confidence and freedom, empowering them to compete naturally in the world on numerous fronts. "Mom always tried to take care of us […] in the sense that no one can make you feel like you're not worth it." The backbone of the family was based on trust. Each of the three entrepreneurs fervently guard their work–family balance: "At 3p.m. we cut off because we believe that it is very important for our mental health and professional development to have a life outside of work."

The extended maternal family (grandfather and extended family of cousins) influenced a culture of collaborative work; during holidays they traveled to their grandparent's farm and worked alongside their cousins on farm chores and in the afternoon they played games at home, making propitious ground to share and a desire to undertake things together: "There was no television, we distracted ourselves by playing together." When one of the sisters moved with her husband to another city, they decided to explore entrepreneurial ventures, creating accessories for the urban mobility and adventure sector. "Ever since we were little girls, the bicycle was our means of transportation […] We knew first-hand what a rider would need." A treasured leather backpack that belonged to their mother and the common means of transportation, the bicycle, became their inspiration.

The founding sisters of Erythina Kapok saw a favorable context—promotion of the bicycle as urban transportation in the city of Buenos Aires and a boom in adventure tourism—to launch their development of bike accessories, leveraging the trust that was always been present in the family. The sisters organized themselves into a team, according to each person's skill (economics, design, and marketing). From the beginning, they outsourced their production to an Argentine manufacturer and relied heavily on digital sales to insert their products into the market. They took advantage of the wide possibilities offered by online sales through Mercado Libre, a giant in the sector in South America, which accounts for 70 percent of their sales. A cousin advised them on financial aspects of their venture. Outsourcing production to a trusted producer allowed them to concentrate on design and sales: "It allows us to have the life we want, finishing the day at the company at 3p.m. and being free to do other things."

4.3.3   Lessons from the Argentine cases

These are cases of women entrepreneurs who, encouraged by their personal and family trajectories, seize the opportunity to start a business, on the one hand, and to journey on a path of self-realization, to fulfill a desire for independence and freedom and to achieve a balance between personal, family, and professional life, on the other. In Campanemia, the endeavor embodies values such as nature conservation and local development (through training and empowerment of employees): "After training them to take care of every detail, I discovered that the team works better when I am not there"; in Erythina Kapok, they developed national production and a sense of pride and confidence: "We wanted to break with the stigma that the Argentinian industry is not viable or reliable. We vindicated confidence in the country. Argentina gave us a lot: a free education at the University of Buenos Aires. Our manufacturer also trusted us."

In both cases, entrepreneurship allowed them to establish new positions within the household: positions of respected women who are heard because of their experiences acquired outside the home. The Campanemia case illustrates the influence that family entrepreneurship can have on the search for equity and empowerment. In the case of Erythina Kapok, the entrepreneurial sisters recognize that they have gained new legitimacy in their respective households.

5.   DISCUSSIONS AND CONCLUSIONS

The central contribution of this research is an understanding of the distinct roles that the family environment has played in the dynamics of IFE in Latin America. We present the results organized by topic.

5.1   Values Influence the Construction of Identity in Female Entrepreneurship

Orser et al. (2013) conducted research into how feminist values are used to recognize opportunity in the venture creation process. The authors associate the identity of the women entrepreneur with feminist values, finding that feminist and entrepreneurship theory are distinct areas; in the framework of our research we connect the two, focusing our study on IFE in Latin America, analyzing the role of family values in the construction of identity and entrepreneurship.

Latin American women entrepreneurs identify with the values of their nuclear family and then strengthen them as they form their own families. The cases emphasized the values of independence, freedom, solidarity, integrity, and trust. This leads us to our first proposition.

P1: In Latin American countries, during the preliminary stages of entrepreneurship, the role of the nuclear family among potential female entrepreneurs lays the foundations for the construction of the entrepreneurs' identity and their orientation toward the type of endeavor. There are common values, with some nuances depending on the context (family and country) in which women entrepreneurs develop.

In Peru, empathy—with a basis in their own experiences (Red Rose) and those of people close to them (Kantuta)—generated a purpose: social change through inclusion. In the case of Colombia, the values of self-confidence (Snowball) and resilience (Sunflower and Snowball) strengthened the dynamics of entrepreneurship, with social and environmental impact outweighing economic impact. In Argentina, family trust (Erithina Kapok) and balance between intercultural values, as well as harmony with the environment (Campanemia), guide the motivations for entrepreneurship.

5.2   Human Capital Development

Human capital is a relevant dimension to analyze the process of opportunity identification in entrepreneurship. Davidsson and Honing (2003) and Arenieus and De Clercq (2005) observe relationships between the level of education attained and the processes of opportunity identification. DeTienne and Chandler (2007) analyze this dimension by studying the role of gender in the opportunity identification process, finding that men and women utilize their unique stocks of human capital (education and experience) following different processes; neither is inherently superior, nor do they differ in innovation opportunity.

Within the framework of the research, we found that innovative female entrepreneurs in Latin America have varied professional and educational backgrounds (undergraduate, master's, PhD) and trajectories in the industry that are related to their entrepreneurial processes (see Table 5.2). Enriched human capital provides competencies for the subsequent identification of opportunities and the organization of ventures supported by the strong ties of the family in the process.

The role of the family context in the formation of human capital is consistently present through empowerment transmitted by the parents to future entrepreneurs, including freedom and confidence to select careers and professions. Entrepreneurs' life trajectories complement their knowledge and are keystones for the type of entrepreneurship they create (socially oriented enterprises, technology-based, wellness, or environmental or nature-based). In extended family enterprises the competencies of the family team complement each other to strengthen the processes of identifying opportunities and generating value. This leads us to our second proposition.

P2: Human capital in the IFE is varied and highly professional, and is fortified by previous work experience related to the enterprise. It is acquired through processes of empowerment of women entrepreneurs in the nuclear family and contributes to the identification of successive opportunities to set up innovative women's enterprises.

5.3   Opportunity Identification (Monitoring and Evaluation)

In the context of emerging economies, continual changes stimulate the identification of opportunities (Andersson & Ronteau, 2017), which are visible to those subjects who have developed sufficient alertness (Kirzner, 1999). This ability has been frequently reported in opportunity identification processes of those seeking work–life balance (Sullivan & Meck, 2012), and in the case of women, those with developed alertness show greater intention to undertake entrepreneurship (Westhead & Solesvik, 2016).

The cases we reviewed provide evidence of the interaction between family values, human capital, motivations, and entrepreneurial alertness. In social entrepreneurships in Peru, the empathy of women directly faced with issues of social inclusion detected in the social context led them to search for alternative methods to address them. In the Argentinian cases, it is trust and family solidarity that triggers the search for opportunities. The search for work–family balance is also a motivation that activates the identification of opportunities.

P3: Our third proposition is that family values (empathy, solidarity, teamwork), human capital, and the search for work–family balance activate entrepreneurial alertness for the identification of opportunities in innovative female entrepreneurship.

5.4   Integration and Learning in the Opportunity Process

The role of networks that leverage tangible and intangible resources has been recognized in the formal training and education processes (Ferro, 2012). The networks of women entrepreneurs have been characterized as strong or trust-based (Granovetter, 1973), and have even been described as less efficient in entrepreneurship processes because they are less diversified (Aldrich et al., 1989). More recent studies (Neumeyer et al., 2019) have found that women are inserted into networks of peers made up of women with a dynamic that bridges social capital, unlike their male colleagues, who efficiently use their networks of weak ties to deliver value in innovation processes.

The IFE research found nuances in the contributions of the entrepreneurs' family networks in the processes of identifying, evaluating, and exploiting opportunities. For example, in one case an investment opportunity arose through a friend of the husband; in another the enterprise was conceived as a husband–wife partnership; in a third, family networks were leveraged, or tangible resources were provided. In view of the above, we formulate the following proposition:

P4: The family leverages networking processes to identify information in training opportunities for innovative female entrepreneurship.

5.5   Virtuous Circles in the IFE

Some women entrepreneurs whom we interviewed indicated that they experience a virtuous dynamic in the family context. One Argentinian entrepreneur said that gender equity issues at home were relatively equal and that "entrepreneurship has helped me to be listened to at home." The serial entrepreneur from Colombia states that gender equity is the norm in her household, responding to a gender ideology shared with her husband (Nikina et al., 2015), which facilitates achieving a balance between work, family, and personal life. The husband's participation as a partner in the company further reinforced the dynamics of virtuous circles, reducing conflict and contributing to the balance sought. Thus, when household activities are shared as a family, the principle of equity favors work–life balance, in line with the findings of Brush et al. (2020). We therefore formulate the following proposition.

P5: The active roles of the couple and awareness of gender equity stimulate changes in the ecosystem and disrupt gender stereotypes to foster virtuous cycles for the IFE.

5.6   Limitations and Future Research

Our research provides new insights for understanding the role of the family environment in the dynamics of IFEs in Latin American countries. We suggest extending the investigation to other Latin American contexts that present great orientation to opportunity, such as Chile, Mexico, and Brazil, to validate the five propositions that have emerged in this study.

In what follows we present an integrative model to represent the role of family environment in the process of innovative female entrepreneurship.

6.   INTEGRATIVE MODEL

As we show in Figure 5.1, there is a reciprocal influence between the family, the social context, and the innovation process of female entrepreneurs. The family is a central informal institution in Latin America; in the three study countries we see evidence of transition from a traditional patriarchal family system to a more matriarchal one where parents empower their daughters to be autonomous and independent and to perceive themselves as actors of social transformation.

The values of the nuclear family (parents, siblings, and grandparents) of potential entrepreneurs strengthen their independence, freedom, empowerment, self-confidence, integrity, solidarity, resilience, and perseverance. Therefore, motivations are characterized in the IFE as intrinsic, aligned with the values, experiences, and life purposes of women entrepreneurs and moderated in a push/pull relationship with constituted families (husbands, children).

The life stories of the Latin American women entrepreneurs in some cases internalize family histories of displacement (Sunflower) and migration (Campanelia) that respond to turbulent environments (social and political). The stories reflect values of resilience inspired by the family (Snowball Flower; Red Rose and Kantuta) or by specific situations in their territorial environments (Sunflower; Red Rose and Kantuta). The cross-cultural exposure that the entrepreneurs have experienced further sensitizes them to environmental and gender equity issues (Campanelia, Erythina Kapok, and Sunflower).

These values shape the identity construction of women entrepreneurs, inspiring their career choices and motivations for entrepreneurship. This acquired human capital is of significant help in identifying innovative oppor-

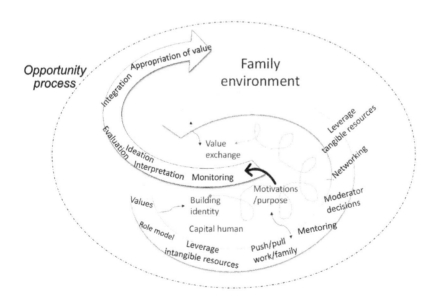

Figure 5.1   Integrative model

tunities with added value. When the entrepreneur expands her family universe to include her husband and children, this new circle is not only a source of new challenges (imbalances and their correction) but also complements her tangible and intangible resources and can even help her to detect new opportunities. Finally—and this is not a minor contribution—the family environment contributes strongly to revising gender postulates in an equitable sense in which responsibilities, satisfactions, and achievements find the desired place.

NOTE

1.   www.hofstede-insights.com/country-comparison/. Hofstede ratings on the individualism dimension measure the degree of interdependence that a society accepts among its members.

REFERENCES

Akter, M., Rahman, M., & Radicic, D. (2019). Revisiting feminism, entrepreneurship, and internationalization foundations to examine institutional factors affecting women-owned SMEs' entry in foreign market. Conference paper given at The 3rd Development Economics Conference.

Aldrich, H.E., & Cliff, J.E. (2003). The pervasive effects of family on entrepreneurship: toward a family embeddedness perspective. *Journal of Business Venturing*, *18*(5), 573–96.

Aldrich, H., Reese, P.R., & Dubini, P. (1989). Women on the verge of a breakthrough: networking among entrepreneurs in the United States and Italy. *Entrepreneurship & Regional Development*, *1*(4), 339–56.

Aldrich, H.E., Brumana, M., Campopiano, G., & Minola, T. (2021). Embedded but not asleep: entrepreneurship and family business research in the 21st century. *Journal of Family Business Strategy*, *12*(1), 100390.

Alsos, G.A., Ljunggren, E., & Hytti, U. (2013). Gender and innovation: state of the art and a research agenda. *International Journal of Gender and Entrepreneurship*, *5*(3), 236–56.

Anderson, A., & Ronteau, S. (2017). Towards an entrepreneurial theory of practice; emerging ideas for emerging economies. *Journal of Entrepreneurship in Emerging Economies*, *9*(2), 110–20. https://doi.org/10.1108/JEEE-12-2016-0054

Ardichvili, A., Cardozo, R., & Ray, S. (2003). A theory of entrepreneurial opportunity identification and development. *Journal of Business Venturing*, *18*(1), 105–23.

Arenius, P. & De Clercq, D. (2005). A network-based approach on opportunity recognition. *Small Business Economics*, *24*(3), 249–65.

Baron, R.A., & Henry, R.A. (2011), Entrepreneurship: the genesis of organizations, in S. Zedeck (ed.), *APA Handbook of Industrial and Organizational Psychology Vol. 1*, Washington, DC: APA, pp. 241–73.

Bauweraerts, J., Rondi, E., Rovelli, P., De Massis, A., & Sciascia, S. (2022). Are family female directors catalysts of innovation in family small and medium enterprises? *Strategic Entrepreneurship Journal*, *16*(2), 314–54.

Bingham, J.B., Gibb Dyer, W., Smith, I., & Adams, G.L. (2011). A stakeholder identity orientation approach to corporate social performance in family firms. *Journal of Business Ethics*, *99*(4), 565–85.

Boly, V., Morel, L., & Camargo, M. (2014). Evaluating innovative processes in French firms: methodological proposition for firm innovation capacity evaluation. *Research Policy*, *43*(3), 608–22.

Bosma, N., & Kelley, D. (2019). Global entrepreneurship monitor 2018/2019 global report. *Global Entrepreneurship Research Association (GERA)*.

Bosman, L., Bartholomew, S., Huber, S., & Amiaya, A. (2021). Using adaptive comparative judgment to promote the entrepreneurial mindset and visual literacy in the engineering technology classroom. *Entrepreneurship Education*, *4*(3), 251–71.

Bourgeois III, L.J., & Eisenhardt, K.M. (1988). Strategic decision processes in high velocity environments: four cases in the microcomputer industry. *Management Science*, *34*(7), 816–35.

Boz, M., Martínez-Corts, I., & Munduate, L. (2016). Types of combined family-to-work conflict and enrichment and subjective health in Spain: a gender perspective. *Sex Roles*, *74*(3), 136–53.

Brush, C.G. (1992). Research on women business owners: past trends, a new perspective, and future directions. *Entrepreneurship Theory and Practice*, *16*(4), 5–30.

Brush, C.G., & Brush, C.G. (2006). Growth-oriented women entrepreneurs and their businesses: a global research perspective. *Women in Management Review*, *21*(8), 690–92.

Brush, C.G., & Cooper, S.Y. (2012). Female entrepreneurship and economic development: an international perspective. *Entrepreneurship & Regional Development*, *24*(1–2), 1–6.

Brush, C.G., Greene, P.G., & Welter, F. (2020). The Diana project: a legacy for research on gender in entrepreneurship. *International Journal of Gender and Entrepreneurship*, *12*(1), 7–25. https://doi.org/10.1108/IJGE-04-2019-0083.

Bruyat, Christian, & Julien, Pierre-André. 2001. Defining the field of research in entrepreneurship. *Journal of Business Venturing*, *16*(2), 165–80.

Calás, M.B., Smircich, L., & Bourne, K.A. (2009). Extending the boundaries: reframing "entrepreneurship as social change" through feminist perspectives. *Academy of Management Review*, *34*(3), 552–69.

Cardella, G.M., Hernández-Sánchez, B.R., & Sánchez-García, J.C. (2020). Women entrepreneurship: a systematic review to outline the boundaries of scientific literature. *Frontiers in Psychology*, *11*, 1557.

Casson, M. (1982). *The Entrepreneur: An Economic Theory*. Rowman & Littlefield.

Casson, M., & Wadeson, N. (2007). The discovery of opportunities: extending the economic theory of the entrepreneur. *Small Business Economics*, *28*(4), 285–300.

Centobelli, P., Cerchione, R., & Esposito, E. (2018). Aligning enterprise knowledge and knowledge management systems to improve efficiency and effectiveness performance: a three-dimensional fuzzy-based decision support system. *Expert Systems with Applications*, *91*, 107–26.

Chatterjee, C., & Ramu, S. (2018). Gender and its rising role in modern Indian innovation and entrepreneurship. *IIMB Management Review*, *30*(1), 62–72.

Cohen, W.M., & Levinthal, D.A. (1990). Absorptive capacity: a new perspective on learning and innovation. *Administrative Science Quarterly*, 128–52.

Daft, R.L., & Weick, K.E. (1984). Toward a model of organizations as interpretation systems. *Academy of Management Review*, *9*(2), 284–95.

Davidsson, P., & Honing, B. (2003) The role of social and human capital among nascent entrepreneurs, *Journal of Business Venturing, 18*(3), 301–31.

De Bruin, A., Brush, C.G., & Welter, F. (2007). Advancing a framework for coherent research on women's entrepreneurship. *Entrepreneurship Theory and Practice, 31*(3), 323–39.

DeTienne, D.R., & Chandler, G.N. (2007). The role of gender in opportunity identification. *Entrepreneurship Theory and Practice, 31*(3), 365–86.

De Vita, L., Mari, M., & Poggesi, S. (2014). Women entrepreneurs in and from developing countries: evidence from the literature. *European Management Journal, 32*(3), 451–60.

Eddleston, K.A., & Powell, G.N. (2012). Nurturing entrepreneurs' work–family balance: a gendered perspective. *Entrepreneurship Theory and Practice, 36*(3), 513–41.

Eisenhardt, K.M. (1989). Building theories from case study research. *Academy of Management Review, 14*(4), 532–50.

Eisenhardt, K.M., & Graebner, M.E. (2007). Theory building from cases: opportunities and challenges. *Academy of Management Journal, 50*(1), 25–32.

Elam, A.B., Brush, C., Greene, P.G., Baumer, B., Dean, M., Heavlow, R., & Global Entrepreneurship Research Association. (2019). *Women's Entrepreneurship Report 2018/2019.*

Fatoki, O. (2014). Parental and gender effects on the entrepreneurial intention of university students in South Africa. *Mediterranean Journal of Social Sciences, 5*(7): 157–62.

Ferro, Luz Marina. (2012). *The Opportunity Formation Process (OFP) in the Context of High-tech (HT).* Montreal, Management Technologique UQAM.

Fletcher, D.E. (2006). Entrepreneurial processes and the social construction of opportunity. *Entrepreneurship & Regional Development, 18*(5), 421–40.

Foss, N.J., Husted, K., & Michailova, S. (2010). Governing knowledge sharing in organizations: levels of analysis, governance mechanisms, and research directions. *Journal of Management Studies, 47*(3), 455–82.

Fuentes-Fuentes, M., Bojica, A.M., Ruiz-Arroyo, M., & Welter, F. (2017). Innovativeness and business relationships in women-owned firms: the role of gender stereotypes. *Canadian Journal of Administrative Sciences/Revue Canadienne des Sciences de l'Administration, 34*(1), 63–76.

Gaglio, C.M., & Katz, J.A. (2001). The psychological basis of opportunity identification: entrepreneurial alertness. *Small Business Economics, 16*(2), 95–111.

Gartner, W.B. (1985). A conceptual framework for describing the phenomenon of new venture creation. *Academy of Management Review, 10*(4), 696–706.

Gartner, W.B. (1990). What are we talking about when we talk about entrepreneurship? *Journal of Business Venturing, 5*(1), 15–28.

Giménez, D., & Calabrò, A. (2018). The salient role of institutions in women's entrepreneurship: a critical review and agenda for future research. *International Entrepreneurship and Management Journal, 14*(4), 857–82.

González-Álvarez, N., & Solís-Rodríguez, V. (2011). Descubrimiento de oportunidades empresariales: capital humano, capital social y género. *Innovar, 21*(41), 187–96.

Granovetter, M.S. (1973). The strength of weak ties. *American Journal of Sociology, 78*(6), 1360–80.

Hechavarría, D.M., Terjesen, S.A., Ingram, A.E., Renko, M., Justo, R., & Elam, A. (2017). Taking care of business: the impact of culture and gender on entrepreneurs' blended value creation goals. *Small Business Economics, 48*(1), 225–57.

Henry, C., Foss, L., & Ahl, H. (2016). Gender and entrepreneurship research: a review of methodological approaches. *International Small Business Journal, 34*(3), 217–41.

Herdjiono, I., Puspa, Y.H., Maulany, G., & Aldy, B.E. (2017). The factors affecting entrepreneurship intention. *International Journal of Entrepreneurial Knowledge, 5*(2), 5–15.

Jain, S., Nair, A., & Ahlstrom, D. (2015). Introduction to the special issue: towards a theoretical understanding of innovation and entrepreneurship in India. *Asia Pacific Journal of Management, 32*(4), 835–41.

Jennings, J.E., & Brush, C.G. (2013). Research on women entrepreneurs: challenges to (and from) the broader entrepreneurship literature? *Academy of Management Annals, 7*(1), 663–715.

Katz, J., & Gartner, W.B. (1988). Properties of emerging organizations. *Academy of Management Review, 13*(3), 429–41.

Kelley, D., Gartner, W.B., Allen, M. (2020). *Global Entrepreneurship Monitor Family Business Report.* Babson College Press.

Kim, P.H., Aldrich, H.E., & Ruef, M. (2005). Fruits of co-laboring: effects of entrepreneurial team stability on the organizational founding process. In *Babson College Entrepreneurship Research Conference (BCERC).*

Kirkwood, J. (2009). Motivational factors in a push–pull theory of entrepreneurship. *Gender in Management, 24*(5), 346–64. https://doi.org/10.1108/17542410910968805

Kirzner, I.M. (1997). Entrepreneurial discovery and the competitive market process: an Austrian approach. *Journal of Economic Literature, 35*(1), 60–85.

Kirzner, I.M. (1999). Creativity and/or alertness: a reconsideration of the Schumpeterian entrepreneur. *Review of Austrian Economics, 11*(1), 5–17.

Langley, A. (1999). Strategies for theorizing from process data. *Academy of Management Review, 24*(4), 691–710.

Leitch, C.M., McMullan, C., & Harrison, R.T. (2013). The development of entrepreneurial leadership: the role of human, social and institutional capital. British Journal of Management, 24(3), 347–66.

Lewis, J. (2013). Disney after Disney: Family business and the business of family. In Disney Discourse, Abingdon: Routledge, pp. 87–105.

Lindvert, M., Patel, P.C., & Wincent, J. (2017). Struggling with social capital: Pakistani women micro entrepreneurs' challenges in acquiring resources. Entrepreneurship & Regional Development, 29(7–8), 759–90. https://doi.org/10.1080/08985626.2017.1349190

Lindquist, M., Sol, J., & Van Praag, C.M. (2015). Why do entrepreneurial parents have entrepreneurial children? Journal of Labor Economics, 33(2), 269–96.

Low, M.B., & MacMillan, I.C. (1988). Entrepreneurship: past research and future challenges. Journal of Management, 14(2), 139–61.

Mmbaga, N.A., Mathias, B.D., Williams, D.W., & Cardon, M.S. (2020). A review of and future agenda for research on identity in entrepreneurship. Journal of Business Venturing, 35(6), 106049.

Muntean, S.C., & Ozkazanc-Pan, B. (2015). A gender integrative conceptualization of entrepreneurship. *New England Journal of Entrepreneurship, 18*(1), 27–40. https://doi.org/10.1108/NEJE-18-01-2015-B002

Nair, S.R. (2020). The link between women entrepreneurship, innovation, and stakeholder engagement: a review. *Journal of Business Research, 119*, 283–90.

Neneh, N.B. (2018). Family–work conflict and performance of women-owned enterprises: the role of social capital in developing countries—implications for South Africa and beyond. *Journal of International Women's Studies, 19*(6), 326–43.

Neumeyer, X., Santos, S.C., Caetano, A., & Kalbfleisch, P. (2019). Entrepreneurship ecosystems and women entrepreneurs: a social capital and network approach. *Small Business Economics, 53*(2), 475–89.

Nikina, A., Shelton, L.M., & LeLoarne, S. (2015). An examination of how husbands, as key stakeholders, impact the success of women entrepreneurs. *Journal of Small Business and Enterprise Development, 22*(1), 38–62.

OECD/Eurostat (2018), *Oslo Manual 2018: Guidelines for Collecting, Reporting and Using Data on Innovation, 4th Edition, The Measurement of Scientific, Technological and Innovation Activities.* OECD Publishing. https://doi.org/10.1787/9789264304604-en

Olson, D.H. (2000). Circumplex model of marital and family systems. *Journal of Family Therapy, 22*(2), 144–67.

Olson, D.H., Waldvogel, L., & Schlieff, M. (2019). Circumplex model of marital and family systems: an update. *Journal of Family Theory & Review, 11*(2), 199–211.

Orser, Barbara, Elliott, Catherine, & Leck, Joanne. (2013). Entrepreneurial feminists: perspectives about opportunity recognition and governance. *Journal of Business Ethics, 115*(2), 241–57.

Patton, M.Q. (2002). Two decades of developments in qualitative inquiry: a personal, experiential perspective. *Qualitative Social Work, 1*(3), 261–83.

Rosca, E., Agarwal, N., & Brem, A. (2020). Women entrepreneurs as agents of change: a comparative analysis of social entrepreneurship processes in emerging markets. *Technological Forecasting and Social Change, 157*, 120067.

Sarasvathy, S.D., Dew, N., Velamuri, S.R., & Venkataraman, S. (2003). Three views of entrepreneurial opportunity. In Z.J. Acs and D.B. Audretsch (eds), *Handbook of Entrepreneurship Research* (pp.141–60). Springer.

Saunila, M. (2017). Understanding innovation performance measurement in SMEs. *Measuring Business Excellence, 21*(1), 1–16. https://doi.org/10.1108/MBE-01-2016-0005.

Saunila, M. (2020). Innovation capability in SMEs: a systematic review of the literature. *Journal of Innovation & Knowledge, 5*(4), 260–5.

Saunila, M., & Ukko, J. (2014). Intangible aspects of innovation capability in SMEs: impacts of size and industry. *Journal of Engineering and Technology Management, 33*, 32–46.

Say, J.B. (1821/1964). *Tratado de economia política.* F. villalpando.

Schumpeter, J.A., & Nichol, A.J. (1934). Robinson's economics of imperfect competition. *Journal of Political Economy, 42*(2), 249–59.

Shane, S., & Venkataraman, S. (2000). The promise of entrepreneurship as a field of research. *Academy of Management Review, 25*(1), 217–26.

Singh, R.P., Hills, G.E., Hybels, R.P., & Lumpkin, G.T. (1999). *Opportunity recognition through social network characteristics of entrepreneurs.* Frontiers of Entrepreneurship Research, Babson College, Wellesley, MA.

Sosa-Sacio, M., & Matos-Reyes, N. (2019). Evaluación de la escala brasileña "grado de innovatividad" en PYMEs peruanas. *Gestão & Regionalidade, 35*(105).

Stevenson, H.H., & Jarillo, J.C. (1990). A paradigm of entrepreneurship: entrepreneurial management. *Strategic Management Journal, 11*, 17–27.

Sullivan, Diane M., & Meek, William R. (2012). Gender and entrepreneurship: a review and process model. *Journal of Managerial Psychology, 27*(5), 428–58.

Terjesen, S., & Amorós, J.E. (2010). Female entrepreneurship in Latin America and the Caribbean: characteristics, drivers, and relationship to economic development. *European Journal of Development Research, 22*(3), 313–30.

Terjesen, S.A., & Lloyd, A. (2015). The 2015 female entrepreneurship index. *Kelley School of Business Research Paper*, 15–51.

United Nations (2020). The World's Women 2020: Trends and Statistics. *Department of Economic and Social Affairs.* 20 October 2020. https://worlds-women-2020-data-undesa.hub.arcgis.com/

Verstraete, T., & Fayolle, A. (2005). Paradigmes et entrepreneuriat. *Revue del Entrepreneuriat, 4*(1), 33–52.

Weick, K.E. (1995). *Sensemaking in Organizations* (Vol. 3). Sage.

Welsh, D.H.B., Kaciak, E., Memili, E., & Minialai, C. (2018). Business–family interface and the performance of women entrepreneurs: the moderating effect of economic development. *International Journal of Emerging Markets, 13*(2), 330–49. https://doi.org/10.1108/IJoEM-03-2017-0095

Westhead, P., & Solesvik, M.Z. (2016). Entrepreneurship education and entrepreneurial intention: do female students benefit? *International Small Business Journal, 34*(8), 979–1003.

Xheneti, M., Karki, S.T., & Madden, A. (2019). Negotiating business and family demands within a patriarchal society: the case of women entrepreneurs in the Nepalese context. *Entrepreneurship & Regional Development, 31*(3–4), 259–78.

Yin, Robert K. (2003). *Case Study Research: Design and Methods*, 3rd Coll. Sage.

Yin, R.K. (2018). *Case Study Research and Applications: Design and Methods* (6th ed.). Sage.

Zhang, J., & Zhou, N. (2021). The family's push and pull-on female entrepreneurship: evidence in China. *Emerging Markets Finance and Trade, 57*(5), 1312–32.

Zheng, S., Zhang, W., & Du, J. (2011). Knowledge-based dynamic capabilities and innovation in networked environments. *Journal of Knowledge Management, 15*(6), 1035–51.

Zou, T., Ertug, G., & George, G. (2018). The capacity to innovate: a meta-analysis of absorptive capacity. *Innovation, 20*(2), 87–121.

Table 5A.1   Snowball flower

Phases	Events description	Environmental dimensions	Evidence of the family environment in the development of the entrepreneur
Family system Norms, attitudes Values	Entrepreneurial father (Biotechnology) and professional mother in nursing, dedicated to the care and education of her four daughters	Matriarchy/entrepreneurship. Family values: • Independence • Perseverance Resilience Self-confidence	"I am from a matriarchal family and my mother, her sisters and my grandmother are strong women […] in Santander, I am from Santander, women are strong […] a matriarchal culture and I grew up with a mother who instilled in us […] to be super independent, never to wait for Prince Charming, she taught me to be resilient […] to give the best of myself, that it was never enough." "I come from super warrior dads who fought hard in entrepreneurship […] I grew up knowing the struggles that entrepreneurship has because my dad was never super successful."
Identity	In a retrospective of 2020, E1 is defined by family attributes.	Identity traits: Mother, wife, and entrepreneur role	"I am a woman who is a mother. I define myself as a mompreneur; always balancing my role as a mom and my role as an entrepreneur. I have three children: AM who is 9 years old […] she was the one who changed me, she was the one who made me take the leap into entrepreneurship; then comes M who is 8 years old and JM who is 4 years old […] that is my personal life. I am also married to an entrepreneur; we are a house of entrepreneurs." E1

Phases	Events description	Environmental dimensions	Evidence of the family environment in the development of the entrepreneur
t0 Background Human capital 1998–2012	E1: Industrial Engineering (1998), postgraduate studies: Finance, Marketing (CESA) and Management (Harvard, 2005–7) Experience in national and international IT (12 years) Acknowledgements in the industry	Self-knowledge: Identify their passions and capabilities to solve problems, innovate, form teams, and so on (intra-entrepreneurship) Gain confidence and legitimacy for their skills and results	"[…] as an engineer and because of my personality I love to solve problems... technology is an enabler, a facilitator to solve problems […] technology solves and improves the lives of all the actors involved... for me it is a passion: to solve problems or to improve." E1 "[…] my infatuation with technology […] I had a successful position with the stock exchange, we were awarded as the best Internet strategy at the time." E1 "[…] although I was not an entrepreneur, I was an intra-entrepreneur, I was given projects from scratch where I had to form the whole strategy part, the marketing part, the operations part, form the team from scratch." E1 "The largest pension fund in Colombia told me 'I do not have anything on the internet, come on […] you, make me the pension fund on the internet'. It was a fantastic experience, again intrapreneurship." E1 Boston: "I helped implement, socialize, met with every director of career services at every school […] I'm fascinated by all things international and making connections." E1

Phases	Events description	Environmental dimensions	Evidence of the family environment in the development of the entrepreneur
t1 **Context perception**	Boston, inspiring for technology and digital-based entrepreneurship Work in academia and corporate environment in the US Leadership positions (VP Latin America, Caribbean, Spain) 1st Maternity Leave	Perceived discrimination at work for being a mother. Resilience Spouse's support for the 1st decision 1ª. Decision to work or to start a business (W/F balance) 2ª. Decision, stay in Boston or leave Family at the center of decisions Identification of two opportunities O1 and O2	"I went to Harvard University, and it was impossible not to feel permeated by high-impact entrepreneurship. Boston was a cluster [...] everyone was talking about technology-based entrepreneurship." E1 (2014) "In Boston everyone is trying to be entrepreneurial, all our friends, everyone is talking about technology, not because it's the fashion, but it goes internal." E2 (2015) "I'm a big believer in the power of networking [...] I brought networking for women to Colombia. At Harvard what we were doing was connecting students. Of the great added values of going to Harvard, is how we help each other, how we support each other." E1 "[...] I took my maternity period and, when I came back [...] there was discrimination, from all my area, they took away like 40%, they never told me anything, I found out was when they appointed, the new president of operations "[...] it was the baby issue. The maternity issue, the issue that she will no longer be able to put so much time in, the issue that she will no longer be able to live on a plane, everything was extremely badly handled." (E1, 2014). "[...] I said: 'I want to start with everything', the only one who supported me was my husband, against all odds [...] I gave up! The cool thing is that I had already started my business at night and on weekends." E1 "Should we stay in Boston [...] it is a super baby friendly city because people go there to have babies because of the policies they must support fertility treatments, the average age is 30 years old. Boston is a divine city, but it has short cycles. People go to Boston, study, work and come back."

Role of the family environment for entrepreneurship

Phases	Events description	Environmental dimensions	Evidence of the family environment in the development of the entrepreneur
t2	Surveillance capability	Networking	"The wonderful thing about one entrepreneurial venture is that it brings you another. And the wonderful thing about an entrepreneur is that it connects you to another […] In Boston, friends are like family." E1 2019
Monitoring information	Connect with the Boston ecosystem	Identify permanent opportunities through their networks, colleagues, friends, and the Boston environment.	"You have to be talking about your company, always. You do not know at a dinner, at a party, at a coffee, you can find the perfect partner, or you can find a client, or you can find an investor. In a meeting, a friend, who was doing his master's degree at MIT, told me: 'E1, you are so entrepreneurial and […] why don't you apply to Wayra?' and I said: 'What is Wayra?', he told me: 'Wayra Colombia is a business accelerator'. […]
Ideation	Understanding unmet need	Evaluate as a couple the best decision for the family (Boston or Colombia?)	O1: Health website development: "[…] what I wanted at that time was to bring that business model to Latin America […] it was a flash health site, a model […] very famous in the United States and Europe." E1
	Second pregnancy	Who will initially provide resources to support the family?	O1: "It was my first failure. I didn't really know who they were bidding for." E1
	Decision to move to Colombia		O2: App development gifts: "Facebook and Amazon, they didn't even have mobile applications, I had to make the Apps for them, it's a technical issue, but neither Facebook nor Amazon were ready to connect mobile applications."
	E1 Apply to Wayra-Colombia call for applications		"In the United States you have to make a decision: either I pay for private school, and it doesn't matter where I live, or I prefer to buy an awfully expensive house near a good public school […] we started to see houses […] I said no, I am moving to the suburbs, and I am staying here, and my family? My sisters, my parents, the family referents, grandparents, uncles, uncles, cousins for the daughters? We should return to have the support system nearby […] E1
			With my husband, we made an agreement: whoever finds a job in Colombia first goes and supports the family, and whoever does not find a job goes to the world of entrepreneurship […] My husband is another brutal intra-entrepreneur. So, we started looking, each of us. And he got a job first […] I got a job at Wayra (the accelerator)."

Phases	Events description	Environmental dimensions	Evidence of the family environment in the development of the entrepreneur
t3 **Evaluation**	Installation of the family in Colombia Connecting to a new ecosystem Reflection on entrepreneurial learning O1 and O2 How to configure a solution to market needs and not to supply? Selling O2 New ventures O3 to O5	Family support in the installation in Colombia Obtaining resources in the ecosystem Identification of new opportunities in technical education for application developers and international partners. Identification of a new segment (children) Pressure to maintain F/W balance	We came to live in Colombia, I started my acceleration process at Wayra, a fantastic experience […] the entrepreneurship ecosystem in Colombia was starting […] I won the Mass Challenge Pitch Competition […] I was a beneficiary of seed capital from Impulsa […] and then I had my first exit, I was acquired." E1 O2: "[…] I made a lot of mistakes, again I focused too much on the product, I closed myself […] to build the most incredible mobile application […] without validating it with customers […] it was the ideal solution for me, not for the market. Although it sold very well […] here comes the other especially critical point in entrepreneurship, you must know how to pivot." E1 O3: Creation of an online education company: "In O2 I had a challenging time finding people who knew how to develop mobile applications, because it was a new topic […] a new language, so we ended up teaching courses in mobile development, algorithms, we formally opened a new company." E1 O4: "It is the first startup incubator in technology and education […] we support three edTech companies." E1 O5: Identification of a niche in science and technology education: "[…] the language of the future is computational, and we have to give kids that same set of skills which is computational thinking and design thinking […] in O5 I find my life purpose, I can consolidate all the learning." E1

Phases	Events description	Environmental dimensions	Evidence of the family environment in the development of the entrepreneur
t4 **Integration & growing**	Niche focus on education for children Consolidates international expansion (10 countries) Set up intercultural team	Reorient: give meaning to the undertakings (E2, the spouse participates in reflection and as a partner, O3, O4, O5) Consolidate social vision	O5: "Education has always been something that I have always liked because with education you bring economic development, you change societies, ...you change lives ...". ... Our mission with children is to awaken the love for science and technology". ... "First we want to make a social revolution, we want children to change their role model, we want scientists to be seen as a role model." E1 I want to leave a legacy" and all this aligned my family part (mother 3 children), my personal part, my life purpose. My husband is a true partner both as a family and as an entrepreneur, he has his expertise *in education*...
Evolution **Roles**	Previous: forge family values, inspire models of independence, perseverance, resilience: t0, while t4 refers to: Give meaning, catalyze and moderate decision making, achieve work–family balance, leverage tangible and intangible resources in processes (knowledge and networks), become embedded in identity building.		

PART III

Leading a business within a family or making up with the family while leading a business: same fight?

6. Strategies for overcoming barriers in women's careers: agency as autonomy and authority-building courage

Mona Haug and Gry Osnes

1. INTRODUCTION

'You know, I was quiet and ignored what happened. I do not care what they said and did but they know it has made me angry.' (US-based female owner and top leader, 35 years old, with two children under three)

Let us consider the context of the statement above, taken from a coaching session in early May 2021. Paula alternated between working online from Miami, where her husband had his business, and from New York, where the business she ran with her father was located. Over several years a coaching process had helped to develop a board, creating a more formal top leadership team and planning exit roles for the senior generation of leaders, including Paula's father. This organisational development process did not accelerate during the pandemic in this business. While Paula was running the business and preparing to take over her father's role as CEO, her male colleagues, in an important Zoom meeting during the pandemic, focused mainly on her role as a parent and her presumed need to be with her children. Her substantial achievements as a leader were ignored in review meetings.

We will explore how women engage strategically with challenges when they encounter barriers in their working environments. We build on a description of power games, reported by the women in this study, and their association with women's experience of gender bias, incongruity, tokenism and being overlooked for promotion, ignored and excluded from networks (e.g., Fletcher 2004; Lines 2007; Sümer 2006; Turner and Hawkins 2016). According to Huse and Solberg (2006), women who are aware of the perception of strong (male) leadership characteristics and their own female traits can change the power game. The main findings reveal the ways in which women, in two different organisational contexts, developed authority and used their power to overcome obstacles and exploit catalysts. Although embedded gender images constitute obstacles, women can use certain catalysts to overcome them (Haug 2016, 2020). Building on this assumption and the success stories described below, we analyse the strategies that women use to advance. Based on the concepts of authority, autonomy, affordable loss, leadership and logics (Osnes 2011, 2020; Osnes et al. 2016), we analyse how individuals can break up power dynamics, decode them and create some agency when the power dynamics that create barriers are closely intertwined (Higgins and Kram 2001; Kram 1983).

Female owners and/or leaders often face questions about whether they are entitled to their roles and leadership, or, more specifically, to the power and authority their roles give them. Women encounter these issues when dealing with colleagues and top leaders of any gender during reviews, evaluations, career paths and the execution of a strategy or ownership vision. According to Vial et al. (2016), issues related to power and legitimacy can represent significant obstacles for women in top positions. A mentoring, supportive dialogue or coaching process can play an important role. Ye et al. (2016) are particularly interested in the relationship between gender, societal culture and managerial coaching: 'globally, female managers may overcome the gender disadvantage by displaying more coaching behaviour towards their subordinates' (p.1792). For women, managerial coaching behaviour, which favours communal traits such as nurturing and listening, appears to correlate well with societal and cultural expectations of their leadership and gender roles.

1.1   Ownership and Leadership Careers in Non-family Businesses

Autonomy and paradoxes within family ownership are associated with emotional ties and the obligation to consider the needs of individual family members during negotiations (Osnes et al. 2017). A sense of autonomy can enable family members to assert themselves while taking up and developing authority, giving them the courage and ability to take risks. We will explore how women owners and women working in non-family businesses rely on support (sometimes provided through coaching and/or mentoring) to overcome obstacles, while also using catalysts to provide leverage. As several authors have pointed out, in certain family-owned firms, women are developing and gaining access to very strong ownership and leadership roles. The advances made by some family-owned and regional companies are more profound than those made by most listed companies. By exploring the emotional ties within families, we can promote a dynamic in which women are given strong or key roles, even in formerly traditional systems, with strongly patriarchal ownership. The family bond enables the review and acknowledgement of embedded gender images and the unconscious biases embedded within them, and a new process of configuring authority.

We illustrate the relevance of this exploration by returning to the coaching client. In doing so, we emphasize the need for a more forensic, in-depth understanding of dynamics and dialogues to help us understand how they are intertwined (Higgins and Kram 2001; Kram 1983) and embedded (Haug 2016, 2020). Paula did not care for the way male leaders treated her in May 2021, when she returned from working digitally. Successful succession and entry into a role are, in themselves, not enough. Like all other employees, she returned to the office in May, when the lockdown regulations were eased. The pandemic had delayed the formal transfer of the company's top leadership role from her father to herself. In effect, she was about to become the top decision maker, a move that has traditionally been made in a favourable transaction atmosphere (Boyd et al. 2015) between two owners. In Paula's case, the transfer involved a delicate dance with a group of male leaders within the business (Osnes 2020). Alongside issues related to successful succession, other gender-based issues also persisted. Strategically, over the previous three years, Paula had, with the support of her father, recruited more women into top leadership roles and as non-executive members of the recently established board. Despite and before this, perhaps accentuated by the pandemic and her parenting and family considerations, the habits, rituals and symbolic actions of her father and other leaders had generally reflected the issue that we will explore here: that of embedded gender images.

2.   THEORETICAL PERSPECTIVES

We will now present the notion of embedded gender images, briefly summarising the ways in which research has revealed advances in women's leadership and relevant topics within the field of family entrepreneurship.

2.1   Embedded Gender

The umbrella term 'embedded gender images' (Haug 2016, 2020) encompasses several concepts and metaphors within a historical, societal and cultural context. One example of embedded gender images is the Howard/Heidi case study (Bohnet 2016; Muir 2012), in which students were invited to evaluate résumés. One group considered a 'man's' résumé, while a peer group evaluated a 'woman's' résumé. The résumé belonging to 'Howard' was evaluated as impressive; the first group felt that Howard was a leader they would like to work for. The second group evaluated 'Heidi' as equally effective, but also rather selfish – someone they would be less eager to work for. In fact, both groups were given the same résumé; the only difference was a slight name change – the non-existent 'Howard' evaluated by the first group simply became 'Heidi' for the second group. This study was repeated by Bohnet

(2016) with the same result. In this way, embedded gender images represent systematic disadvantages for women.

Embedded gender images derive from our perceptions and evaluations of people, our conscious or unconscious bias (Fan et al. 2019), and implicit bias, which is firmly anchored in our minds (Tetlock and Mitchell 2009). They may be regarded as a cultural imprint, since we are unconsciously shaped by our culture and socialisation (Hummelsheim and Hirschle 2010). Within the male-breadwinner model, gender roles and tasks are clearly outlined: men are employed full-time, while female carers are responsible for running the household and raising children (Cooke 2006).

2.2   Women in Top Leadership Roles

Embedded gender images are perceived characteristics, competences and associations (such as being 'emotional' or 'decisive') which we unconsciously align with male and female leaders, regardless of their effectiveness. Ample research has revealed the way in which gender influences women's career paths and their ability to access and achieve top leadership roles (e.g. Ely et al. 2011; Swartz et al. 2016). Studies have also considered discrepancies in the perception of women's and men's performance and potential, highlighting the challenges that women face when pursuing careers towards top positions. These barriers also include the existing wage gap (Kunze 2008), the limited pipeline of qualified women versus hierarchical responsibility 'at a macro-contextual layer' (Graham et al. 2017, p.251), and domestic responsibilities (Cooke 2006; Eagly and Carli 2007), which still represent a prominent research area. The common denominator involves discrepancies in the perceived performance and potential of women and men, highlighting the challenges that women encounter on their career paths towards top positions.

2.3   Family Entrepreneurship

Undeniably, family business research is a vast field. Our work shows that ownership is evolving, significantly influencing a new generation of competent women as they take on ownership roles (Osnes 2016). Not only do women create more distributed leadership systems with their siblings (Gronn 2002), but (if disadvantaged, or as a part of a family tradition) they also start new ventures, which may become part of the main business at a later date. We consider it important to capture both new and old forms of entrepreneurship within the family ownership field (Gronn 2002; Tsabari et al. 2014). The most agile and long term-focused family owners often incubate new ventures, outside (or in addition to) the succession process. Members of the senior or next generation may change their roles or enter into business life, starting new ventures that are partly funded by or connected to a family office or established business. When researching the complexities of women's family ownership trajectories, new ventures, whether built on or linked to the original family business, are important for research.

Bringing together the above research fields, we build on embedded gender images, in the form of unconscious bias towards women in ownership and top leadership roles. Using two different research projects, we investigate how women accept authority and relate to barriers, including embedded gender images. Based on earlier research on the factors that foster women's access to top leadership and ownership roles, we explore how certain unique factors can help women gain important roles in such organisations.

2.4   Research Aims

Based on our findings, we argue that there is a need to raise awareness of embedded gender images, which act as barriers to female entrepreneurs and managers (as proxies for stereotypes, biases, prejudices and barriers) and are often firmly established in a historical, cultural and societal context. We also address the importance of strategic career coaching, mentoring and sponsorship as catalysts for female entrepreneurs and managers on their career paths toward top positions.

Based on a selected group of top leaders (Research Project 1) and family owners (Research Project 2), we set out to explore how women overcame barriers when ascending to top leadership positions. The research questions focused on the strategies they employed. The initial data analysis found that support, in the form of formal or informal coaching or mentoring, was a key contributing factor. We used family ownership cases to explore how such support increased the women's ability to address biases, which are often unconscious. In doing so, we explored how support, built on emotional ties with others (such as coaches and family members), could increase women's autonomy and give them a stronger sense of authority when addressing obstacles based on embedded gender biases.

3.   METHODOLOGY

There are many possible explanations for the continued relative absence of female managers in top positions. However, we were curious about aspects of the issue that numbers could not easily explain – a puzzle piece seemed to be missing. We therefore used semi-structured interviews and narratives from two different research projects to gain a better understanding of women's roles and trajectories and the critical incidents they experience. First, we used 4 out of 16 interviews transcribed during dissertation research. Second, we investigated a global family-business project, the 'Learning from Family Ownership project' (Osnes et al. 2016). Each project is described below, with details of the cases and interviews.

3.1   Project 1: Exploring the Relationship between Tokenism and Gender Quotas through the Concept of Embedded Gender Images

3.1.1   Selection and participants
Dissertation interviews were carried out with ten female managers who were contacted via social networks, including XING and LinkedIn; at conferences; and via snowball sampling. These women were chosen for interview based on their roles, their positions and the size of their organizations. All held more or less equivalent positions and were responsible for managing a team or project. Notably, 90 per cent of participants worked for a current or former German automotive family business. In terms of seniority level, the women ranged from reporting directly to a CEO to being responsible for 25,000 employees as an HR representative on the management board. This analysis draws on biographical narratives and semi-structured interviews with four female managers in leading positions in the German automotive industry.

3.1.2   Structure and content of the interviews
Each interview consists of two parts. The first part involves biographical-narrative themes, while the second consists of a semi-structured interview (Kvale and Brinkmann 2009; Schostak 2006). Each semi-structured interview lasted 60–90 minutes. For both projects, the interviews followed an interview guide and research protocol; all semi-structured interviews were transcribed and translated into English.

3.2   Project 2: Learning from Family Ownership

3.2.1   Selection and participants
The Learning from Family Ownership project is a global study of several family-owned businesses conducted collaboratively by an international research team. Interviews with four to eight family members and top leaders in each business were carried out in Sweden, the US, Israel, Norway, China and Germany by researchers who spoke the interviewees' mother tongues (Osnes et al. 2016). We have focused on the barriers and catalysts facing four female entrepreneurs, based on a heritage of male-dominated leadership, which had been in place for some for four generations.

3.2.2 Structure and content of the interviews

Family members were initially asked about the roles they played in the family, business or other contexts. They also discussed the history of key roles. Critical incidents were a focal point, seen as milestones and key events and explored for their significance in relation to learning, tension, conflicts and family implications. Succession dynamics, leadership and inheritance, selling a company, health issues and expansion were typical critical incidents. Most interviewees were asked to share their experiences and stories. All significant events in the family or family business and the individuals' thoughts, feelings and reflections on their experiences were followed up with questions about the implications of those experiences for the family and family business.

3.3 Treatment of Data

In both projects, the interviews were recorded using a digital voice recorder. This was essential to ensure accuracy in processing the data and conducting subsequent comparison studies across different countries. Any details or combinations of details that could have disclosed the interviewees' identities, such their names, addresses or ages, were replaced appropriately to ensure that all cases were anonymous.

3.4 Ethical Considerations

In addition, draft versions of the case descriptions and subsequent publications were given to the interviewees for evaluation to ensure that their preferred level of anonymity was preserved and that no unintentional reference was made that could affect or offend others.

3.5 Analytic Approach

The objective was to gain knowledge of 'a rich and detailed, yet complex account of data' (Braun and Clarke 2006, p.5) and to understand those data at a deeper level (Galletta 2013). Initial findings from Research Project 1 were applied to materials from the family ownership project. This deductive analysis made a comparative analysis possible. It further enabled an inductive analysis of the common denominator linking various obstacles. An abductive analysis (Timmerman and Tavory 2012) allowed us to explore strategies and establish a more nuanced sense of 'doing' or agency.

3.5.1 Deductive analysis

The barriers and catalysts (Haug 2020) that female managers, owners and leaders encounter on their career paths towards top positions illustrate the stark influence of embedded gender images within the historical, cultural and societal background of a male-dominated environment. The barriers listed by women managers include the following: being the only woman (token); being considered 'exotic'; having to fight for access to information; feeling excluded from influential networks; getting their voices heard; the concept of (potential) motherhood; and stereotypes such as emotional relatedness. Other barriers include the classical perspective on the division of roles and tasks, sexual harassment and negative gendered power experiences. The following catalysts were crucial for women working toward top positions: influential networks, such as alumni networks; being in an eligible pool; critical factors influencing, for example, policy outcomes; critical mass in top positions; and female managers acting as role models in top positions (Haug 2020). Strategic career coaching and mentoring impacted the way they addressed and leveraged these; in addition, these tools were in themselves a catalyst. For working mothers, support also came from external networks, including partners, nannies and domestic help. For female entrepreneurs the family network proved to be the most important asset, in relation to role ownership, information flow, the exchange of business strategies and re-entry into the family business.

3.5.2   Iterative and abductive analysis

An abductive analysis allowed us to explore a given phenomenon (in this case, the success of certain strategies) and what it would take to create this outcome (Timmerman and Tavory 2012). We have therefore selected strong, surprising and positive outcomes from our data to explore the factors that made these outcomes possible. The first stage of analysis involved deducing barriers and the emergence of catalysts. To develop more in-depth insights into the inductive aspect of this analysis, we parsed the relationship between autonomy, authority, courage and aspects of intermediate space, assessing what the catalysts did to help women overcome barriers.

4.   FINDINGS

The findings are presented in two sections: strategies for engaging with barriers and in-depth research on transitions and the participants' autonomy and authority. The strategy section introduces four top leaders and their strategies for addressing the following barriers: (i) overcoming tokenism and informal/ male networks; (ii) negative gendered power experiences; (iii) power issues and sexual harassment; and (iv) motherhood. Lastly, we describe the shifts made by these women (v) after support was received and authority acquired.

The research section explores transitions and the development of autonomy and authority. In the case of the four families described below, emotional bonds, a sense of autonomy and a process of authority-building were part of the family dynamic, resulting in strong female ownership and leadership roles: (i) a collective family effort in Germany succeeded in addressing invisible female leadership roles; (ii) a co-entrepreneur couple in Israel shared autonomy and authority; (iii) a second-generation entrepreneurial succession consisted of a father–daughter relationship; and (iv) a mother–daughter relationship spun off a new business, based on the main business.

4.1   Part I: Strategies for Engaging with Barriers

The women who participated in this study were highly qualified managers, and all had developed a range of survival strategies within their work environments. What follows focuses on four of the ten women and the strategies they used to engage with particular barriers. The important question to explore further is how the support provided by husbands, coaches, mentors and parents strengthened the women's sense of autonomy and courage. What factors helped them develop strategies for liberating themselves and, in some cases, even stepping out of the system?

Katharina was born in 1970. She is hard-working, dedicated to everything she does and proactive across several different jobs. She remembers her same-level colleagues viewing her as an inconvenience and feeling uncomfortable in her presence. After the CEO left and three lower-level managers moved up, her situation changed dramatically. These managers had not supported her before and did not support her after their promotions.

Jasmin was born in 1968. Being straightforward and outspoken, she raised the alarm with colleagues and offered solutions when a project was at risk. Her male managers warned her not to speak out, but she decided to ignore them and prepared a presentation for a supervisory team member. Her efforts were successful and she received resources, support and a budget.

Ulrike was born in 1965. She has risen to a top leadership position, one level beneath the supervisory board. Her journey to the top reveals her inner strength, perseverance, value-based leadership style, well-honed fighting skills, intelligence and strategic approach. Often, she is the only woman in a hostile, male-dominated arena.

Stephanie was born in 1970. Her first years as a working mother with two children were awful. In 2008–9, her supervisors had the unspoken expectation that, even though she was working only 25 hours, she would somehow achieve the performance of a full-time manager. She had to grow a thick skin – especially among her colleagues, who included other women without children, as well as men.

4.1.1   Strategies for overcoming the barriers of tokenism and informal male networks

Katharina was the only woman in her firm to hold a top management position. As the HR Global Director, she held the highest-ranking position in her company. She was on the road 36 out of 52 weeks and would often meet her (fully supportive) husband at the airport between business meetings. She was responsible for 24,000 employees and an international rollout programme for 14 plants in 14 different countries. Although she enjoyed her international leadership role, in 2014 she decided to become self-employed, after experiencing the playing of power games and feeling that she could not continue to live by her values. Given the power games she had witnessed, Katharina was strongly convinced that men would not support the promotion of women onto executive boards. For this reason, Katharina decided to set up her own company.

In the beginning, Katharina had to fight for access to general information and discussions. As the only woman in a circle of men, she felt that she did not exist to them. They talked to each other as if they were a group of male friends drinking beer together. She recalled a few incidents which suggested that no one took her seriously at the beginning. As long as she talked about HR they were fine, but as soon as she spoke about strategy or organisational development she lost their confidence and felt unwelcome. Although they did not express hostility, their non-verbal communications made her feel excluded. Katharina noticed this non-verbal behaviour in meetings and workshops and said it conveyed a certain message: 'Just let her talk. What is she doing this time? They would cross their arms to express scepticism: Let's see what she's talking about.'

Katharina remembered how challenging it was to be accepted as an equal partner by her male colleagues. Initially, she was denied timely information, which the men shared within their 'informal, male information network'.

> If you are the only woman in a circle of men it feels as if you do not even exist. Of course, I went with them to events, went to a bar and watched a football game. You have to do it step by step until they realise I'm interested in it as well and that I'm not disturbing them. But you really have to be at the same level with them and you have to be knowledgeable about the topic.

When Jasmin was excluded from the 'male information network', she applied a different strategy. She collected all the information she needed by visiting a range of different premises to inquire about technical requirements and the actual state of the project: 'I was an exotic person. I had always been different. I was guided by my father's behaviour who taught me to be open and friendly.'

Katharina's strategy for countering the impact of perceived culturally embedded gender images within the German automotive industry was to prove that she was an equal. After her lower-level colleagues accepted her, she moved on to the decision-makers. Her chosen strategy was to convince and engage with male CEOs, who began to fully support her ideas and projects. Her new position – supported by the CEO and CO, who acted as mentors – enabled her to roll out an international benchmark and achieve high levels of positive visibility. Strong support from her superiors encouraged her to succeed in her powerful new role. However, her same-level colleagues viewed her as an inconvenience and felt uncomfortable around her:

> I had the impression that they could now work against it. They didn't have the power to work against the initiatives before, but now they could. All of a sudden, they demonstrated immense resistance. It was overwhelming. That was the moment when I decided not to be part of it anymore. I did not need it. I had the feeling that I had to fight even more than before. It wasn't something I wanted any longer.

Ulrike was the first woman in the back office. She was also the first woman sales representative and the first woman to become an inhouse broker for another company. Today she has risen to a top leadership position, one level beneath the supervisory board.

> I was not meant to be successful in a job. My male colleagues would be wondering why I was so dedicated to my job since my position in life would be another one. When those people realised that I was not only good at my job, but also cooked well and liked it, it didn't fit into their worldview at all.

The right to succeed in a somewhat hostile environment was central to the story and identity of every female manager.

4.1.2   Strategies for overcoming the barriers created by negative gendered power experiences

Jasmin describes her parents as strong personalities, with her father as the family alpha male for many years until his health deteriorated and the roles were switched, with her mother becoming the alpha partner. Jasmin had a strong and close relationship with both of her parents. She drew on them as mentors throughout her life. In her professional career, she referred to a work mentor who supported her as treating her like 'his daughter'. She also worked with a female mentor when she was launching a new company. Attacks on her authority marked her life as a sales manager. Fighting for her core values and struggling to live by them within a hostile, mainly male environment was a repetitive business pattern for many years. When Jasmin was a manager and new to the job, she identified weak points and critical loopholes in several projects, and made the decision to forward this information to high-ranking company decision-makers. As she told her husband, she would either survive or be fired. However, her action had more long-term implications, as her male colleagues took steps to undermine her. 'My strategy to inform my big boss about the poor state of the project saved the company's reputation. The project has been very successful and the product is No. 1 amongst the competition', she said. Apparently she did not anticipate any backlash from her actions, which undermined the company hierarchy by going over the heads of her immediate bosses. However, these male managers may have perceived the actions of this young woman as risking a loss of power, control and reputation, leading them to turn against her. At one point in her career, Jasmin decided to take a sabbatical year; later, she became self-employed.

Ulrike left her company, where she was part of a program for employees with high potential, because she could not support the company's values. She had learned during her life that it was important to stay true to one's own convictions, regardless of other people's expectations. She drew strength from staying true to her beliefs and holding on to her values: 'What I have witnessed is that very often men recruit other men rather than women because they know what to expect. I believe that women are extremely powerful in times of uncertainty and crisis situations. More women are needed to become significant decision makers on supervisory boards.'

The recession in 2009 prevented Stephanie from participating in a programme for employees with high potential. However, she had a male mentor who supported her, and a friend of her parents also mentored her. She loves her job, in which she is responsible for a budget of 70 million euros, a flood of information and meeting the needs of staff members:

> I wouldn't know of one position which was occupied at my company where the responsible manager would recruit someone he hadn't known before. Men only recruit someone who is from a hierarchy level below. There are enough women who could be in a higher position at my company, but it would require a bottom-up approach. Women do not get developed into higher positions. At the moment there is a blockage from above that hinders it.

Stephanie still wonders whether she could have made it to the top had she been able to participate in the programme for employees with high potential. Although the strategies introduced by the female managers were generally successful, all of these women faced a backlash at some point in their careers.

4.1.3   Strategies for overcoming barriers related to power issues and sexual harassment

Ulrike favoured a different survival strategy in her male-dominated environment. Her successful strategy for career advancement was to identify the key decision-maker in each project or company and to ensure that she was visible to him: 'I have learned to identify the grey eminence in the room. The silver-back (gorilla) who is an influential decision-maker. I build a relationship, find out their points of view, make them interested in me and my projects and keep them informed about my development.'

When it comes to power issues, Ulrike prefers to address a threat head on:

> I have very seldom met a woman trying to wield power over me. Mostly men. I have learnt to recognise it when someone tries to wield power over me. Today, power is active and not reactive any more. That makes the difference, due to what I have experienced in life and have been able to overcome emotionally.

When she perceives a misuse of power she refuses to back down, given what she has learned from the coaching process and her own life experiences. The coaching process has empowered her to find new ways of dealing with 'doing power and doing leadership' other than those she has experienced in the German automotive industry. For more than six years she worked with a coach, learning from her how to be a warrior but not how to be her authentic self. Although she knew she had a warrior within her, she felt that she was missing a female identity and did not know who she truly was. The second coach who entered her life helped her get in touch with herself. Finally, after working with the coach for quite some time, Ulrike was capable of putting the missing puzzle pieces together. Nowadays, she accepts that her life will have ups and downs: 'If the sea is rough, I'll find a way and if the sea is calm, it is ok with me too. I am at peace with myself.'

Katharina remembers her first apprenticeship as a negative power experience, which she decided to end early and move on from. She has had several jobs in the course of her career and some experiences were better than others. However, she was fortunate to have two great mentors and a husband who consistently supported her. She was always financially independent. After many years of working for large organisations, she finally decided enough was enough and set up her own company. Since then, she has been hiring employees; her social media presence in 2021 suggests that she is happy to be her own boss:

> My first boss was someone you wouldn't want to work with. He was narcissistic and self-assured and did not treat the team well. As an apprentice one is placed lowest in the ranking. I remember that I was completely terrified by him and had great respect for him. I did not trust or look up to him even though his professional competence was enormous. He was not empathetic and one could not talk to him. He wrote notes instead of speaking. He would avoid conflicts by hiding behind his post-its.

4.1.4   Strategies for overcoming barriers to motherhood

At times, Stephanie thought she would never be able to regain her previous professional reputation. In her circle of friends, a man who didn't know that she was working said nasty things about a woman who worked and put her child in childcare. He called her 'Rabenmutter', a term used to criticise working mothers. Stephanie had to decide quickly how to cope with the situation because there wasn't much time to react:

> I told him that I too was what he called 'Rabenmutter' and that I had better leave the discussion because I didn't think I had to put up with it. The automotive industry has a history of 100 years or rather 150 years and is marked by men who will not be changed overnight.

While Jasmin was going to school she helped a neighbour with her children, and experienced childcare as very stressful. Jasmin's neighbour, a young mother, could not handle her situation, with three young children, and her marriage suffered as a result. Later, this mother was diagnosed with cancer and died at a young age. Jasmin supported the widower as best as she could, often spending half a day with one of the children. Ultimately, Jasmin decided to remain childless, although people in her social environment could not understand or accept the fact that she did not want children:

> The real reason for me was that I had seen my mother being very tight in regard to money. My mother sacrificed a lot for me. I have a different expectation of my life with children. I would want to be able to afford a nanny and a nice lifestyle for my children, myself and my husband.

Jasmin's arguments for not having children taught her that people would not respect her decision. However, when she explained that parenthood had just not worked out for her husband and herself, the discussions and inquiries stopped because people accepted this as a legitimate reason.

Katharina was grateful to her boss, who smoothed the path for her, enabling her to combine her career ambitions and family plans. After three months in a top leadership job, Katharina realised she was pregnant. She went to her German boss, who had a degree in social education, and explained the situation. Her boss advised her to train an assistant to support and back her up, enabling her to work part-time at first and build up gradually to full time. By using the latest technology she could work from home, avoiding the need to travel so much. She began working part-time, for 20 hours a week, and then moved up to 30 and 40 hours. She stayed with the company for four years and successfully combined motherhood with being a manager in a top leadership position. Having a male mentor act as an enabler made all the difference to

Katharina's career. With his support, she successfully managed the demands of her varied roles as a manager, mother, wife and daughter-in-law:

> My job involved a lot of strategic decisions, like closing plants and opening new ones. My four years at Kolobi were the icing on the cake. I could bring in all my ideas and my boss and his colleague supported everything. My husband first swallowed hard at the thought of me being away for three days a week. I knew he would be able to manage the child with the in-laws. He had taken on a position as CEO and did not have to travel so much anymore. He left the house at 9 in the morning and came home at 7 in the evening. To him it was more important to see his son growing up than it was to me. I was fine with not seeing our son for three days a week.

4.2 Part I Findings: The Role of Autonomy, Courage and Authority in Creating a Shift

This section will examine the Part I findings in more depth. First, we examine the narratives above, analysing how these professional managers were able to shift from a sense of autonomy to a new sense of authority. We explore four such shifts among female owners, based on the sense of autonomy, the freedom of choice that autonomy imparts and the way it can be used to develop authority. We explore a German case in which such a shift was created for the next generation after three generations of assumed male leadership. We also explore female co-entrepreneurship in Israel, a father and daughter collaboration in the US and a mother and daughter in China who created a spin-off new venture, which later became a merger. Appendix 6.1 presents an extract from the data analysis of the Israeli and American cases, in the form of a data matrix; this shows how we built inductively on strategies for addressing obstacles, exploring autonomy, courage and authority in more depth.

4.2.1 Shifts in autonomy and authority among female managers

The participants focused on implementing innovative ideas successfully. They negotiated over issues that were vital for them, such as resources and budgets. They also rescued projects in crisis, changing the context by demonstrating high commitment, passion and endurance. They achieved this by applying a multi-stakeholder strategy, involving key decision-makers, great determination and threats addressed head on. The participants displayed the agentic traits typically associated with male managers: they delivered top results, achieved top performance and demonstrated endurance, perseverance and courage. It could be argued, however, that some of these positive outcomes were achieved with the help of protective mentors or superiors or via long-term support networks.

4.2.1.1   *Katharina's progression from an informal to a formal role*

Katharina's new role as HR Global Director and the support she received from the CEO and CO enabled her to achieve significant positive visibility, fulfilling her formal role as an official international change agent:

> I was really lucky to have two members of the supervisory board who supported my projects. If they hadn't backed me up and I would have had to push through the projects all by myself, I think I would have experienced more resistance. Those two executive board members and I were on the same page. They knew that the projects I was committed to were significant for the company. They weren't the driving forces themselves, but were content to go along with it. The issue was how I developed the organisation strategy. How I broke the organisation strategy down to the department strategy.

4.2.1.2   *Jasmin's progression from an informal to a formal role*

Jasmin was just 30 years old and had been with the company for three months when she had to tell her 'big boss' that all of his other employees were dishonest, that they had done a lousy job, and that the project on which they were working would not succeed. Jasmin's role within the department changed as soon as she found the courage to reveal to the boss what other managers had done wrong. She was given full authority over a project that was vital to her company. 'But do you know, Mrs Haug, with this, I have again hit many, really many men against the shinbone in their positions. They bear a grudge against me to this day because I believe that it has done harm to their careers.'

Jasmin's professional behaviour is proactive, determined, open and honest. She lives by the values her father taught her.

4.2.1.3   *Ulrike's progression from an informal to a formal role*

Ulrike's informal role as a regular employee changed completely when her boss asked her to implement an idea she had proposed for strengthening the company. He trusted her and gave her the necessary resources to achieve it. The business has achieved significant profits because of her innovations. The processes are still in place and working well after seven years. 'My boss has never understood what I actually implemented, but he trusted me completely. He was courageous enough to give me a chance. He earned an extreme amount of money with it and I could test my idea.'

Looking back at the various different companies for which she had worked, Ulrike commented that power games were still in place and had not changed at all. However, the opportunity she was given to test her idea resulted in a win–win situation for her boss and herself.

4.2.1.4   Stephanie's progression from an informal to a formal role

Stephanie recalls losing team members in her first leadership role because she was unaware of her own leadership style. She did not lose team members because they applied for other positions, but because they felt she was too remote. A leadership seminar and her children taught her that she could choose what kind of person and leader she wanted to be:

Team: You are the locomotive, but at the very back are the wagons and you have just lost them. We would like to work together with you.

Stephanie: I enjoy motivating others to go the extra mile and showing them how to break down an immense workload into small manageable chunks.

She read a book about power and applied some of that knowledge, which ultimately worked for her. She now has a good relationship with the members of her team and often knows about their private lives.

4.2.2   A family in Germany acknowledging invisible female leadership roles

One case of family ownership discussed here involves a four-generation family which founded a medium-sized German utilities company in 1952, after the Second World War; the company had approximately 140 employees and 39 million dollars in revenue. With a tradition of passing down ownership from father to son, the business is now preparing for a shift to a gender-balanced leadership, which will be continued by the coming generation. What was once the founder's vision has become the company's leading strategy and main financial, socio-emotional and symbolic advantage. Preserving a company that family members see as their 'real home' motivates their actions, according to the current leader of this family-owned business. The interdependent aspects of their group identity reveal themselves in statements such as 'we try to hold on to our strengths as a family-owned business'. Various financial failures and safety issues experienced by the company over the past 40 years have placed the current male leader in a strong decision-making position. Now, with a long-term perspective in mind, the present leader has recognised the need to pass on the baton to the fourth generation. He will be joined by one of his female cousins on the executive board. In addition, the following generation will consist of his son and niece.

Developments in the socio-political landscape after the 1940s and 1950s have increased the entitlement of female entrepreneurs with family businesses. The daughters of a business family working in the German utilities industry were free to have children, received support from the entire family and were able to stay up to date on all business-related issues and re-enter the family business whenever they chose. These female entrepreneurs did not have to choose between family and career, only when to return to the company. At the same time, our findings highlight several embedded images that have guided the family for four generations. These suggest that female entrepreneurs should consider taking steps to develop their gender-specific potential and increase the number of women on their executive boards.

This German case illustrates the way in which emotional bonds and women's informal leadership roles can act as a catalyst, enabling a female successor to take up a leadership or ownership role. The three cases further illustrate how emotional ties within a family can generate support and coaching/mentoring relationships.

4.2.3   A co-entrepreneurial couple in Israel, with female authority

This case study involves a husband-and-wife team in Palestine/early Israel. The business in question was co-owned initially by the husband and wife, and later by their sons. When the interviews took place, a succession plan was developed for three of Wada's grandchildren. What we will show is the unusual level of support between husband and wife. In particular, the husband supported his wife in her role as co-entrepreneur. They both came from a Christian Arab background and a strongly patriarchal culture.

Wada: In 1957 and 1958, we had lots of these individual tours and archaeological digs for American professors and very educated people who really used to come, not just to see the country, but to go through history. The work started with the good service of my husband. And everybody who used to come I used to take them here, to my home, to give them tea. And every tourist who comes would then like to go to a native home and see how people live. You know, these professors and priests who used to come, they were happy here and they used to go home and talk about it with their friends or at school or in churches. And since my husband was driving and guiding I had to organise it.

Interviewer: And your husband didn't mind? I mean, he liked it or he …

Wada: Who?

Interviewer: Your husband.

Wada: Oh. No, I mean, there was a big difference between my husband and me, I was 17 [and] he was 32. He was much older. But he was very free minded, very […] Working with foreigners makes quite a difference. He was not a very strict minded man. He gave me the freedom to do whatever I wanted.

When Wada was in her early eighties, she was still the head of accounts. She had oversight of a large tourism agency (the main business), with one son as the majority owner, and a chain of hotels, with another son as the majority owner. In addition, they owned a bus company, which was part of the tourism agency and linked to the hotel business. As the work and career she had chosen were highly unusual, there was a price to pay. Not only was tourism in Jerusalem a volatile and risky business but it also had social implications, as she was isolated from her female peer group:

> Oh yes. Oh yes. Lots of people gossip. I didn't care, I didn't mind. I did, I am not from here, I am from Bethlehem, from Beit Jala. I was born in Beit Jala, so I didn't care. I didn't know anybody and until now I don't know anybody. I don't visit people and nobody visits me because I didn't have time. First it was with the kids and then with the office. So, I don't care what people say. As long as I am satisfied and I know myself.

This grandmother represents a visible leadership model for several of her granddaughters, while the cross-generational emotional bonds, initially with her sons but then also across the generations, enable the necessary support, mentoring and knowledge transfer. This structure sets the stage for future diversity, with women in top leadership roles and other positions:

> We have one female top leader who is not in the family. It was Dalia, Hani's daughter, who employed her. We – I mentioned before that we opened a Rome office for her, after she graduated. First, she wanted to work and we had another manager in the Amman office, who was not a good man. He was good at promoting the business but he was a thief. He really robbed us. We nearly lost that office. So when Dalia came, we thought that she would learn from the beginning. We put her in the Amman office. And she met that girl, she was a guide. She met her and saw her; she is capable. And when she went to Rome, she took over that office. Dalia learned from her father how to do things, how to do a programme. And this girl, being a guide, she knew every corner in Jordan and that helps. And this is, she is smart. She just took over and everything […] It is, for this part of the world in our culture, not […] Of course, you will find many girls working in offices. And we have in our office about 12 or 13. It wasn't like this before, when I started working. Only men were managing the whole thing.

4.2.4   A father–daughter team in the US: building authority

> The separation was hard, but it was best for all concerned. We shared ideas in the beginning. At least we did back then, we don't much anymore. My mother is, well, she's not a hands-on operator any longer. She pretty much lets the people she has hired run it. But she still has a presence there – through today's technology she supervises the business using a TV camera over the register, a little TV monitor at home, and she calls them any time that she's not satisfied with something. But as far as us sharing ideas, that probably hasn't taken place for a few years now. But we,

at one time or another, would share ideas with each other: what would work for one and what was working for the other to enhance her business or mine. Our businesses are different now.

The statement above comes from a second-generation entrepreneur: the father of a family in which three generations have been serial entrepreneurs. In the quotation above he describes the moment of 'separation' when he set up his own business after having worked for several years, alongside his wife, for his mother and stepfather. It was the start of a story about emotional ties, and also one of healthy separation and new ventures with continued cooperation across the generations. After the family sold the original business and leveraged the profits, the father built increasingly large businesses. Working with his wife and a younger brother, he guided his daughter in starting her own business. She described her initial engagement and sense of autonomy as she became involved and grew up with the business during her childhood and young-adult years:

> I guess I always felt a part of the BBQ business, as soon as I was able I would help out by wiping down tables and when I was old enough, I would run the cash register. But when I got further into high school, I got an independent streak and I decided I wanted to work for somebody else for a while. I just wanted to have the experience of working in a different environment so I got a job at a chicken finger place. I liked it; it seemed like a really simple, neat, popular concept and I just saw how packed it was all the time. I was 18 and graduating high school and I went to daddy and said I wanted to open a chicken finger restaurant. It gave me a greater appreciation even working for someone else. I saw, you know, how good daddy was to his employees. He was never just a boss and not just because I was his daughter. He is that way with all of his employees. He cares about them and wants to be a part of their lives and to influence them. I had a very deep appreciation for him as a business owner and a boss.

The father, along with all the family, welcomed the new venture and appreciated his daughter's desire to balance her emotional ties with a need and drive for autonomy. For both father and daughter, this new venture involved risk and worry. However, they both believed that they could see the project through and manage the risk. They had the courage to take an affordable risk, building on existing family support and emotional ties:

> It was actually Gail who came up with the new idea for a restaurant and she sold us on it. But [...] we all had to work together to get the ball rolling. I remember how we learned how to cook chicken. We got a deep fat fryer and put it out on the back porch. We already had our bank loan approved and everything. When the first big batch came out green and greasy, I thought to myself, 'Oh, my goodness, what have we gotten ourselves into, we don't know how to do this!' And so, I said, 'I'm glad the bankers are not in our back yard watching this or they would take back the loan

they promised us.' But anyway we did test cooking almost every day, it seems like for weeks, but eventually we came up with a product we all really liked.

Also, when I was there before, that was when we first opened 20 years ago and it was me, my ex-husband, my mom and my dad so we all just had our positions. When I came back this time I had a lot to learn. The ex is gone, so I am responsible for the bookwork, the employees, ordering, everything. So it was very overwhelming to do all of that by myself. I had to overcome that and be like daddy.

4.2.5   A mother and daughter supporting each other in China

The He family from southern China has run a wooden toy business for more than three generations. The company dates back to 1973, when China began a process of dramatic social, political and economic change. Even during communism, when the communes owned all businesses, the business still had a 'co-founder couple', namely a husband and wife. The first-generation wife had an invisible leadership role. The second-generation wife was also involved, both as an employee and in an invisible leadership role. Although the first two generations did not own the business, leadership roles were still passed down from father to son, based on a staff vote.

When capitalist ideas and private ownership were introduced into the economy, several family members created spin-off businesses. New ventures, launched and owned by members of the younger generation, produced competing products and more modern designs; some also acted as suppliers to the main business. Although these companies sometimes cooperated on larger contracts, they also competed against each other. In addition, the family launched and invested in a business designed as a small-scale incubator for new design ideas and product development. One next-generation family member, the future owner of the main business (in what had become a cluster region in China), was a young woman, the sister of an owner and top leader. She was not given the opportunity to work in the business and settled in Beijing. Her mother had been one of the earlier-generation wives who had worked in the business and held an informal leadership role.

In 2005 the daughter started a business, initially in bamboo coal, a sustainable product. She learnt how the budding internet trade operated and realised that the low margins and distribution difficulties would make it difficult to earn much money:

> Yes. It was fun. I set up my own e-shop on Taobao.com (the Chinese equivalent of eBay). In 2005, I just gave birth to a baby and was quite boring at home. The only entertainment was surfing the Internet. One friend of mine sold children's clothes online at home, which inspired me. There were credit grades for buyers and sellers on Taobao.com and I felt like I was playing some game. I bought a lot of stuff online and had a very good record as a buyer, so I wanted to have credit as a seller too. So

at the beginning, I was selling bamboo charcoal, but there is no bamboo charcoal production in Yunhe County.

My mother saw my business and said: 'Why don't you sell our wooden toys online at home? If, sometimes the client was not satisfied with our wooden toy or there was some unexpected situation, plenty of toys were back in stock. Why don't you give it a try and see if anyone is interested in them?' I thought my mom was right. Besides, I have nothing much to do so it won't hurt to give it a try. So I took pictures of the toys and uploaded them online. The toys were made of original wood and the style was quite trendy. Some Japanese clients placed orders with our company but they could also withdraw them for many reasons, even after paying the deposit. Cooperation was suspended while the toys had to be returned to stock. I later on found that many customers like Japanese-style wooden toys. So the online sales were quite good.

After five years, the daughter's online store received the top 'Imperial Crown' rating as a trusted seller. In 2010 she sold her online business to her brother, finalizing an ownership and credit transfer and keeping only around 10 per cent as a minority shareholder in her own venture. In this way she increased the family assets more broadly and developed her own financial independence. The experience and learning she created would make her an owner with a choice and a proven reputation as an innovative entrepreneur and owner. Her brother had always appreciated her efforts and achievements but was more strategic as a top leader. His support, and the purchase and integration of the online business, came at a crucial time. This transition occurred just before 2009, when the global recession set in. Global buyers suddenly had less need for wooden toys. Instead, these global companies sought distribution networks within China, with the main company as a new market. Suddenly, the main family firm and assorted smaller ventures were able to sell their own designs and products in the local Chinese market. The global companies became suppliers rather than buyers.

5.   DISCUSSION

Despite the barriers that still exist, our research findings show that the following factors help more women ascend to active and top ownership roles. The stories of successful women share one common feature: they all received some type of support, which enabled them to overcome obstacles and leverage catalysts. Supportive dialogues were provided by formal mentors, coaching relationships or informal family mentors and coaches. We will discuss three aspects of these findings, which relate to social changes, ways of challenging barriers and the use of catalysts. Women who learned to use catalysts to create a shift had access to supportive dialogues with mentors or coaches; the dialogue became an intermediate space, in which the 'other' provided support and the women learned to treat obstacles as determining moments, offering options and choices. The dialogues, and their reflections or aftereffects, built autonomy, courage and the authority to act. Autonomous authority-building changed the roles and authority assigned to the company leader and/or owner. Coaching and mentoring, whether provided by family members or a formal coach, acted as a catalyst for building an awareness of their own choices and autonomy. They provided understanding, built authority and helped the new entrepreneur develop courage by exploring affordable loss.

We will start with a surprising finding: that family business owners may be ahead of societal gender-inclusivity trends. We also discuss aspects of the courage that the women appeared to need to create shifts in their careers.

Our findings support the documented obstacles and biases that woman encounter (Sümer 2006; Huse and Solberg 2006). We contribute a more in-depth understanding, revealing new aspects of the ability to use catalysts. These show what it takes to develop the courage to challenge barriers to female leadership and ownership.

The present study has some limitations. Multiple interviews with each participant would have allowed us to probe specific areas further. Ideally, we could have returned to themes that emerged from the data. Despite this limitation, however, the fully transcribed interviews and data analysis provide a strong argument for the role played by embedded gender images and other themes in both projects. Another limitation involves the number of participants in the two research projects. However, 90 per cent of the participants worked for a current or former family businesses and 10 per cent worked for a non-family business, thus mirroring the high percentage of family businesses in the German economy. The female entrepreneurs represented the fourth generation of a family-owned business in Germany. In addition, both projects would have benefited from member checks, external coders or third-party analyses by the participants themselves.

5.1   Ahead of the Times amidst New Gender Dynamics

The increasing number of women in powerful roles, as top leaders and/or business owners, is accentuating various conflicting images and notions of women in positions of authority and power. When Ulrike, one of the study participants, was developing her own agency, her strategy was to (a) approach the threat by confronting it directly and (b) make sure that she was noticed by influential multi-key stakeholders (Turner and Hawkins 2016). The strength of her approach shows that a person who decides to fight back develops a self-in-relation (Fletcher 2004) and determination. Other strategies that include less confrontation, such as complementarity or following another set of considerations, are also explored in our data. The common denominators, based on inductive and abductive analyses, relate to the fact that agency existed in different types of strategies that were built on a sense of autonomy. In addition, women who developed authority in their roles were able to assess risk and develop courage.

Within the family dynamic, both invisible and visible leadership roles can act as the main catalyst. In many of the family businesses discussed here, the family narrated out female roles. Rewriting or discovering those roles could provide catalysts for future generations. Collinson has argued that embedded images guide both men and women in their decision-making (Collinson 2011). As the German case shows, one of the most surprising results is the fact that, over the past 10–15 years, a new cohort of female owners has emerged. They are negotiating owner and leadership roles and advancing rather quickly. Family ties seem to force through a more radical shift. It seems typical, as in the German and Chinese cases, that the interviewees did not initially consider their grandmothers, the female co-founders, to be noteworthy.

Earlier entrepreneurship research has shown that autonomy is a crucial driver or aspect of entrepreneurship processes. Studies have called for a stronger focus on the way in which family dynamics affect fundamental entrepreneurial processes (e.g. Aldrich and Cliff 2003: 573–4). The traditional approach to exploring family dynamics has been to focus on the family's strategy for managing life stages and succession; this becomes less relevant given the conditions on the variables discussed here.

5.2   Courage: Autonomy, Authority and Affordable Loss

Coaching and mentoring, whether from a family member or a formal coach, can act as a catalyst, raising awareness of one's choices and autonomy, building understanding and authority and developing courage by exploring affordable loss. Building on Ye et al. (2016), our findings confirm that women on career paths towards top positions should adopt managerial coaching behaviour to mitigate the impact of embedded gender images. Such concepts can capture the lived experience of female entrepreneurs and leaders and prove useful to aspiring women entrepreneurs and their coaches and advisors.

5.2.1   Awareness of choice and autonomy
Female managers see various power games being played during the course of their business lives. As Sümer (2006), Huse and Solberg (2006) and Vial et al. (2016) have pointed out, each power game has its own locked-in dynamic, which embeds and intertwines (Higgins and Kram 2011; Kram 1983) with gender bias. These dynamics include tokenism, exclusion from networks, lack of promotion and incongruity, to name just a few. According to Huse and Solberg (2006), awareness is the key to changing power games. Our findings reveal, in depth, how women create career advances. They include an

awareness of the rules that provide access to power and authority. As various succession studies have shown, the process of shifting leaders in and out of roles requires an established or renewed process of decoding the dynamic and logic of leadership (Osnes 2020). During any transition into an established role, there is a process whereby the logic of leadership determines what constitutes access to power and how it bestows legitimacy. Understanding the game creates a choice: to be a part of a system, or to leave or challenge it.

5.2.2 Risking an affordable loss to gain courage

It is also worth asking what price an individual must pay for bending or breaking the rules of the game. Dialogue and mentoring within interrelationships make such analysis possible, allowing each individual to understand the effect of the game on herself as a person and on the organisation. Like the family dynamics in family ownership cases, dialogue and mentoring lead to a sense of autonomy and the ability to consider choices. In venturing into a new business, as the daughter did in China, a sense of autonomy can lead to risk taking but also to a successful venture, which gives the entrepreneur authority, power and a strong ownership position.

Non-family members can also benefit from such dialogues, in the form of coaching, to create shifts and develop courage. Ulrike's experience with two female coaches, one of whom was an external consultant to her company, focused on developing her inner strengths. The coaching process helped her become stronger, more self-confident and tougher (Rogers 2012). She also mentioned the management and business skills (Lines 2007) that she learned from her first coach, arguing that every leader in a work environment requires professional learning (Turner and Hawkins 2016). The affordable loss that Ulrike faced was the risk that her boss would be unwilling to consider or annoyed by her idea of changing the entire IT system. He also had to estimate the risk and determine what he was willing to lose to follow Ulrike's proposed course of action. The women discussed in this study all benefited from coaching, developing strategies to develop support for their projects, resources and ideas.

5.2.3 Authority and carving out role(s)

At the practical level, some participants struggled to understand what they had the authority to do or felt guilty for aspiring to or accepting the authority and power that came with ownership or top leadership roles. If they or others experienced themselves as powerful or strongly influential, they framed themselves as merely 'supportive'. Since 'supportive' is a term that reflects traditional female roles within the home or society, it bears the cultural imprint of approval. A supportive function is often seen as enabling others, while staying in the background. Based on this logic or modus operandi, women's actual decision-making and influence has been hidden behind their supporting roles. Further research should focus on the way in which roles at the top of an organisation, such as on the board or leadership team, are assigned to leaders, and how this differs from less formal initiatives such as dialogues about needs and tasks, which, over several discussions, can become a process of carving out a new role. As the latter is a more innovative process, it can be carried out with ease within family systems (Osnes 2016). This finding also supports Tsabari et al. (2014) by confirming that new roles and ventures have an important impact on career trajectories.

6.   CONCLUSION

The empirical evidence gathered through these research projects reveals that embedded gender images are deeply ingrained in historical, societal and cultural attitudes. This evidence should not be restricted to a single theoretical domain: it can apply to several, including role authority, gendered leadership, entrepreneurship theory, gender diversity and barriers to women in general. We have presented our findings across several case studies. Coaching or advising should use the concept of embedded gender images, allowing female entrepreneurs and managers to benefit from targeted awareness training, which can help them respond to the embedded gender images rooted in their culture and work environments. The findings on coaching, mentoring and sponsorship show that women need to be taught and trained by mentors and coaches. To start this process, universities and training schools could offer tailored programmes of strategic coaching and mentoring for career advancement.

To conclude, this chapter has addressed a number of significant issues, all of which raise the following question: what does it take to navigate around the challenges and barriers most likely to impede female leadership?

REFERENCES

Aldrich, H.E. and J.E. Cliff (2003), 'The pervasive effects of family on entrepreneurship: Toward a family embeddedness perspective', *Journal of Business Venturing*, 18(5), 573–96.

Bloomberg, L.D. and M. Volpe (2018), *Completing your qualitative dissertation: A road map from beginning to end*, Newbury Park, CA: Sage Publications.

Bohnet, I. (2016), *What works*, Cambridge, MA: Harvard University Press.

Boyd, B., S. Royer, R. Pei and X. Zhang (2015), 'Knowledge transfer in family business successions', *Journal of Family Business Management*, 5(1), 17–37.

Braun, V. and V. Clarke (2006), 'Using thematic analysis in psychology', *Qualitative Research in Psychology*, 3(2), 77–102.

Collinson, D. (2011), Critical leadership studies, in A. Bryman, D. Collinson, K. Grint, B. Jackson and M. Uhl-Bien (eds), *The Sage handbook of leadership*. London: Sage.

Cooke, L.P. (2006), 'Policy, preferences and patriarchy: The division of domestic labor in East Germany, West Germany and the United States', *Social Politics: International Studies in Gender, State and Society*, 13(1), 117–43.

Eagly, A.H. and L.L. Carli (2007), 'Women and the labyrinth of leadership', *Harvard Business Review*, 85(9), 62.

Ely, R.J., H. Ibarra and D.M. Kolb (2011), 'Taking gender into account: Theory and design for women's leadership development programmes', *Academy of Management Learning and Education*, 10(3), 474–93.

Fan, Y., L.J. Shepherd, E. Slavich, D. Waters, M. Stone, R. Abel and E.L. Johnston (2019), 'Gender and cultural bias in student evaluations: Why representation matters', *PloS One*, 14(2).

Fletcher, J.K. (2004), 'The paradox of postheroic leadership: An essay on gender, power and transformational change', *The Leadership Quarterly*, 15(5), 647–61.

Galletta, A. (2013), *Mastering the semi-structured interview and beyond: From research design to analysis and publication*, New York: NYU Press.

Graham, M.E., M.A. Belliveau and J.L. Hotchkiss (2017), 'The view at the top or signing at the bottom? Workplace diversity responsibility and women's representation in management', *ILR Review*, 70(1), 223–58.

Gronn, P. (2002), 'Distributed leadership as a unit of analysis', *The Leadership Quarterly*, 13(4), 423–51.

Haug, M. (2016), Das Coaching der weiblichen Herausforderer im 21. Jahrhundert, in *Coaching als individuelle Antwort auf gesellschaftliche Entwicklungen* (pp.247–54), Wiesbaden: Springer Fachmedien.

Haug, M. (2020), 'Exploring the relationship between tokenism and gender quotas through the concept of embedded gender images' (Doctoral dissertation, University of the West of England).

Higgins, M.C. and K. E. Kram (2001), 'Reconceptualizing mentoring at work: A developmental network perspective', *Academy of Management Review*, 26(2), 264–88.

Hummelsheim, D. and J. Hirschle (2010), 'Mother's employment: Cultural imprint or institutional governance? Belgium, West and East Germany in comparison', *European Societies*, 12(3), 339–66.

Huse, M. and A.G. Solberg (2006), 'Gender-related boardroom dynamics: How Scandinavian women make and can make contributions on corporate boards', *Women in Management Review*, 21(2), 113–30.

Kram, K.E. (1983), 'Phases of the mentor relationship', *Academy of Management Journal*, 26(4), 608–25.

Kunze, A. (2008), 'Gender wage gap studies: Consistency and decomposition', *Empirical Economics*, 35, 63–76.

Kvale, S. and S. Brinkmann (2009) *Interviews: Learning the craft of qualitative research interviewing*. London: Sage.

Lines, R. (2007), 'Using power to install strategy: The relationships between expert power, position power, influence tactics and implementation success', *Journal of Change Management*, 7(2), 143–70.

Muir, S. (2012), 'Heidi versus Howard – perception barrier to be hurdled: Commissioner', *Agriculture Today*, accessed 13 August 2014 at www.dpi.nsw.gov .au/content/archive/agriculture-today-stories/ag-today-archive/march-2012/heidi -versus-howard-perception-barrier-to-be-hurdled-commissioner.

Osnes, G. (2011). 'Succession and authority: A case study of an African family business and a clan chief', *International Journal of Cross Cultural Management*, 11(2), 185–201.

Osnes, G. (2016), 'Strategic avenues for succession' in G. Osnes (ed.), *Family capitalism: Best practices in ownership and leadership*. Abingdon, UK: Routledge, pp. 179–92.

Osnes, G. and A. Wilhelmsen (2020), *Leadership and strategic succession: the how and why for boards and CEOs*, Abingdon, UK: Routledge.

Osnes, G., A. Uribe, L. Hök, O.Y. Hou and M. Haug (2017), 'Autonomy and paradoxes in family ownership: Case studies across cultures and sectors', *Journal of Family Business Management*, 7(1), 93–110.

Osnes, G., L. Hök, O.Y. Hou, M. Haug, V. Grady and J.D. Grady (2018), 'Strategic plurality in intergenerational hand-over: Incubation and succession strategies in family ownership', *Journal of Family Business Management*, 9(2), 149–74.

Ostner, I. (2010), 'Farewell to the family as we know it: Family policy change in Germany', *German Policy Studies*, 6(1), 211.

Rogers, J. (2012), *Coaching skills: A handbook*, London: McGraw-Hill Education (UK).

Schostak, J. (2006), *Interviewing and representation in qualitative research*. Berkshire, UK: Open University Press.

Sümer, H.C. (2006), 'Women in management: Still waiting to be full members of the club', *Sex Roles*, 55(1–2), 63–72.

Swartz, E., F.M. Amatucci and S. Coleman (2016), 'Still a man's world? Second generation gender bias in external equity term sheet negotiations', *Journal of Developmental Entrepreneurship*, 21(03), 1650015.

Tetlock, P.E. and G. Mitchell (2009), 'Implicit bias and accountability systems: What must organizations do to prevent discrimination?' *Research in Organizational Behavior*, 29, 3–38.

Timmerman, S. and I. Tavory (2012), Construction in qualitative research: From grounded theory to abductive analysis, *Sociological Theory*, 30(3), 167–86.

Tsabari, N., R. Labaki and R.K. Zachary (2014), 'Toward the cluster model: The family firm's entrepreneurial behavior over generations', *Family Business Review*, 27, 161–85. doi:10.1177/0894486514525803.

Turner, E. and P. Hawkins (2016), 'Multi-stakeholder contracting in executive/business coaching: An analysis of practice and recommendations for gaining maximum value', *International Journal of Evidence Based Coaching and Mentoring*, 14(2), 48.

Vial, A.C., J.L. Napier and V.L. Brescoll (2016), 'A bed of thorns: Female leaders and the self-reinforcing cycle of illegitimacy', *The Leadership Quarterly*, 27(3), 400–414.

Ye, R., X.H. Wang, J.H. Wendt, J. Wu and M.C. Euwema (2016), 'Gender and managerial coaching across cultures: Female managers are coaching more', *International Journal of Human Resource Management*, 27(16), 1791–1812.

Table 6A.1   Appendix

Emotional bond in family ownership	Autonomy	Authority	Courage and affordable risk
CHINA: support from mother to daughter *Barrier:* patriarchal culture *Catalyst:* invisible leadership roles	'The first order I placed was for original wood buttons, which could be pinned on a bag or sweater. They sold so well that I thought, why not put other patterns on the wood buttons? With this thought, I went to the factory and asked if they could put strawberry patterns or colourful patterns on the wooden buttons? They said yes.'	'This one customer bought more or made a wholesale deal each time and then I would be very pleased. For me, it was a great win if I sold it out. After all, these toys were in stock and we could at least cover the original cost. There was one client who bought a lot from my store and then resold it on his own store and did well. Every time he put the new products online, the next day they would be gone.'	'The first order I placed was for original wood buttons, which could be pinned on a bag or sweater. They sold so well that I considered why not put other patterns on the wood button? With this thought, I went to the factory and asked if they could put strawberry patterns or colourful patterns on the wood button. They said yes.'
ISRAEL: support between husband and wife; from grandmother/ father to granddaughter *Barrier:* (for woman in focus) a patriarchal culture *Catalysts:* poverty and need; female leadership role-modelling	'Well, I have been in that office since 1963. My husband, when he was a guide, when he started having groups coming and the Jordanian, we were under the Jordanian regime and they said, "you cannot be a guide and a travel agent without an office. Either you be this or that." So of course when we had groups coming, we had to have an office. And we used to work from home.'	'Yeah. When he was a guide and we used to have groups coming, I used to hand in everything from our home. I used to make the correspondence and he would meet the groups in Turkey, in Jordan and bring them over. And then we thought, when he couldn't do any more guiding we had to open an office. And we opened an office. Not this office, it was in A-Zahra street. I was the head of the office.'	'The tourist business is very interesting. But in this country, I always say, working in the tourist business is like cards, it is like gambling. You can never say what will happen tomorrow. Anything that happens in the Middle East affects the tourist business.'

Emotional bond in family ownership	Autonomy	Authority	Courage and affordable risk
	'To be frank, if I stayed in Beit Jala, I would have married a boy from Beit Jala and I would have been nothing. Just sitting there and having more and more kids. But marrying my husband has great influence on me. He really helped me a lot and encouraged me.'		
USA: support from father to daughter *Barrier:* historic patriarchal culture *Catalysts:* poverty and need; visible female leadership role-modelling	'I have always been impressed how well mother and dad work so well together. Mother is, like I said, the brains behind the financial part of it and knowing what will work there and you know, how much you can spend to build it and what you would need to make – and kind of thinking through all of that.	'I guess I always felt a part of the BBQ business. As soon as I was able, I would help out by wiping down tables and when I was old enough, I would run the cash register. But when I got further into high school, I got an independent streak and I decided I wanted to work for somebody else for a while.	'But I learned a lot. I saw the way they did things and it worked for them but I saw where I could also make improvements and have different things in the meal. They only had fried chicken. I thought that it would be good to have grilled chicken because everybody was becoming more health conscious at that time

Emotional bond in family ownership	Autonomy	Authority	Courage and affordable risk
	She is very much the strength behind him and both of them are very strong people with very good character. They are people-oriented so they are very good with customers. They always want to please the customer and that is very important and obviously, in the restaurant business, the customer is always right.'	I just wanted to have the experience of working in a different environment so I got a job at a chicken-finger place. I liked it; it seemed like a really simply, neat, popular concept and just saw how packed it was all the time. I was 18 and graduating high school and went to Daddy and said I wanted to open a chicken-finger restaurant. It gave me a greater appreciation even working for someone else. I saw, you know, how good Daddy was to his employees. He was never just a boss and not just because I was his daughter. He is that way with all of his employees. He cares about them and wants to be a part of their lives and to influence them. I had a very deep appreciation for him as a business owner and a boss.'	and just some things like that and just a very simple, easy-to-fix menu and daddy was interested but I was so young and I wasn't married and I needed to go to college and all of that so we kind of put in on the back burner for a while. About that time, daddy came and said that if we wanted to go ahead and open one instead of taking all those years to finish college that he and momma would put up the money to do that. My husband really took to the idea of doing that. So we went ahead and dove in—Mom and Dad put up the money and owned the restaurant and we ran it together. I was very proud to be in business with Daddy and that he would trust us enough to do a good job. We would then buy it from them.'

7. Female entrepreneurship in the wine sector: the role of family and identity in Italian small and medium wineries' strategies

Cinzia Colapinto, Vladi Finotto and Christine Mauracher

1. INTRODUCTION

One of the many under-investigated facets of the entrepreneurial phenomenon, female entrepreneurship has gained prominence in the past 15 years. The reasons are manifold. As the genesis of the Diana Project shows, women founders face a unique set of challenges in establishing and guiding their firms, such as lack of access to capital and limited power in decision-making in the venture capital industry. Brush et al. (2006) suggested that tackling these issues might have helped to overcome obstacles to women's participation in firm creation and their contribution to economic and job growth. Mainstream entrepreneurship research dedicated a limited amount of attention and effort to understanding the intersection between gender and entrepreneurship, thus producing an under-representation of the phenomenon and a substantial delay in transferring scientific evidence into policy-making and practical support (Brush and Cooper, 2012; Foss et al., 2019). The marginal position of women entrepreneurs in scientific accounts of firm founding and activity stems from two main assumptions. The first is that entrepreneurship has no gender. The second, partially orthogonal to the first, is that women found and conduct firms whose nature clashes with the high-growth focus of much entrepreneurial literature: female firms were often perceived as not having the size or the growth orientation of their male-led counterparts (Brush et al., 2006, 2019).

These two assumptions actually delayed the mainstreaming of female entrepreneuring. More important – and urgent – as Brush et al. (2020) and Jennings and Brush (2013) suggest, there might be a specific, gendered, way of founding firms that could harbinger alternative ways of interpreting and navigating the entrepreneurial story. Tackling these specificities could contribute to changing our understanding – and practice – of entrepreneurship, adding novel perspectives to the palette that would also be available to male founders.

Looking for evidence in extreme contexts could contribute to the aim of documenting the obstacles women face and how they circumvent them, and to that of capturing the peculiarities of entrepreneurship interpreted in a feminine way. The wine industry represents such an environment: an industry that has been culturally masculine for many years (Bryant and Garnham, 2014) and whose firms were eminently male-led is currently experiencing a sudden wave of female entrepreneurship. A cursory view of the phenomenon helps to suggest its dimensions. Italy, the country of our study, has more than 30 per cent female entrepreneurs running agricultural firms with vineyards or wineries (115 thousand firm owners) (Borsa Italiana, 2016). California, the US hotbed of quality wine production, has seen a rise in the number of women-owned wineries: up to 14 per cent in 2021, from 10 per cent in 2011 (Gilbert and Gilbert, 2021). Numerous studies in fields such as marketing and consumer research have documented the quantitative rise of female wine-drinkers.

Such a dynamic opens up a variety of avenues for research trying to assess how the industry's categories and meanings (Giorgi et al., 2015; Lounsbury et al., 2019a, 2019b) could be impacted by its increasing feminization. In this chapter we investigate the different paths through which women take control, conduct and guide firms in a male-dominated field. We focus in particular on how women gain legitimation as creators of new wineries or as the harbingers of transformation of family firms. We then consider how they manage internal resources and how they leverage their social networks.

The chapter aims at answering the following research questions: what are the paths followed by women in founding or managing the generational passage in wineries? How are they mobilizing providers of valuable resources – capital, labour, intangibles – to project their firms along paths of growth? Our inductive study is based on a sample of wineries located in the North East of Italy selected from the national list of members of the Association of Women in Wine. Based on a multiple-case study conducted in Italy and involving both new and extant firms, our chapter proffers a stylized description of the factors and strategies allowing female firms to subvert the typical logics of male-dominated fields. We work at the intersection between women entrepreneurship and family business, since the wine industry is one wherein the control of firms by women is largely dependent on generational handover.

The rest of the chapter is organized as follows. Section 2 reports the overall situation of the wine industry, sketching its characteristics as well as the presence and role of female entrepreneurs. Section 3 reports background literature and research focus, questions and method. Section 4 reports our methodology and describes our sample. Section 5 discusses our findings resulting from the interviews and Section 6 concludes.

2.   THE EVOLUTION OF A 'MASCULINE INDUSTRY': THE ITALIAN WINE INDUSTRY

In the postwar period, the Italian wine sector has been characterized by a strong increase in production and structural changes supported by national and European agricultural policy. An increase in yields and consumption was paralleled by a drastic decline in the number of farms. Wine, traditionally made by farmers for self-consumption, was increasingly produced in rationally organized wineries. From 1970, the export orientation of the sector and the phenomenon of wine of certified origin became increasingly important. After the methanol scandal of 1986 that caused a number of deaths, wine production fell dramatically in volume and came to focus on quality and exports. This led to a reorganization of the sector with the development of high-quality wines, the adoption of new techniques and the modernization of production processes.

Nowadays Italy is among the world's main wine producers; the national wine industry leads the domestic agrifood sector, with the largest contribution to Italian agrifood exports. In particular, viticulture is an important part of Italian agriculture. In 2018 vineyards covered 658,000 hectares and estimated production was about 48 million hectolitres. Italy is the foremost wine producer in the world in quantitative terms (about 18 per cent of world production), although France overtakes Italy in terms of value. According to the last Agricultural Census, there were 369,000 farms growing wine grapes, but if we consider only professional operators, grape production is carried out on about 197,000 farms. Wine-growing farms in Italy are predominantly small businesses, mostly family-operated. The average size of vineyards is very small (less than 2 hectares); Italian viticulture includes a share of relatively large farms. Winemaking is carried out by several operators (farms processing self-produced grapes, cooperative wineries, winemaking industry) and this phase is very heterogeneous, both with reference to the nature of the operators and to their economic size. Winemaking is performed by nearly 46,000 wineries (ISMEA, 2019), mostly belonging to the agricultural phase.

The Italian wine industry comprises a large number of operators: most of them are professional producers, but many only produce for self-consumption or as a hobby. The presence of such a large number of operators is a typical feature of the wine supply chain in Italy compared to other countries. In terms of turnover, in the Italian wine industry many micro companies represent a small share of production, and a few large companies cover most of it.

The production system is complex in terms of number of operators, forms of organization and differentiated forms of supply based on how they relate to the territory. In Italy 408 wines receive a PDO (protected designation of origin) and 118 wines a PGI (protected geographical indication), more than in Spain or in France. This designation system based on territorial origin is adopted by all traditional European producing countries, but in Italy it is widespread given the high number of grape and wine varieties.

The wine industry is an interesting research setting in terms of socio-environmental performance because it has recently adopted proactive sustainable practices in various business functions with an impact at the strategic level (Santini et al., 2013). Socio-environmental choices are impacted by consumer attitudes towards sustainable wine (Bonn et al., 2016; Forbes et al., 2009; Pomarici et al., 2015). Social practices can be externally oriented, if companies for instance consider new generations and support for local communities, or may instead focus on internal dimensions: in this case companies are interested in improving working conditions for employees or in providing developmental training, just to mention few examples (Pullman et al., 2010; Santini et al., 2013; Szolnoki, 2013). Thus, the wine industry is a changing business environment engaged in sustainability.

Looking at the behaviours adopted by wineries, Casini et al. (2010) propose a classification of wineries' orientation towards sustainability, ranging from devoted to laggards, that we can associate with the walk–talk approach. The walk–talk approach describes how much companies invest in communication and marketing (talk) and/or in actions and strategic plans (walk). The authors identify that 'devoted' wineries have a strong orientation towards sustainability, which they emphasize in customer communication. This leads to investments in customers' education and employees' training on one side, and the need to align their corporate and managerial visions on the other. The intermediate category is the so-called unexploiters, which adopt sustainable practices (thus they walk) but do not inform other people, even their clients, about their decisions (they do not talk). Consequently, they receive limited benefits from their sustainable orientation.

The opposite of unexploiters are the opportunists, wineries that do not have a particular interest (walk is moderated) in sustainability, but tend to heavily highlight the few sustainable practices introduced (high level of talk). Finally, the so-called laggard wineries are those who will never adopt sustainable practices (they do not walk or talk).

As far as governance aspects are concerned, the similarities in ownership and management imply a concentrated corporate governance model in Italian wineries. We briefly report the data from the Mediobanca Reports (2019, 2020). On average, a company's board is composed of four members. The wine sector has a predominance of mature managers (aged over 73), more than in most other sectors, while the presence of young managers aged between 18 and 39 is low. Baby boomers – aged between 54 and 73 – are the most represented generational group. About 60 per cent of respondents have a CEO belonging to the owner family and 50 per cent declare the presence of independent members on the Board of Directors. Boards with a single director are reported by 20 per cent of companies; a further 30 per cent have a Chief Executive Officer who also holds the position of President. Overall, therefore, 50 per cent of the major wine producers present a governance structure in which the operating powers are concentrated in the hands of a single entity.

Finally, moving on to the gender analysis of managers, men are predominant at managerial level is predominant: 85 per cent of managers are men and 15 per cent are women. According to the most recent studies, women are increasingly entering the wine industry as winemakers, winery owners, cellar managers, sommeliers or entrepreneurs, indicating the evolution of this traditionally masculine world.

2.1   Women and Wine

The role of women in the wine industry has emerged as a topic for study over the past decade. Traditionally this has been a male-dominated industry. Indeed, as highlighted by Discua Cruz et al. (2013), agricultural property, professional qualifications and the status of business leader are, in most cases, passed on to male heirs. Female heirs may operate a family business only under exceptional conditions, especially in the absence of male siblings.

Bryant and Garnham (2014) explain that women active in wine leadership programmes have voiced concerns regarding existing structural and cultural issues associated with gender. Nevertheless, the representation of women in the wine industry has seen a change: nowadays wine industries all over the world feature women's participation at various levels and country cases illustrate that women are gaining extensive exposure in their professional pursuits (Fookes, 2019).

In the extant literature we found insights on female entrepreneurship in the wine industry in specific geographical contexts. Galbreath (2014) analyses the Australia and New Zealand Wine Industry Directory data from 2007 to 2013 and makes use of 'social identity theory' because, as stated before, this industry is highly characterized by a 'male identity'. As a result of this identity and its corroboration in media and public discourses, women can be disinclined to try to enter the sector and might perceive it as elitist or exclusive; moreover, their career aspirations may be affected and frustrated. Galbreath was able to prove that when a company has a woman CEO, the presence of women in other roles (such as viticulturists, marketers, winemakers) is more likely to be found. Furthermore, the highest percentage of women was found in marketing roles, followed by the CEO role. Women are greatly represented in young and small companies, specifically in those producing fewer than 20,000 cases per year. Finally, women-led firms are less oriented towards exporting their wines.

Another study on the topic is that of Insel and Hoepfner (2018), based on Californian data. They selected 106 winemakers with production superior to 10,000 cases/year. Their findings show that women represent only 38 per cent of leadership positions, always lower-paid; moreover, as the size of the winery increases, the proportion of women decreases. The roles that 'fit' women best are considered to be in human resources, marketing and sales, while they are underrepresented in the line and lead positions such as viticulture, CEO or COO. The gender pay gap becomes greater as the work position grows in prestige; in senior positions women are expected to receive 77 per cent of the amount of salary received by men.

The study by Santos et al. (2019) provides an important contribution to the literature on female entrepreneurship and, more specifically, on networks of entrepreneurial women in the wine sector. The authors assess women wine-makers' motivations for and objectives in creating a formal, horizontal and inter-organizational network. The results indicate that networks can generate more advantages through formalization, namely, in the sharing of knowledge and experiences and the level of internationalization and networking. The strategy of coopetition promotes unity among network members.

In the previous section we pointed out the attention devoted to sustainability in the wine industry. Considering the link between women and sustainability, it is worth mentioning the paper by Galbreath and Tisch (2020). The study shows that women in the operations manager role frequently promote environ-mentally sustainable practices, while women in the CEO role do not. However, when women are in both CEO and operations manager roles in the same firm, the relationship with environmentally sustainable practices is positive.

A final element that is interesting to consider is the impact of women on the quality of wine, or on the perception of higher quality of wine produced by women. Research from Gilbert and Gilbert (2012) conducted in California and based on Opus Vino and Wines & Vines databases revealed that wine produced by females has higher quality features.

2.2   Bridging Family and Female Entrepreneurship Literature

Since the 1980s scholars have been studying whether and how gender influ-ences entrepreneurial processes and careers, thus calling for a distinction of female entrepreneurship from 'general' entrepreneurship investigations (Rey-Martí et al., 2015). More than two decades of analyses (Allen et al., 2008; Malach Pines et al., 2010) show that women are largely underrepresented in the population of individuals starting, running and guiding the growth of firms. A lively debate on the reasons for this gap pointed to a host of factors hindering creation and ownership of firms by women: culture, lack of support and social capital, lack of competences and lower entrepreneurial intentions (Malach Pines et al., 2010).

A reason to seek to understand the inner workings of female entrepreneurship lies in the apparent desirability of women-created and -led organizations, to bring about many societal benefits. Claims regarding the apparent better performance of women-led organizations in terms of job creation, financial performance, organizational climate, and employee satisfaction periodically make the news (see for instance Castrillon, 2019). Sound scientific confirmation of potential correlations between women leadership and heterogeneous and desirable impacts is not yet available. In some areas, more robust evidence of an impact of gender on business sustainability emerged recently, indicating that the avenue is worthy of further exploration (Glass et al., 2016). Recent studies on female-led ventures have found that the leadership style of women entrepreneurs brings advantages in stretching the human resource base in growth processes, since women show a higher propensity to facilitate and encourage interpersonal communication in organization, often display a transformative leadership style and have a higher propensity towards empowering managers (Devine et al., 2019; Eagly et al., 2003).

Our chapter aims at contributing to a fine-grained understanding of female entrepreneurship through a qualitative research design focusing on a specific industry and a limited geographical area: the production and commercialization of wine in the North East of Italy. The research design choices are key to the contribution the chapter aims at making. First, the qualitative research design: often research on entrepreneurship tends to point to the 'how much' in an effort to measure either the dimensions of a phenomenon (such as how many firms are created and conducted by women) or how much a series of determinants impact on the creation and conduction of a firm. There is a risk that knowledge of the subtleties of the process is overlooked. Despite the burgeoning of the field, much literature states that the nuances of the entrepreneurial process are not yet understood (Feldman, 2014; Sarasvathy, 2001). We aim at shedding light on the process of creation and conduct of the firm, trying to account for factors that pertain to the social and cultural context wherein entrepreneurship emerges.

Second, the scope of the analysis is limited. We espouse the recent critical assessment of the advancements in entrepreneurship: the disproportionate attention given to a specific portion of the phenomenon – high-tech, high-growth start-ups – might be misleading policy-makers, convincing them it is feasible to replicate success stories like that of the high-tech sector in Silicon Valley.

3.   METHODS

We opted for an inductive research design. Despite the authors' familiarity with entrepreneurship and female entrepreneurship literature, the field was entered with no preconceived theoretical framework in mind. We aimed at reconstructing the story of these firms and the personal histories of the women guiding them, with the aim of understanding the critical moments, actions and stakeholders that allowed the creation, control and growth of selected companies.

The research protocol consisted of a preliminary analysis of secondary data sources followed by semi-structured interviews. All interviews were recorded and transcribed. The authors then coded manually and autonomously all the transcribed passages. After a first wave of coding, we confronted our code structure and, through various iterations, reached an agreement by following the indications of Gioia et al. (2012). The Gioia Method, a qualitative approach (Gioia et al., 2012), was adopted to investigate the role of social ties during critical moments in the lives of the wine firms, focusing on origin, growth, management and future prospects. Because of Covid-19 all semi-structured interviews were conducted through videoconferencing applications (Google Meet, Skype, WhatsApp and Zoom). We conducted follow-up interviews after a first round to collect more information or clarify parts of the conversations. The interviews took place in 2020, starting on 11 March. Our sample comprises small and medium winemaking firms located in northeastern Italian regions (Veneto and Friuli-Venezia Giulia): the two regions are characterized by a population of small and micro firms and their winemaking traditions. Our sample comprises informants who have different family histories and manage firms of varying dimensions.

4.   WOMEN-RUN WINE FIRMS IN THE NORTH EAST OF ITALY

The northeast corner of Italy is home to three major wine-producing regions: Veneto, Friuli-Venezia Giulia and Trentino-Alto Adige. Our analysis focuses on this area and allows us to gain insights on female wineries. Focusing on how a woman got to be the head of a company, we identify two such methods: because of a generational shift or through the creation of a new venture (start-up). In the former, we distinguish between a planned shift and an involuntary and sudden generational change. Our results are consistent with the findings in Discua Cruz et al. (2013): female heirs may operate a family business only under exceptional conditions, especially in the absence of male siblings. In particular, we can observe that this phenomenon has in the past

Table 7.1   *Demographic information of participants and their wineries*

Entrepreneur	Type	Province	Woman's age	Business volume	Employees
Anna	Female-run	Treviso	69	~ 400,000 bottles/year	6
Giulia	Female-run	Verona	31	~ 60,000 bottles/year	5
Maria	Start-up	Padua	52	~ 27,000 bottles/year	4 seasonal workers
Alessandra	Start-up	Treviso	58	~ 25,000 bottles/year	0
Elena	Female-run	Treviso	39	~ 15,000 bottles/year + 1200 hl of bulk wine	3
Piera	Female-run	Pordenone	57	€12,649,131	27
Marcella	Start-up	Vicenza	65	~ 16,000 bottles/year	4
Antonella	Female-run	Treviso	60	€2,229,363	10
Manuela E.	Start-up	Treviso	30	€200,000	3
Elvira	Female-run	Treviso	62	€13,800,000	28
Elisa	Start-up	Padua	44	na	na
Silvia	Start-up	Padua	40	€325,000	8
Marilisa	Female-run	Verona	67	€26,000,000	32

three decades prepared the path and the environment for women start-ups in the wine industry. Observation of the histories of the different firms displayed the increasing space occupied by women in the wine industry.

The first path is common to Maria, Alessandra and Marcella. They moved with their husbands to a new location that was in some way a trigger for their entrepreneurial idea. Moreover, the involvement of women's husbands was clear, as well as the balance with family needs: the couple preferred to leave the frantic pace of city life and moved to the countryside. Passion drove the entrepreneurial idea development. Not surprisingly, the results of the research by Brush et al. (2010) show that women are more likely to accept and ask for family advice before deciding on an opportunity. In the case of Elisa and Silvia, the male supporting figure is played by the father who was backing their passion.

The closest family members can be considered the cause and the obstacle at the same time. While Marcella expressed the need to slow the development of her project because both daughters had given birth and she did not wish to neglect her family, Alessandra's daughters reaching adulthood was key to her relocation from the city. Nine of the interviewed women (not only the start-uppers) have children but only one of them started managing the business while her children were toddler-age, and highlighted a conflictual relationship.

The women's previous experience proved crucial even if not linked to the sector: these women were coming from other careers and their skills or professional networks were essential to the winery's development. Entrepreneurs who have founded a business are more likely to found others afterward (Davidsson and Honig, 2003; Wright et al., 1997), as in the cases of Alessandra and Marcella. Social ties can support the identification of opportunities (Elfring and Hulsink, 2003; Singh et al., 1999), as highlighted by the collaboration between Marcella and her oenologist; networks also favour the collecting of assets (Garnsey, 1998), such as capital, labour, skills and tacit knowledge (Stuart and Sorenson, 2005), as in the case of Alessandra, who exploited her husband's wines to open her business.

Moving to female-run wineries, Anna, Giulia and Antonella shared a similar story concerning generational change. They gained control of the company after finishing their studies, spending their childhood and adolescence in the company, helping and learning. Anna had already acquired production and marketing skills and had been involved in travel abroad for a decade: she repeatedly stressed the need to gain experience for many years before becoming the owner and running a company – something that happened in her case, and which she is replicating with her son. We can see a planned shift, and our interviews revealed passion and pride in following the steps of the family.

Sometimes, a critical and sudden generational change occurs (Elena B. and Piera) and the woman heir is prepared and trained to drive the winery: thus, the need for training emerges as a strong precondition in the generational turnover of the company. For instance, Elena made use of the advice of a trainer, because she was dissatisfied with the company's performance: she understood how to change the business model and this experience also helped in her approach and in the way of communicating with colleagues. Piera felt the need to resort to external training to evaluate situations, to weigh activities, to learn to reflect and to be rational but also emotional within the company.

The second characteristic shared by this last group of companies is the decision to produce and focus on local wines and on the value of the territory. Elena B.'s passion for territoriality can be seen in the decision to limit the production of Prosecco: given the high competition and the frequent use of discounting, conflicting with her philosophy, she prefers to sell and produce the wines of her land. This is an internally controversial decision, not well accepted by the men in the company; however, she has been proving her capacity and passion in pursuing this strategy.

4.1   New Markets and Tools

An interest in international markets can be found in start-ups as well as in the new business models of some established wineries. Start-ups invested in creating great recognition of their wines abroad, through important awards, as pointed out by Maria, or fairs, as suggested by Marcella and Alessandra. They looked for less mature markets, characterized by greater purchasing power, such as Northern Europe and Asia. Also, some woman-run wineries (Anna, Elisa, Giulia) perceived the need to go abroad because the Italian market was not receptive to, and was saturated with, wine companies (Pomarici, 2005): thus, they all changed the previous business model. Their wines met the international tastes of customers while remaining tied to the characteristics of the territory and increasing the focus on quality. A second aspect to be pointed out is the use of technology and social networks as a means of communication and sales. Giulia recognized the usefulness of social media, especially to understand which areas to explore based on the feedback received from online comments: she exploits the commercial potential that technology can offer and controls the risks involved in detaching from the father's sales approach.

Another detachment from the paternal approach can be observed when technology concerns new machinery, steel equipment and labellers, as well as the renewal of the cellar, as in the case of Antonella and Anna.

However, the role of communication is seen in all companies, with different nuances and motivations. Piera engaged herself in training to improve her communication skills. As communication to clients is essential nowadays, Anna wanted to transmit her passion and respect for the product to the final consumer and she exploited new technologies.

Marcella's nephew asserts that they address the curiosity of those who want a new wine in their portfolio, because the Colli Berici area is little known for wine both in Italy and worldwide. They focus heavily on the combination of the Palladian villas and the city of Vicenza in their advertisements to attract customers; it is a recent trend in the wine sector, in fact, connecting cultural references to products so they become an integral part of the competitive strategy is a recent trend in the wine sector (Rizzo, 2015).

We can consider the specific values, concepts and elements that characterized the communication strategies. Wine is an expression of a country's culture and its traditions. Italy is a country with a long tradition in wines, where we can observe a strong relationship with the cultural heritage, as the wines (as well as other local gastronomic products) are presented with labels and branding which prove their origin. For instance, the website and Instagram page of Anna's company refers to two elements: 'the heritage of tradition' and 'the strength of innovation'.

4.2   Covid-19 and Female Wineries

The Covid-19 pandemic might represent one of the most significant environmental changes in modern marketing history, with a great impact on marketing logics and communication strategies, in particular when the relevance of corporate social responsibility is considered (Hongwei and Lloyd, 2020). The pandemic has had social and economic consequences at a global level. The wine industry has been heavily impacted. Marketing microenvironments have been changed by social distancing and forced lockdowns that impacted on the supply chain and marketing investments. In the marketing macro environment, Covid-19 measures closed entire sectors, forced industries to move mostly online and transformed consumer spending. In particular, the wine industry was impacted by changes in food purchasing by consumers and by the interruption of the Horeca (Hotellerie–Restaurant–Catering) channels at national and international levels (Coluccia et al., 2021). Indeed, 2020 data show a sharp decline of wine sales (−37 per cent) in these channels, an unprecedented fall to numbers not seen in more than 30 years: this was a consequence of the closure of bars, restaurants and hotels (Cardebat et al., 2020). Despite the downturn in sales, the wine supply chain was resilient and original prices remained essentially stable, especially thanks to the fact that wine is a storable product and to the focus on quality (ISMEA, 2020).

To establish how the Covid-19 pandemic affected women entrepreneurs and how resilient their firms were, we interviewed some of the studied entrepreneurs between December 2020 and March 2021 in order to explore how female wineries changed direction or deployed new strategies. We find that women weigh strategic choices such as using e-commerce with the need to maintain extant relationships, make decisions influenced by the need to preserve communities and rely on peer networks to provide mutual support.

We observed that the digital approach has been embraced but not without issues, the main one relating to competences and resources able to exploit the digital component. Indeed, most firms had to rely on external resources – mainly professionals, but also young family members. The scientific background of entrepreneurs led them to focus more on the production and management challenges rather than on the communication and marketing ones.

Despite the growth of wine e-commerce in Italy (Nomisma, 2021), it was not a solution adopted by the generality of firms – also among those we interviewed – for many reasons. First, the adoption of an e-commerce strategy was seen by firms as a potential trigger of channel conflicts and a potential source of friction with the networks of agents and resellers that are key in guaranteeing small business the opportunity to be present in large retail chains. Specifically, if the product portfolio offered on the website is the same as the one that is distributed through traditional channels, channel conflicts can be generated, especially if the pricing policies or promotional offers are not well managed. We found that women entrepreneurs acted and made decisions as if they were part of an extended family, in the words of one of the interviewees: a network of wineries and suppliers that had to be protected and had to be characterized by mutual help and understanding. This is consistent with the female tendency to compassion (Weisberg et al., 2011). Literature suggests female entrepreneurs may focus primarily on the internal negative effects of the pandemic and how it may be affecting their employees and close partners: as expected, the decisions taken reflect an interest in maintaining employees' well-being and developing them, and this was emphasized by Alessandra, Anna, Elvira and Elena B.

Moreover, the platform set-up and operating costs, together with the indirect costs on processes and warehouses, were perceived as too high by micro- and small firms: they opted to join e-commerce platforms managed by several companies of small wineries. Other smaller wineries used digital technology (emails, WhatsApp and Facebook) to collect orders from customers located close to the winery's plant. Orders were then delivered to consumers' houses thanks to food and wine delivery services either offered by commercial platforms or by wineries. On the contrary, larger and more structured companies had mostly already had e-commerce websites in place before the pandemic; thus they declared that the channel was simply strengthened and played an important role in sales in 2020. In the case of newly founded companies, e-commerce does not seem to be a useful tool to launch the product: our informants said that the experience dimension of products and places is key to gain a new company legitimacy and credibility and that establishing a relationship with consumers from scratch via digital channels is too expensive and difficult to manage. Product information is essential to allow the consumer to better assess the wine.

Most wineries integrated digital marketing innovations by creating virtual remote wine-tasting experiences (Alessandra and Elvira) and using social media to produce and distribute narratives that were more elaborate than those they had previously replied upon. Changes affected especially means and tools, and most of all the content of messages delivered via social media. One common element is the desire to bring the customer to the centre and to care about individuals and their families. As in-person tasting rooms were not an option, many places brought tastings, classes and events directly to living rooms instead.

In terms of content, from the interviews it emerged that it was important to avoid going dark and to convey optimistic (Alessandra, Anna and Elvira) and simple (Anna and Giulia) messages. Social media users are more inclined to positively engage with content if they understand it (Scorrano et al., 2019), so most entrepreneurs pointed out the relevance of language style.

As Forbes et al. (2009) pointed out, consumers are becoming increasingly concerned by the effects of conventional agricultural food production practices on human health and environmental well-being. Covid-19 brought this to the fore. Indeed, wineries aligned with the mood and emotional needs of consumers during the pandemic. In general, we saw many brands replacing planned campaigns with messages of empathy and commitment, and with messages pointing out specific values (attention to quality and the environment, and the fact that consumers are looking to be more health-conscious, such as in the cases of Anna, Giulia, Elena and Elvira).

5.   CONCLUDING REMARKS

Based on a narrative analysis of the life stories, we were able to reconstruct the changes and to observe the main characteristics of female entrepreneurs in the wine industry in northeastern regions of Italy. Indeed, in Italy, until recently, the wine industry was dominated by a masculine mentality: it was certainly not usual or expected that women would work in, let alone guide, a winery. The male succession rule has been questioned recently, as we observed. The generational shift has shaped a more favourable environment for start-ups led by women. All the businesswomen managed their company differently at first glance, but upon a more profound consideration we identified three types of evolutionary strategies, namely: geographical displacement as a trigger of the entrepreneurial idea; generational change leading to the use of technology; and generational change leading to a focus on local wines.

Our analysis revealed that wine companies can be managed in a feminine way: with workers' evaluation based on soft skills rather than educational background, and a great respect for the product, which sometimes leads to organic/sustainable production methods. Second, we observed the role of family and tradition: most of the interviewees stressed the importance of family approval, complementarity among family members and the necessity to stick together for business continuity, recalling the findings by Brush et al. (2017). This sense of family was a central theme of the communication during 2020, along with images and content related to sustainability and future projects.

Considering how some Italian wineries fared in the face of the pandemic, we observe that what could have been a dramatic story has instead been a tale of resistance, and of the reinvention and creativity of women-owned wineries. Women entrepreneurs have been leveraging the female management style to cope with the challenges related to Covid-19: we refer to the role played by heritage elements and environmental passion (from sustainability to healthy lifestyle). As expected, wineries with more advanced multi-channel distribution systems had more developed ambidexterity capabilities to cope with the 2020 restrictive measures. Their ambidexterity stems from the ability to simultaneously maintain relations with distributors and innovate and search for creative ways to establish online direct communication with consumers' sales systems. Relationships and ties with all stakeholders were transferred to an online setting to pursue the continuity of all educational, commercial experiences and collaborations. To sum up the themes emerging as distinctive traits of women-owned wineries' response of to the crisis: first is an increasing focus (and investment) on sustainability as a lever to cater to the novel consumer coming out of the current pandemic; second is renewed attention to collaboration with the younger generation, in particular students, perceived as the harbingers of a new perspective on business that is more respectful of social and environmental concerns; and third is a determined search for high-level positioning to escape from price competition, sustained by substantial investments in socially and environmentally responsible processes and strategies and renewed attention to novel forms of communication emphasizing the values of the firm.

REFERENCES

Allen, I.E., Elam, A., Langowitz, N. and M. Dean (2008), 'Global entrepreneurship monitor: 2007 report on women and entrepreneurship', Wellesley, MA: Babson College.

Bonn, M.A., Cronin Jr., J.J., and M. Cho (2016), 'Do environmental sustainable practices of organic wine suppliers affect consumers' behavioral intentions? The moderating role of trust', *Cornell Hospitality Quarterly*, 57(1), 21–37.

Borsa Italiana (2016), *Il vino è sempre più donna*, accessed 26 June 2021 at www .borsaitaliana.it/notizie/italian-factory/food/donneevino.htm.

Brush, C.G., and S.Y. Cooper (2012), 'Female entrepreneurship and economic development: An international perspective', *Entrepreneurship & Regional Development*, 24(1–2), 1–6.

Brush C., Ali, A., Kelley, D., and P. Greene (2017), 'The influence of human capital factors and context on women's entrepreneurship: Which matters more?' *Journal of Business Venturing Insights*, 8, 105–13.

Brush, C.G., Bruin, A., de Welter, F. and I.E. Allen (2010), 'Gender embeddedness of women entrepreneurs: an empirical test of the 5 "M" framework', in *Frontiers of Entrepreneurship Research*, Wellesley, MA: Babson College.

Brush, Candida G., Carter, Nancy M., Gatewood, Elizabeth J., Greene Patricia G., and Myra M. Hart (eds) (2006), *Growth-oriented women entrepreneurs and their businesses: A global research perspective*. Cheltenham, UK and Northampton, MA, USA: Edward Elgar Publishing.

Brush, C., Edelman, L.F., Manolova, T. et al. (2019), 'A gendered look at entrepreneurship ecosystems', *Small Business Economics*, 53, 393–408.

Brush, C.G., Greene, P.G., and F. Welter (2020), 'The Diana project: A legacy for research on gender in entrepreneurship', *International Journal of Gender and Entrepreneurship*, 8(12), 7–25.

Bryant, L., and B. Garnham (2014), 'The embodiment of women in wine: Gender inequality and gendered inscriptions of the working body in a corporate wine organization', *Gender, Work and Organization*, 21(5), 411–26.

Cardebat, J.M., Masset, P., and J.P. Weisskopf (2021), 'COVID-19: What is next for the market for fine wines?', AAWE Working Paper No. 250, Economics, https:// wine-economics.org/wp-content/uploads/2020/05/AAWE_WP250.pdf.

Casini, L., Corsi, A., Cavicchi, A., and C. Santini (2010), 'Hopelessly devoted to sustainability: Marketing challenges to face in the wine business', paper presented at the 119th EAAE Seminar 'Sustainability in the Food Sector: Rethinking the Relationship between the Agro-Food System and the Natural, Social, Economic and Institutional Environments'. Capri, Italy, 30 June–2 July.

Castrillon, C. (2019), 'Why women-led companies are better for employees', *Forbes*, 24 March, accessed 4 June 2021 at www.forbes.com/sites/carolinecastrillon/2019/03/24/why-women-led-companies-are-better-for-employees/.

Coluccia, B., Agnusdei, G.P., Miglietta, P.P. and F. De Leo (2021), 'Effects of COVID-19 on the Italian agri-food supply and value chains', *Food Control*, 2021(May), 123:107839.

Davidsson, P., and B. Honig (2003), 'The role of social and human capital among nascent entrepreneurs', *Journal of Business Venturing*, 18(3), 301–31.

Devine, R.A., Molina-Sieiro, G., Holmes, R.M., and S.A. Terjesen (2019), 'Female-led high-growth: Examining the role of human and financial resource management', *Journal of Small Business Management*, 57(1), 81–109.

Discua Cruz, A., Howorth, C., and E. Hamilton (2013), 'Intrafamily entrepreneurship: The formation and membership of family entrepreneurial teams', *Entrepreneurship Theory and Practice*, 37(1), 17–46.

Eagly, A.H., Johannesen-Schmidt, M.C., and M.L. van Engen (2003), 'Transformational, transactional, and laissez-faire leadership styles: A meta-analysis comparing women and men', *Psychological Bulletin*, 129(4), 569–91.

Elfring, T., and W. Hulsink (2003), 'Networks in entrepreneurship: The case of high-technology firms', *Small Business Economics*, 21, 409–22.

Feldman, M.P. (2014), 'The character of innovative places: Entrepreneurial strategy, economic development, and prosperity', *Small Business Economics*, 43(1), 9–20.

Fookes, T. (2019), 'Wine industry looks to improve jobs and leadership opportunities for women', *ABCNews Online*, 8 March, accessed 26 July 2021 at www.abc.net.au/news/2019-03-08/women-in-wine-industry-emerging/10870916.

Forbes, S.L., Cohen, D.A., Cullen, R., Wratten, S.D., and J. Fountain (2009), 'Consumer attitudes regarding environmentally sustainable wine: An exploratory study of the New Zealand market place', *Journal of Cleaner Production*, 17(13), 1195–9.

Foss, L., Henry, C., Ahl, H., and G.H. Mikalsen (2019), 'Women's entrepreneurship policy research: A 30-year review of the evidence', *Small Business Economics*, 53(2), 409–29.

Galbreath, J. (2014), 'Women in top roles in the wine industry: Forging ahead or falling behind?' *American Association of Wine Economists*, 150, 1–36.

Galbreath, J., and D. Tisch (2020), 'The effects of women in different roles on environmentally sustainable practices: Empirical evidence from the Australian wine industry', *Australasian Journal of Environmental Management*, 27(4), 434–51.

Garnsey, E. (1998), 'Theory of the early growth of the firm', *Industrial and Corporate Change*, 7, 523–36.

Gilbert, L.A., and J.C. Gilbert (2012), 'Evidence of women winemakers' success in a male-dominated field', paper presented at the Meeting of the Association for Psychological Science, Chicago, IL, 24–27 May.

Gilbert, L.A., and J.C. Gilbert (2021), 'Facts and figures gathered in our on-going research on California women winemakers', Women Winemakers website, accessed 1 May 2021 at https://webpages.scu.edu/womenwinemakers/facts.php.

Gioia, D.A., Corley, K.G., and A.L. Hamilton (2012), 'Seeking qualitative rigor in inductive research: Notes on the Gioia Methodology', *Organizational Research Methods*, 16(1), 15–31.

Giorgi, S., Lockwood, C., and M.A. Glynn (2015), 'The many faces of culture: Making sense of 30 years of research on culture in organization studies', *Academy of Management Annals*, 9(1), 1–54.

Glass, C., Cook, A. and A. Ingersoll (2016), 'Do women leaders promote sustainability? Analyzing the effect of corporate governance composition on environmental performance', *Business Strategy and the Environment*, 25(7), 495–511.

Hongwei, H., and H. Lloyd (2020), 'The impact of Covid-19 pandemic on corporate social responsibility and marketing philosophy', *Journal of Business Research*, 116, 176–82.

Insel, B., and A. Hoepfner (2018), 'The presence of women in leadership positions in California's wine industry: A survey', *American Association of Wine Economists*, 231, 1–25.

ISMEA (2019), *Il settore vitivinicolo alla sfida della PAC post-2020: complementarietà degli interventi tra I e II pilastro e prospettive*. RRN, Rome.

ISMEA (2020), https://www.ismea.it/istituto-di-servizi-per-il-mercato-agricolo -alimentare

Jennings, J.E., and C.G. Brush (2013), 'Research on women entrepreneurs: Challenges to (and from) the broader entrepreneurship literature?' *Academy of Management Annals*, 7(1), 663–715.

Lounsbury, M. Cornelissen, J., Granqvist, N., and S. Grodal (2019a), 'Culture, innovation and entrepreneurship', *Innovation*, 21(1), 1–12.

Lounsbury, M., Gehman, J., and M. Ann Glynn (2019b), 'Beyond homo entrepreneurus: Judgment and the theory of cultural entrepreneurship', *Journal of Management Studies*, 56(6), 1214–36.

Malach Pines, A., Lerner, M., and D. Schwartz (2010), 'Gender differences in entrepreneurship', *Equality, Diversity and Inclusion: An International Journal*, 29(2), 186–98.

Mediobanca (2019), *Indagine Sul Settore Vinicolo*, accessed 26 June 2021 at www .mbres.it/sites/default/files/resources/download_it/Indagine_vini_2016.pdf.

Mediobanca (2020), *Indagine Sul Settore Vinicolo*, accessed 26 June 2021 at www .mbres.it/sites/default/files/resources/download_it/Indagine_vini_2020.pdf.

Nomisma Wine monitor, https://www.nomisma.it/servizi/osservatori/osservatori-di -mercato/wine-monitor/

Pomarici, E. (2005), 'Il mercato mondiale del vino: tendenze, scenario competitivo e dualismo tra vecchio e nuovo mondo', *VQ*, 0.

Pomarici, E., Vecchio, R., and A. Mariani (2015), 'Wineries' perception of sustainability costs and benefits: an exploratory study in California', *Sustainability*, 7, 16164–74.

Pullman, M.E., Maloni, M.J., and J. Dillard (2010), 'Sustainability practices in food supply chains: How is wine different?' *Journal of Wine Research*, 21(1), 35–56.

Rey-Martí, A., Porcar, A.T., and A. Mas-Tur (2015), 'Linking female entrepreneurs' motivation to business survival', *Journal of Business Research*, 68(4), 810–14.

Rizzo, L.S. (2015), Wine cooperatives in the east of the Verona province. Company consolidation and networking: an update. *Proceedings-AIEA2 VII Congresson Internazionale*.

Santini, C., Cavicchi, A., and L. Casini (2013), 'Sustainability in the wine industry: Key questions and research trends', *Agricultural and Food Economics*, 1(9), 1–14.

Santos, G., Marques, C.S., and V. Ratten (2019), 'Entrepreneurial women's networks: The case of D'Uva – Portugal wine girls', *International Journal of Entrepreneurial Behaviour and Research*, 25(2), 298–322.

Sarasvathy, S.D. (2001), 'Causation and effectuation: Toward a theoretical shift from economic inevitability to entrepreneurial contingency', *Academy of Management Review*, 26(2), 243–63.

Scorrano, P., Fait, M., Maizza, A., and D. Vrontis (2019), 'Online branding strategy for wine tourism competitiveness', *International Journal of Wine Business Research*, 31(2), 130–50.

Singh, R.P., Hills, G.E., Lumpkin, G.T., and R.C. Hybels (1999), 'The entrepreneurial opportunity recognition process: Examining the role of self-perceived alertness and social networks', paper presented at the Academy of Management Meeting, Chicago, IL, 6–11 August.

Stuart, T., and O. Sorenson (2005), 'Social networks and entrepreneurship', in Sharon A. Alvarez, Rajshree R. Agarwal, and Olav Sorenson (eds), *Handbook of Entrepreneurship: Disciplinary Perspectives*. New York: Springer, pp.233–51.

Szolnoki, G. (2013), 'A cross-national comparison of sustainability in the wine industry', *Journal of Cleaner Production*, 53, 243–51.

Weisberg, Y.J., DeYoung, C.G., and J.B. Hirsh (2011), 'Gender differences in personality across the ten aspects of the Big Five', *Frontiers in Psychology*, 2, 178.

Wright, M., Robbie, K., and C. Ennew (1997), 'Venture capitalists and serial entrepreneurs', *Journal of Business Venturing*, 12(957), 227–49.

PART IV

Women's practices to realize themselves while entrepreneuring

8. Women's entrepreneurship practices of context and sustainability

Kim Poldner, Mónica Grau-Sarabia and William B. Gartner

1. INTRODUCTION

Context is not only given, but also made (Goodman, 1978; Herman, 2009; Sarasvathy, 2009). As given, context in entrepreneurship studies is increasingly inclusive of the environmental and social embeddedness of the enterprise (Welter, 2011). Entrepreneurs are no longer seen as autonomous agents, but rather as rooted in their environments and social contexts (Blackburn et al., 2015). Yet entrepreneurship, by its nature, is transformative and emancipatory (Jennings et al., 2016; Rindova et al., 2009), whereby context can be socially co-created (Sarasvathy, 2009; Fletcher and Selden, 2016).

This chapter offers an approach that both recognizes the constraints of context and shows how context is created and shaped. We employ a critical perspective (Tedmanson et al., 2012) that invites scholars to recognize differing understandings of what entrepreneurship is and can be (Bacq and Janssen, 2011). A critical studies approach perceives entrepreneurship as a gendered activity (Ahl, 2002; Bruni et al., 2005); that is, gender is, inherently, 'socially constructed' (Ahl, 2006, p.596). We build on this perspective, which challenges dominant perceptions of the entrepreneur as a Western white male in search of economic opportunity (Gherardi and Perrotta, 2013). Specifically, we take an entrepreneurship-as-practice approach (Johannisson, 2011) to circumvent fundamentally gendered discourses of dominant entrepreneurship constructs such as economic action, risk, legitimacy and opportunity recognition (Gherardi, 2015; Marlow, 2015). Entrepreneurship-as-practice focuses on the contextual relation between actors and the learning processes to which they are exposed (Fletcher and Selden, 2016).

To explore practices that would surface the 'gendering' of context, we study a sample of women entrepreneurs who are based in Southern Europe and focus on sustainable return on investment (blended value). Unravelling the value of apparently marginal practices (Calás et al., 2009) of women sustainable entrepreneurs in South European countries enables us to redefine the outcomes of entrepreneurial action and expand its 'emancipatory potential' (Jennings et al., 2016; Rindova et al., 2009). According to recent Global Entrepreneurship Monitor (GEM) findings, 'females are more likely to engage in social and environmental activity than males' (Hechavarria et al., 2012, p.144). In work on motivations of nascent entrepreneurs, both men and women valued financial success but women had other motivations that went beyond financial ones, whereas men's motivations were primarily financial (Cassar, 2007; Manolova et al., 2012). Thus far, only a handful of case studies have been conducted at the intersection of women's and sustainable entrepreneurship (see for example Datta and Gailey, 2012; Goss et al., 2011). Whereas most sustainable entrepreneurship research has copied economic models and strategic approaches from the commercial world to understand societal problems (Nicholls and Young, 2008, p.xiv), critical studies expand entrepreneurship to be a societal rather than just an economic phenomenon (Calás et al., 2009, Steyaert and Hjorth, 2003; Steyaert and Katz, 2003). By focusing on a sample of women sustainable entrepreneurs, we aim to answer the call for diversification in research settings and perspectives (De Bruin et al., 2006; Jennings and Brush, 2013) and position our study as critical in both approach and choice of phenomenon.

The chapter identifies three core practices that women sustainable entrepreneurs in Southern Europe enact to sustain their business and themselves, namely: reconnecting the entrepreneur's own aspirations with the needs of others; resourcing their human, social and financial capital by staying close to their origins; and recharging themselves, personally, through reflection and ownership of their situations (the 3Rs). These three practices help them to address the obstacles to women's entrepreneurship identified in the literature: lack of condition, credibility and confidence (we call them the 3Cs). First, lack of condition (or status) refers to the fact that women are traditionally defined by their primary role as caretakers of children with domestic responsibilities (see for example Aidis et al., 2007). Second, women entrepreneurs experience a lack of credibility when they cannot access finance, networks and resources (Yousafzai et al. 2015). As a result of lack of condition and credibility, women tend to have lower self-esteem when it comes to setting up a business and trusting their own skills and potential (Yousafzai et al., 2015). A lack of confidence is often a major barrier for women in the process of setting up and running their business. Comparing the 3Cs with the 3Rs leads to a reinterpretation of context: from women entrepreneurs being marginalized by their context, to women entrepreneurs as co-creators of their own contexts. Women develop solutions to their situations on terms that are defined, in meaningful ways, by themselves, rather than by an evaluation of outsiders using standards that ignore these women's specific contexts.

The chapter is structured as follows. In the literature review in section 2, we will problematize women's sustainable entrepreneurship through a critical, entrepreneurship-as-practice lens. In section 3 we will describe the methodology and analysis, after which the findings will be presented in section 4. Section 5 will discuss the results and implications of the study, followed by a conclusion.

2.   LITERATURE REVIEW

2.1   Sustaining the Entrepreneur in Sustainable Enterprise

In a world experiencing financial crises, resource scarcity, wealth inequality and climate change, sustainable entrepreneurship offers more effective models of sustainable economic development (Nicholls, 2006). The field of sustainable entrepreneurship is commonly approached from a blended-value logic of people, planet and profit (Zahra and Wright, 2016). Most publications conceptualize sustainable entrepreneurship as a variation of the discovery, creation and exploitation of economic opportunities to create goods and services towards a more sustainable society (see for example Dean and McMullen, 2007, p.58; Hockerts and Wüstenhagen, 2010, p.482; Pacheco et al., 2010, p.471; Patzelt and Shepherd, 2011, p.632). Many of these articles question how entrepreneurs blend the '3Ps' (people, planet and profit) to sustain their enterprise, but little is known about how entrepreneurs sustain themselves. That is, it would seem important to take into account these entrepreneurs themselves in the blended-value logic. To have enterprises that focus on sustainability would also necessitate ensuring that the entrepreneurs involved in these efforts are sustained. Therefore, this study focuses on how entrepreneurs sustain themselves in the process of creating blended value through a critical, entrepreneurship-as-practice perspective.

2.2   Moving Beyond the Ideal Image of the Entrepreneur

Although literature on women's entrepreneurship has increased considerably (Ahl, 2002; Bruni et al., 2005; Calás et al., 2009; Essers and Benschop, 2009), most entrepreneurship research still considers the stereotypical image of the male, Western, white, Calvinist entrepreneur (Gherardi and Perrotta, 2013) in search of economic opportunity. This functionalist perspective positions the 'entrepreneur as hero' in the centre of the analysis (Jones and Spicer, 2009; Williams and Nadin, 2013), focusing on personality traits and neglecting all 'other' entrepreneurs, including those who fail. A critical perspective seeks to question the category of the entrepreneur by focusing on the politics and regimes of domination that are constructed under the name of the entrepreneur

(Nicholls, 2006). Instead of asking how entrepreneurs create utility, we try to understand how entrepreneurs create meaning (Gartner, 1993) and aim to expand the concept of entrepreneurship itself. By doing so, we challenge dominant perceptions of *the* entrepreneur and of entrepreneurs as heroes endowed with unique qualities (Williams and Nadin, 2013). We might find out that, when we study the stories narrated by an alternative group of entrepreneurs, the dominant character of the entrepreneurship discourse is not so dominant (Gherardi, 2015, p.663).

Calás, Smircich and Bourne reframe entrepreneurship 'from positive economic activity' to 'entrepreneurship as social change' (Rindova et al., 2009) using a feminist analytical lens (Calás et al., 2009). Contemporary society is historically built on not only ideologies of patriarchy, but also on ideologies that sustained industrial capitalism. These ideologies thrived on the assumption that women and other beings should be subordinated (Calás et al., 2009). The critical researcher is challenged to bring about a different perspective to such biases by unravelling the value of apparently marginal (entrepreneurial) practices (Calás et al., 2009). A feminist lens on entrepreneuring (Calás et al., 2009) suggests that gender destabilizes interpretive categories and encourages a plurality of meaning. Yet little work has so far explored the processes of how people grow into becoming entrepreneurial, while accounts of gendered practices of such entrepreneurial 'becoming' are even scarcer (Poldner et al., 2011, p.226). A critical perspective invites us to not simply look at if the entrepreneurs under study are men or women, but rather to perceive entrepreneurship as a *gendered* activity (Ahl, 2002; Bruni et al., 2005). We use the term gender in the original sense of the word, that is, as socially constructed (Ahl, 2006, p.596). The concept of 'the entrepreneur' is thought to be neutral, but a critical, gendered perspective on entrepreneurship reveals that the 'ideal' entrepreneur is a man.

2.3 Three Contextual Obstacles to Women's Entrepreneurship Practices

Comparing characteristics of masculinity and femininity with the characteristics ascribed to entrepreneurs reveals how entrepreneurship is considered to be a masculine activity (Ahl, 2006). In other words: entrepreneurs exhibiting more characteristics that are masculine-coded are considered closer to the ideal image of the entrepreneur. As a result, studies on women entrepreneurs often define obstacles to their entrepreneurship, which has 'stunted understanding of the factors that contribute to the flourishing and optimal functioning of women entrepreneurs' (James, 2012, p.237). With that realization in mind, three contextual obstacles were identified (lack of condition, credibility and confidence;

Bruni et al., 2005) that served as sensitizing concepts in subsequent analyses (Jennings and Brush, 2013).

The first obstacle is that women are traditionally defined by their primary role as caretakers of children and the domestic realm, which inflicts a *lack of status* or *condition* (Bruni et al., 2005, p.19). Studies on women's entrepreneurship often examine work–home conflict, while hardly any studies examine work–home conflicts of male entrepreneurs (Hughes and Jennings, 2010). In fact, most categorizations of women entrepreneurs are built around the reproductive life cycle: the majority of typologies mentioned in the literature relate to childlessness, childbearing, empty-nest syndrome and extended motherhood. The assumption is that family duties take priority in women's lives and therefore that women can never be trustworthy entrepreneurs (Bruni et al., 2005, p.18).

The second obstacle is that women entrepreneurs sometimes experience scepticism by potential clients, suppliers and business partners and must be more persistent to prove their knowledge, skills and capacities. Implicit in the obstacles to access to, for example, finance (Marlow and Patton, 2005; Wu and Chua, 2012; Saparito et al., 2013), information (DeTienne and Chandler, 2007) and networks is the *lack of credibility* of women seeking to build a thriving business (Bruni et al., 2005, p.19). A lack of access to finance (Coleman and Robb, 2012; Marlow and Patton, 2005; Saparito et al., 2013; Wu and Chua, 2012) is based on the prejudiced view of women as being unable to handle money (Bruni et al., 2005; Marlow and Swail, 2014). This prejudice is sometimes reflected in the argument that women start less viable businesses as they are often in the low-profit service sector (Jennings and Brush, 2013). In addition, educational choices and skills are often mentioned as obstacles to women entrepreneurship (DeTienne and Chandler, 2007). These obstacles discourage women from work in technical sectors, while a lack of access to finance forces women into low capital-intensive activities (Jennings and Brush, 2013). As such, academics and practitioners use male entrepreneurship as a benchmark for entrepreneurship, assessing women entrepreneurs according to masculine values. Third, lack of access to networks points to the 'old boys' networks'; that is, a reliance on informal contacts when doing business. Many traditional business networks eschewed women and even nowadays, informal business networks seem to be less open to women (Bruni et al., 2005). Women spend less time attending network meetings, while their involvement in special networks for women may lead to ghettofication.

The third main obstacle that hinders women's entrepreneurship is a *lack of confidence*. As a result of lack of condition and credibility, 'women tend to perceive themselves and their business environment in a less favourable light compared to men' (Langowitz and Minniti, 2007, p.356). Women are less likely to become entrepreneurs, tend to see fewer business opportunities and have lower entrepreneurial self-efficacy (Gupta and Turban, 2012), especially in well-developed countries (Shinnar et al., 2012). These three obstacles to women's entrepreneurship serve as a conceptual departure point for our study.

2.4   Entrepreneurship-as-Practice

We adopt an entrepreneurship-as-practice approach (Johannisson, 2011) to circumvent fundamentally gendered discourses of entrepreneurship such as economic action, risk, legitimacy and opportunity recognition (Gherardi, 2015; Marlow 2015). As such, the three obstacles are seen as challenges that can be co-creatively reimagined and co-constructed. Thereby, gendering contexts through an entrepreneurship-as-practice approach is a way to reveal how women create value and meaning inter-subjectively, that is, on their own terms. Such a perspective focuses on practices 'as the objects to be followed', disclosing connections to other activities, products and humans (Nicolini, 2009, p.121). We specifically study the practices that women sustainable entrepreneurs enact as embedded in a Southern European context. Entrepreneurship-as-practice focuses on the relation between actors and the learning processes to which they are exposed (Fletcher and Selden, 2016). The focus on practice no longer considers actors as isolated entities, but rather as 'bundles of practices' (Schatzki, 2005). Entrepreneurship-as-practice helps to move beyond defining *who* the entrepreneur is towards *how* entrepreneurship is *enacted*. The conceptualization of entrepreneurship can thus be seen as a mundane occurrence that invites researchers to study the processes and practices of daily entrepreneurial activity (Steyaert, 2007). This perspective spotlights everyday practices and how actors interpret and reflect on these activities. A practice approach helps to broaden the definition of entrepreneurship beyond sustainable and economic opportunity, to address the unsuccessfulness of most entrepreneurs and to predict situations where entrepreneurship may arise (Jones and Spicer, 2009, p.12). Unravelling the value of apparently marginal practices (Calás et al., 2009) enables us to redefine the outcomes of entrepreneurial action and expand the 'emancipatory potential' (Jennings et al., 2016; Rindova et al., 2009) of entrepreneurship theory and practice.

3.   METHOD

3.1   Data

This research study focused on questions of *how* women entrepreneurs sustain their businesses and themselves within the context of the three obstacles (condition, credibility, confidence) defined in the literature. The sample of entrepreneurs for this study was specifically drawn from countries in

Southern Europe since unemployment – particularly of women – thrives in this region; many people who lose their jobs consider becoming entrepreneurs as their only alternative. According to data from the European Employment Policy Observatory, the European member states with the highest rates of unemployment in 2012 were Spain and Greece (26.6 per cent and 26 per cent respectively[1]). Unemployment rates for women are generally higher: in Spain, 29.2 per cent for men compared to 31.9 per cent for women; in Greece, 21.7 per cent for men compared to 28.9 per cent for women in 2012. The European Commission prioritizes both social and women's entrepreneurship as a way to stimulate the economy and create jobs and sustainable growth. We selected women entrepreneurs who had started sustainable businesses in Greece, Spain and Croatia, as these three countries have the highest unemployment rates in Europe.[2] In collaboration with organizations such as The Impact Hub, we gained access to a network of women entrepreneurs who had started sustainable businesses. Through purposeful sampling (Patton, 2001), we selected entrepreneurs from different stages of the venture life cycle, including early start-ups, established enterprises and failure cases.

We conducted 28 semi-structured interviews with women who were all business founders between 25 and 65 years, with the majority being between 30 and 50 years old (see Table 8.1 for an overview of the 28 interview respondents). They had a variety of backgrounds, ranging from dentists and economists to artists, teachers and engineers. Founding years were between 1990 and 2014. Two women had businesses in the fashion industry, three in construction, three in food and/or body care, four in tourism and two in media industries. We spoke with two women who run businesses in youth work and three in childcare. Four women had started a type of incubator supporting specific groups such as artists or social entrepreneurs. In addition, we interviewed five women in businesses that involved mentoring companies.

The interview guide consisted of ten open-ended questions focusing on the process of becoming an entrepreneur and the everyday practices that entrepreneurs perform in building their ventures. The interview guide, which was developed in English, was translated into Greek, Spanish and Croatian.

The interviews were performed face-to-face, via Skype and over the phone in Spain, Croatia and Greece. The interviews took between 30 minutes and an hour and were audio-recorded and transcribed. In addition, two face-to-face focus groups were held with a total of 16 participants to enable group dynamics to bring out more in-depth information about the practices of women sustainable entrepreneurs (Morgan, 1997). The focus groups lasted up to two hours and were audiotaped, while additional field notes were taken. We acknowledge that as all interviews were done in the original languages, some information might have gotten 'lost in translation'. Upon request, we can

Table 8.1   Interview respondents

Nr.	Location	Name	Age	Background	Enterprise	Founded
1	Croatia	Theresa	38	Business coach	Online magazine about the NGO sector	2012
2	Croatia	Ornela	33	Psychologist	Support for long-term unemployed	2013
3	Croatia	Ana	25	Food technology engineer	Connecting sustainable agriculture with tourism on the Adriatic coast	2013
4	Croatia	Keli	29	Web designer	Developing constructing material out of recycled plastics	2014
5	Croatia	Zelika	32	Designer	Circular bus/tram shelter	2014
6	Croatia	Anka	44	Economist	Life coach	2012
7	Croatia	Valentina	36	Music teacher	Music school for kids	2008
8	Spain	Sandra	41	Artist	Sustainable fashion brand	2005
9	Spain	Catarina	44	Manager	Organic food delivery	2009
10	Spain	Sonia	36	Graphic designer	Incubator for entrepreneurs in the creative industry	2011
11	Spain	Nuria	49	Marketing	Organic soaps and bodycare	1999
12	Spain	Almudena	30	Social worker	Working with vulnerable groups	2013
13	Spain	Laura	25	Model	Sustainable bags	2015
14	Greece	Stella	39	PR	Promotion of free evens in the city of Athens	2013
15	Greece	Myria	29	Controller	Finance education for kids	2012
16	Greece	Pia	37	Manager	Social enterprise hub	1990
17	Greece	Yannia	34	Mechanical engineer	Youth leadership training	2008
18	Greece	Pepy	48	Economist	Barter economy online platform	2006
19	Greece	Dritsa	45	Lawyer	Youth empowerment training	2000
20	Greece	Barbara	65	Tour guide	Pottery workshop	1997
21	Greece	Antonia	49	Architect	Sustainable buildings	2001
22	Greece	Kleopatra	53	Policymaker	Training and mentoring for women in the job market	2003
23	Greece	Susanna	58	Yoga teacher	Supporting the island	2005

Nr.	Location	Name	Age	Background	Enterprise	Founded
24	Greece	Chrystianna	31	Secretary	Refugee children	2011
25	Greece	Lea	43	Dentist	Web mentoring	2009
26	Greece	Yolanda	33	Salesperson	Social enterprise hub	2010
27	Greece	Natalia	42	Chef	Promoting local gastronomy	2006
28	Greece	Lola	28	Artist	Arts hub for young people	2012

provide the original notes and audio recordings to track transparency of our data and approach.

3.2   Analysis

A team of seven researchers was involved in first and second-order coding of the interview transcriptions (Glaser and Strauss, 1967, p.5). The analysis, conducted with the help of NVivo software, took place in three stages: Table 8.2 provides an overview of the three analytical steps taken to analyse the data. First, with the 3Cs as an analytical lens, two or three researchers in each country coded the transcriptions of interviews and focus groups, leading to first-order codes (Gioia et al., 2013). Then the three teams discussed the first-order codes in an international meeting, following the method of participatory group analysis (Flicker and Nixon, 2014). The leading question during the analysis was 'How do women sustainable entrepreneurs sustain their business and themselves?' In a process of constant comparison and deliberation, three second-order themes surfaced: 'community', 'personal balance' and 'developing skills'. In the second stage of the analysis, a team of three researchers compared the three main obstacles for women's entrepreneurship derived from the literature with the themes that emerged. The leading question was: How do women sustainable entrepreneurs tackle the obstacles defined in the literature in relation to community, developing skills and personal balance? Through clustering second-order themes, three practices emerged that women sustainable entrepreneurs enact to create and sustain their enterprises and themselves: reconnecting, resourcing and recharging.

The third stage of the analysis consisted of a comparison between the three practices that were revealed and the dominant entrepreneurship discourse. We looked specifically at how the three practices contributed to an emancipatory understanding of entrepreneurship, thereby reframing the ideal type of *the* entrepreneur. Figure 8.1 shows the data structure, with first-order codes and second-order themes that – linked to the obstacles that were adopted as a conceptual lens – led to delineating the three practices. During data collection and analysis, the research process abided by four criteria for qualitative studies: credibility, transferability, dependability and confirmability (Lincoln and Guba, 1985). First, credibility was enhanced through a triangulation of methods (interviews and focus groups) and of researchers (analysing and interpreting the data in groups). Second, regarding transferability of findings to other settings, describing the context as well as methods of the study in a precise manner 'enables someone interested in making a transfer to reach a conclusion about whether the transfer can be contemplated as a possibility' (Lincoln and Guba, 1985, p.316). Third, this study enhances dependability by providing quotes to support the traceability of arguments (Flick, 2006). Fourth, confirmability refers to the extent to which others can confirm the research results (Lincoln and Guba, 1985). The research protocols, interview transcriptions and audiotapes of focus groups, as well as reflective field notes, can all be provided upon request and give insight into the process of analysing and interpreting the raw data. To safeguard anonymity, respondents are quoted under pseudonyms.

4. RESULTS

The process of analysing the data revealed how gender acts as a mobilizer for creating novel contexts for women sustainable entrepreneurs. We found three core practices that support a reconceptualization of women entrepreneurs as co-creators of their own context rather than being shaped by their context. These practices can be perceived as a way to reframe the three obstacles to women's entrepreneurship that are commonly identified in the literature. It is important to note that all practices are interlinked: the process is iterative and not a closed loop from one to the other; entrepreneurs constantly navigate between them. Finally, as the fundamental question driving this research focused on ways that women entrepreneurs sustained themselves in the process of entrepreneuring, these three core practices are not only ways to sustain their businesses but also, critically, ways of becoming self-sustaining.

4.1   (Re)connecting

The first core practice points to the observation that building a business is primarily a relational activity. As one woman indicated: 'Before anything starts, I need to first connect. It is good to create together' (Anka, Croatia).

The practice of connecting relates both to business and to private life. There is no division between work and life, as clients become friends and husbands become mentors. Therefore, 'community' becomes a generic term for all the connections women social entrepreneurs make. Seven connections are highlighted: with self (i), partner (ii), family (iii), team members (iv), mentors (v), peers (vi) and the wider community (vii).

Table 8.2   Analytical steps

	What	How	Assumptions	Questions asked	Outcome
1st stage of analysis	Identifying 3 core themes key to the entrepreneurial process of women sustainable entrepreneurs	Empirically derived	Women sustainable entrepreneurs prioritize aspects other than 'dominant' ones in the process of entrepreneuring	How do women sustainable entrepreneurs sustain their businesses and themselves?	3 themes that are key to the entrepreneurial process of women sustainable entrepreneurs: Community Personal balance Developing skills
2nd stage of analysis	Linking 3 core themes with 3 obstacles Delineating 3 strategies for sustaining the entrepreneur in sustainable enterprise	Conceptually informed framework development based on 1 and 2a	Women entrepreneurs suffer from a lack of: Credibility Condition Confidence	How do women sustainable entrepreneurs tackle the obstacles defined in the literature in relation to community, developing skills and personal balance?	3 (multiple layered) practices that differ in their application in relation to associated obstacles: Reconnecting (self, partner, family, team, mentors, peers and wider community) Resourcing (people, materials, knowledge and finance) Recharging (space – physical/emotional, time and beauty)
3rd stage of analysis	Comparing the 3 layered practices to the dominant discourse	Conceptually informed and empirically 'tested'	The 3 practices offer an alternative understanding of the dominant entrepreneurship discourse	How do the 3 practices inform the discourse of (sustainable and women) entrepreneurship? How can they contribute to an emancipatory perspective?	A framework that links the 3 practices to reframing the 'ideal type' and an emancipatory perspective of entrepreneuring

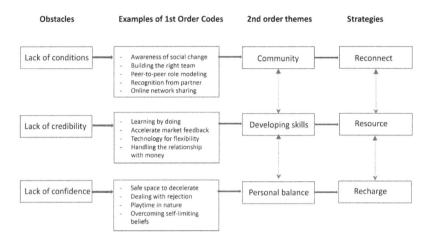

| Obstacles | Examples of 1st Order Codes | 2nd order themes | Strategies |

Figure 8.1   Data structure

First, but often forgotten, is the relationship of women entrepreneurs to themselves: connecting to their values and dreams, knowing their strengths and weaknesses. This is the basis of all connections they make. Second, especially when they have children and when a business is (partially) run from the home, a woman entrepreneur needs time and (physical/emotional) space to dedicate to her business. Entrepreneuring and 'running/having a family' are ongoing activities and time-slots need to be sought not just during 'business and babysitter hours' but also during the evenings, at weekends and in the early morning before kids wake up. Even when (paid) help around the house is available, without trust, recognition and support from a partner, a woman entrepreneur will struggle to survive. The 'space to enterprise' needs to be mainly provided by a spouse, as one entrepreneur mentioned: 'Support from my partner is essential' (Nuria, Spain).

Third, many women operate their business as well as their family in one relational space: a dichotomy between work and family does not exist, as our respondents perceive entrepreneuring as a life project with entrepreneurs embedded in a rhizomatic network of relationships. As one entrepreneur narrated: 'Being a mother and an entrepreneur means always being late for everything. One day my car was full of samples for a new collection and I had to pick up the kids from school. When I arrived, I realized I did not have space in my car for them!' (Laura, Spain).

This often creates a tension, then, as many women perceive a conflict between the roles of entrepreneur and mother: 'Sometimes I think all this running around raising capital to be able to deliver my mission and have social impact is a waste of energy away from my own child' (Chrystianna, Greece).

Fourth, finding people that connect to the cause in the same way the founder does might be unrealistic, but choosing team members wisely is important for the economic success and sustainability of the business. One of the main problems reported by women entrepreneurs is the issue of building the right team: connecting people to your values and message is crucial to a flourishing enterprise. Intuition in attracting the right people needs to be combined with a pragmatic approach, which is not easy. A common mistake is the tendency to choose team members based on a feeling of sharing similar passions, but leaving a blind spot for what skills are missing in the team. 'I thought you just needed a team of enthusiastic people, but now I realize that I needed a team of expert people with complementary expertise' (Barbara, Greece).

Fifth, connections to mentors and experts help entrepreneurs to bounce off ideas, provide for emotional support and to share the passion. As one entrepreneur mentioned: 'I need mentoring, knowledge exchange with a person who has a more technical profile, an expert on the topic' (Željka, Croatia).

Sixth, peers are essential to the well-being of women sustainable entrepreneurs. 'The biggest support that I get is from peers that have the same passion as I do' (Stella, Greece).

Seventh, connections to the wider community of customers, collaborators and competitors (or rather comparables) are essential in resourcing and transforming. In the focus groups, the women social entrepreneurs shared stories of how difficult it is to run a business in a Southern European country. The similarities between Greece and Croatia, and, to a lesser extent, Spain, are that gender stereotypes inhibit women to fully participate in the business community. Bureaucracy and informal 'rules' make it difficult for women entrepreneurs to navigate the landscapes of funding and investments. A greater emphasis on informal relationships and networks – to which women entrepreneurs usually have lesser access – causes business to stagnate. As one entrepreneur expressed: 'Written support is one thing, reality is another' (Theresa, Croatia).

Sustainable entrepreneurship is a novel concept in many Southern European countries and people have difficulty taking it seriously, often thinking it is just another type of social project. The continuous challenge to prove one's worth as a woman makes the sustainable entrepreneurial journey even harder: 'They think women are for work related to the housekeeping [...] when they hear five women created a social enterprise, they ask if we are making sweets' (Pepy, Greece).

Women sustainable entrepreneurs in Greece reported cases of extreme jealousy: women entrepreneurs who were economically successful often experienced aggressive attacks (by both men and women) on their businesses, but also on their private belongings such as houses and cars. Many women sustainable entrepreneurs are willing to support each other and find partners in key male stakeholders while manoeuvring through the stormy waters of running a social business in a country such as Greece, where unsustainability seems to take precedence, as one woman explained: 'We have a long Greek tradition in social cooperatives; our resistance during the Second World War was based on social cooperatives but we then forgot this tradition and that is why our societies lost their strength and stability and sustainability' (Yolanda, Greece).

Their only guide in such an endeavour is a strong connection to their authentic self, which can be used as a compass in dealing with other people. The energy given to and received from the whole network is reported to be crucial to their economic success. A focus on trust, nurturing, an ethic of care and harmony is essential. As one entrepreneur puts it: 'I feel that people in my working environment should trust each other, take care of each other and have harmonious relationships. This is how I want people to view me' (Susanna, Greece).

The social capital nurtured by a strong network of people sharing in each entrepreneur's values, passion and goals appears to be the strongest asset that these women had in seeking to create a context where the obstacles of condition are neutralized.

4.2   Resourcing

The second practice, resourcing, means that entrepreneurs are resourceful in how they develop their businesses, particularly in terms of how they tackle challenges. The study discloses the connective essence of tapping into the entrepreneurs' relationships to derive the resources and skills necessary to build and sustain their businesses. The women sustainable entrepreneurs we interviewed tended to feel inadequate when embarking on new challenges. They often believed they needed to obtain a new degree before they could apply a learnt skill. This lack of confidence can be an immense obstacle in getting a business up and running. We distinguish four types of resources that are crucial for women sustainable entrepreneurs to flourish: (A) people, (B) materials, (C) knowledge and (D) finance.

First, being resourceful in *how* entrepreneurs source (the right) people is a key practice in entrepreneuring. Many of the women with whom we spoke originally were stuck in the idea-and-dream phase of starting their sustainable businesses and were reluctant to go out and talk to potential customers. One entrepreneur mentioned: 'If I could start all over, I would talk with clients first before developing our product' (Natalia, Greece).

What often holds these entrepreneurs back from interacting with potential customers is their fear of negative feedback: they avoid criticism as it directly affects their self-belief. Most women sustainable entrepreneurs build a business around their passions and their personal values. Criticism can be interpreted as a direct attack on who they are, and without proper preparation – and self-confidence – to face such feedback, an entrepreneur's fear of discouragement can prevent efforts to reach out in the first place. Unfortunately, the desire to 'stay in a safe space' is not beneficial and keeps many women in the dream stage. Excessive fear of disappointment can lead to a position of despair, as one woman cried out during a focus group: 'From the phase "No one can steal my idea!" I have moved on to the phase "Please steal my idea to make it a reality!"' (Valentina, Croatia).

The second resource that is highly valued by women entrepreneurs is access to materials. For example, entrepreneurs active in the fashion industry shared that sourcing sustainable textiles is difficult as fabrics can only be purchased in large quantities. In other sectors, such as sustainable building, materials play an equally important role: 'We wanted to revive the construction based on natural materials such as straw and clay' (Antonia, Greece).

The third type of resource commonly mentioned as crucial to sustaining the entrepreneur and her enterprise is knowledge. Women sustainable entrepreneurs often mention a lack of information and expertise: 'We need training in raising our own funding, in achieving commercial goals, in the management of every activity from production to marketing, sales, accounting…' (Yannia, Greece).

Being resourceful in acquiring meant that these entrepreneurs reached out to experts, enrolled at institutions that offer specialized training and sought mentors as ways to 'source' the knowledge women do not (yet) have themselves. Technical knowledge is one of the types of knowledge commonly mentioned by the entrepreneurs: 'We need technical knowledge now as our whole business relies on it and I have no clue about it. Not about the software itself nor about how to work with the people who develop it' (Kelli, Croatia).

The fourth type of resource that women sustainable entrepreneurs mention is money. First, they often underestimate their own worth and charge too little for their contribution to society. One entrepreneur explained: 'I do not really know how to promote/sell myself or charge for my services' (Ornela, Croatia).

In addition, the women sustainable entrepreneurs we interviewed reported a tendency to shy away from financial management as it is 'too boring', and from sales because it is 'too aggressive'. The inclination for 'sales' to take over the entire business leaves women with the feeling that there is no space for what they actually love to do, such as new product creation. The perceived entrance of competitors made many women who were afraid of losing market share driving the focus of their businesses come to focus solely on sales: 'At first, we were the only ones doing this, but now we have many competitors, so we need marketing and sales, sales, sales' (Catarina, Spain).

Building a business driven by strong values is a challenging endeavour that constantly confronts entrepreneurs with choices between financial and social sustainability. Being a woman in the sustainable entrepreneurship sphere can make this task even more difficult, as women most often develop hybrid and non-profit business models while their male colleagues rely on conventional business models. Many women indicated that, ironically, social investors prioritize investments in conventional business models, which disadvantages women focusing on sustainable enterprises (Segran, 2010). These women's capacity to prioritize the social risked the possibility of financial gaps which could ultimately lead to the loss of their businesses. This might be the reason why equal numbers of women and men start social enterprises, but male social enterprises are more likely to survive. 'As we grow, I get scared, I don't want this to become commercial and lose its values [...] You have to remind yourself every day, what is my scope and where do I want to get' (Sonia, Spain).

Motives ascribed to economically successful entrepreneurs, such as a focus on growth and making more money, do not resonate with the view of non-commercial organic growth articulated by these women social entrepreneurs. In addition, women social entrepreneurs do not automatically go after 'large' and 'successful'. Instead, they seem to be driven by the desire for an impact that is tangible to them: 'My most important achievement, to offer the best services to my patients and, at the same time being sustainable, not with the profit margins the public knows of the dentists in Greece' (Lea, Greece); 'We have to stop being afraid to say that non-profit organizations need to raise capital to survive' (Dritsa, Greece).

Believing that operating from the heart will attract sufficient funds is naïve. To avoid the value trap, women social entrepreneurs in this study needed to give priority to hard skills such as financial and business management.

In today's globalized world, almost everything can be learnt through the internet, via online courses, videos, games and many more tools that are often free of charge. A variety of resources can be found on anything from how to write a business plan or get social media to work for you to market research and sales strategies. There are experts who offer webinars on 'healing your relationship with money' and books are appearing on business modelling for the social enterprise sphere. Social media plays a crucial role in obtaining knowledge, but its limits seem to have been reached: 'I feel social media is falling into the mainstream and I want to find new ways of doing things' (Sandra, Spain).

Outside of the online world, women sustainable entrepreneurs seek out training and mentoring (sometimes for free) through local chambers of commerce, NGOs and educational institutions. Participation in the training program on which this study is based was one way for women to take charge of their own resourcefulness. 'I would like to become more confident and to gain necessary knowledge and skills, to be successful in business. I would like to meet other women and develop friendships and business relationships and find out how it works in other countries and what problems they have encountered. I would like to be given the opportunity to learn about myself and the way I can make a difference in my local community' (Almudena, Spain).

The women sustainable entrepreneurs in this study learned how to cross the (internal) bridges that separated them from the information, networks and knowledge they needed to develop their business. Nurturing themselves as the main resource driving their vision and venture was key to their sustainable enterprising and to sustaining themselves in the process.

4.3   Recharging

Women sustainable entrepreneurs are aware that time to 'recharge their batteries' is crucial to their enterprise and should not be pushed to the margins of their lives. Whether through a massage, doing sports, spending moments with their kids or other recreational time, recharging creates balance in their lives. As one entrepreneur clearly expressed: 'My business needs are constantly changing, but my need for personal balance, for inspiration and rest, remains the same' (Pia, Greece).

Recharging includes getting/having the 'space to enterprise' – physically as well as emotionally – as mentioned before with regard to the practice of reconnecting. Recharging also means the process of constantly renewing: giving space and time to feel and deal with the emotions that are inherent to the process of sustainable enterprising. Continuous reflection on activities (through connecting to themselves and others) helps to restore power in taking charge of their business with a clear intention in mind. This is especially valuable in societies that suffer high levels of unemployment. 'Since there are no employers to employ us, we will create an employer' (Kleopatra, Greece).

Economic instability represents a big challenge for the women sustainable entrepreneurs, who are struggling to keep up with constantly altering regulations and timelines. The upside is that anger and frustration can result in enormous energy to create change. It also trains women's resilience in weathering the ebbs and flows of running a business with which they are emotionally engaged. 'The greatest societal impact would be that Greek women would feel again that they have the right to dream about their professional course and go out and do these things and demand them' (Myria, Greece).

In such difficult situations, seeing, stimulating and surrounding themselves with beauty supports women sustainable entrepreneurs in recharging. It can also provide them with the confidence to act without being prohibited by self-limiting beliefs, given that 'it seems to be easier for men to demand things and achieve their goals. For women because of our nature, we analyse everything and when we face a first obstacle we are panicking' (Lola, Greece).

It appears that women are aware that they are evaluated against the ideal image of the entrepreneur as a man. One respondent commented: 'I am young, a woman and blonde – no one will take me seriously' (Ana, Croatia).

For most women their enterprise is a mirror of who they are in the process of becoming themselves, thereby dreaming up new possibilities and drafting novel ideas. Practices of recharging encourage women to see the beauty in themselves and the world around them, which makes them receptive to reconnecting and resourcing, with the sustainable impact of their venture at its heart.

5.   DISCUSSION

This chapter reconceptualizes women entrepreneurs as co-creators of their own context rather than as being shaped by their context. We disclose three practices that women sustainable entrepreneurs in Southern Europe enact to address the obstacles that commonly hinder building and sustaining their enterprises. Their practices of entrepreneuring involve an alternative set of values than those ascribed to 'the ideal typical entrepreneur', namely relationships, the importance of support and balance, compared to autonomy, independence and drive. Our results offer three avenues to consider blended value in a more contextual way. First, 'status' (or condition) needs to be redefined when relationality becomes the core of sustainable enterprising. Second, the crafting of knowledge and co-creation of resources can renegotiate a lack of credibility. Third, we need to account for the 'person' in the blended-value proposition of 'people', 'planet' and 'profit' as an avenue for fostering confidence. Table 8.3 provides an overview of how our findings contribute to reframing the 'ideal' entrepreneur.

Table 8.3   Reframing the 'ideal-type entrepreneur'

Practice	Application	Associated obstacle	Reframing the 'ideal type'	Emancipatory perspective
Reconnecting	When relating to themselves and others	Lack of condition	'Status' redefined – relationality is core characteristic of sustainable enterprising	Feminine values contribute to a contextual approach of entrepreneurship
Re-sourcing	When pursuing knowledge creation	Lack of credibility	Knowledge creation becomes knowledge crafting and co-creation of resources	
Recharging	When striving for personal balance	Lack of confidence	Addition of the fourth 'p' to the triple-P proposition	

5.1   Condition Redefined

A critical perspective on women entrepreneurs addresses the lower-status role of caretaker as a culturally constructed discourse, and probes work–family questions from a different angle. First, our analysis views balancing an entire network of relationships – between family, team and community members; between mentors and peers and spouses – as a valuable high-status skill. Earlier research suggested that a need for security, harmony and peace, as well as a desire to take care of and be cared for, opposes entrepreneurial characteristics such as independence, assertiveness and risk-taking (Ahl, 2006). The gender subtext underlying the ideal typical entrepreneur prohibits understanding how feminine values contribute to sustainable enterprises. We argue that values such as connectedness and embeddedness – considered feminine characteristics – are key to understanding women's sustainable entrepreneurship in Southern Europe.

Second, most research on work–family balance has focused on how family intervenes with entrepreneurial success (Bruni et al., 2005; Hughes et al., 2012). Our analyses found no separation between work and family, but rather a *continuation*. This follows up on studies that have reframed work–family balance as a resource rather than an obstacle to entrepreneuring (Gherardi, 2015; Jennings et al., 2013). Family relationships might nourish entrepreneurs in their endeavours (Eddleston and Powell, 2012, p.435), while entrepreneurial practices could be seen as 'complementary to reproduction and home centrality' (Gherardi, 2015, p.662). Our analyses show how a regional context of high unemployment and cultural challenges adds to the mix of contextual factors crafting the enterprise as a love object amid a life project.

5.2   Credibility as Co-created

Building, and being embedded in, a community enables women entrepreneurs in Spain, Greece and Croatia to be resourceful in crafting the knowledge they need to develop and sustain their businesses. Our results show that the strong connectedness of women sustainable entrepreneurs in Southern Europe has the potential to overcome the perceived lack of credibility that hinders their access to finance, information and networks (Bruni et al., 2005, p.19). Research has shown that 'social factors' and 'social relationships' contribute to the 'information asymmetries and cognitive differences' that influence opportunity identification (Shane, 2012, p.17). Our focus on women sustainable entrepreneurs in a Southern European context discloses positive aspects of the social embeddedness of opportunity identification: the better the quality of a (potential) entrepreneur's relationships, the more likely it is these social relations might spark opportunities. The success of crowdfunding campaigns in this group of entrepreneurs is based on their communities, not their business plans. With regard to access to networks, Facebook, Instagram and other social media are rapidly replacing traditional networks (Kelley et al., 2012), enabling women entrepreneurs in Southern Europe to tap into circles of friends of friends. And finally, knowledge that is not taught via formal education but is co-created (such as intuition, creativity, relationality) might be way more beneficial for women entrepreneurs than what is generally considered to be necessary for sustainability. As such, the crafting of knowledge through social networks becomes more credible and valuable.

5.3   Confidence by Adding the 'P' of Person to the Triple-P Proposition

The focus in sustainable entrepreneurship is commonly on blending people, planet and profit (Zahra and Wright, 2016), thereby focusing on factors *outside of* the entrepreneur (Hoffman, 2016). Our proposal is to bring the *person* – and specifically the practices to sustain the entrepreneur, herself – into the definition. The practices enacted by women sustainable entrepreneurs in Southern Europe are interlinked via 'care of self'. Women sustainable entrepreneurs, in a context of high unemployment and cultural emphasis on traditional femininity, enact practices of reconnecting, resourcing and recharging and consider self-care a necessary condition to prevent burnout, relationship breakdown and/or depression. In particular, they perform the practice of recharging as a prerequisite to be able to (re)connect and be resourceful. When conscious of and connected to their own values, motivations and needs, women entrepreneurs are able to better connect to, and have impact on, their context, but also co-craft their contexts in such a way that these contexts work for them.

First, only by keeping themselves balanced are women entrepreneurs able to care for others – whether it is the community their business serves, their family members or their friends. Caring for themselves leads to confidence that will foster entrepreneurial self-efficacy (Gupta and Turban, 2012), see more opportunities arise and indeed enable the initial steps on the entrepreneurial path. Confidence helps these women entrepreneurs to reach out and ask for support, which is then perceived as a sign of strength rather than weakness. Second, through an inherent feeling of embeddedness (Welter, 2011) and deriving their values from their regional context, women entrepreneurs nurture their environment. Third, a strong sense of self-worth translates to generating the financial means to live the life they want to live. Even though profit might not be their first objective – it is social/environmental impact they are striving for (Hechavarria et al., 2012, p.144) – without it, they themselves and their business will not be sustained. Only when women entrepreneurs first take care of themselves can they take care of the blended-value proposition of people, planet and profit. The 'value of the care of self' contributes to the blended-value proposition, or in other words, the 'person' becomes the fourth P in the triple-P proposition (Zahra and Wright, 2016).

It is crucial to note that in bringing the 'person' back into the equation, we are not aiming to draft a new 'hero entrepreneur' who possesses unique qualities (Williams and Nadin, 2013). A critical, entrepreneurship-as-practice perspective takes entrepreneurial practices as the centre of the analysis – entrepreneurial becoming is a result of those practices, not the other way around (Steyaert, 2007; Steyaert and Katz, 2004). A gendered lens (Calás et al., 2009) supports seeing women sustainable entrepreneurs 'in context' – in the context of their regional and national culture and of 'masculinized normality' (Marlow and McAdam, 2013). By taking a practice perspective, we have aimed to explain how women entrepreneurs develop sustainable businesses in a Southern European context (Croatia, Greece and Spain). The contribution of our study is the reconceptualization of women entrepreneurs as shaping their own contexts instead of being only impacted by those contexts.

5.4   Reframing the 'Ideal' Image of the Entrepreneur

Creating alternatives to a masculine working environment appears to be an important driver for women sustainable entrepreneurs to start out on their own. In this respect, the gender characteristics of their sustainable enterprises, and in particular the main values that guide their processes of becoming an entrepreneur, are relevant. Women sustainable entrepreneurs prioritize feminine values over the masculine values typically attributed to entrepreneurship, thereby bringing 'the silent, feminine personal end of the entrepreneurial process' (Bird and Brush, 2002, p.57) under closer scrutiny. In line with earlier work (Gherardi, 2015, p.663), 'the exploitation of economic opportunities' – an expression often used to conceptualize sustainable entrepreneurship (see for example Dean and McMullen, 2007; Patzelt and Shepherd, 2011, p.632) – was less present in the narratives our entrepreneurs provided. We found that women sustainable entrepreneurs in Southern Europe narrated values such as aiming for a personal balance; connecting with their customers, colleagues and families; using resources to build bridges; and reflecting in order to adapt to new circumstances. These values may be classified as feminine (Ahl, 2006), but they are not passive: women sustainable entrepreneurs are actively looking for connections, taking charge of their situations and seeking to combine their own needs with those of others. In that respect we conceptualize women sustainable entrepreneurs as co-creators of context. The practices of recharging, resourcing and reconnecting provide an alternative conceptualization of entrepreneurship to the hegemonic, masculine ideal.

5.5   Practical Implications

Through adopting a critical, entrepreneurship-as-practice approach, this study offers insights into key practices women sustainable entrepreneurs in Southern Europe enact to sustain their business and themselves. Implications for practice are three-fold. First, the skill of reflecting on one's own sustainability ('care of self') should be included in entrepreneurship training and education. Their desire to make the world a better place can turn against entrepreneurs when they fail to take care of themselves in the process. Especially in high unemployment contexts such as Southern Europe, the focus might be on financial survival of the business, but we have seen that a business cannot survive financially when the entrepreneur does not honour her own needs. Second, considering family a resource for entrepreneurial activities should challenge policy makers to co-create childcare and other social care services, making them more adaptable to entrepreneurs' needs and aspirations (Ahl and Nelson, 2015). Third, our results inform the emancipatory potential of small and medium-sized entrepreneurship (Jennings et al., 2016; Rindova 2009) in building thriving societies.

6.   CONCLUSION

Starting from a critical entrepreneurship perspective, and using a qualitative inductive analysis, our conceptualization of women sustainable entrepreneurs as co-creators of context challenges dichotomist understandings of entrepreneurship (Marlow, 2015) and considers entrepreneurship as a departure point to focus on the influence of a 'gendered' context that is positive, creative, beautiful and reflexive. Moreover, we suggest that this approach is an affirmative perspective on entrepreneurship (Weiskopf and Steyaert, 2009, p.200) that moves beyond the dichotomy between masculine and feminine values of entrepreneurship and between economic and sustainability motives (Poldner et al., 2015). Such a 'beyond' critical perspective views the entrepreneur as a catalyst who brings together (bridges) human and non-human actants such as people, networks, artifacts, spaces, money, ideas, resources and nature. An affirmative perspective 'favours an inventiveness that increases the possibilities of life that are not yet known' (Weiskopf and Steyaert, 2009, p.200). Creativity, curiosity and imagination are key components of such a view of entrepreneurship (Gartner, 2011; Steyaert et al., 2011). An affirmative perspective on the study of organizations can draw our attention to forms of knowledge creation that are tacit and sensorial, rather than *a posteriori* constructed (Strati, 2000, p.13). An affirmative perspective focuses on the aesthetics of women social enterprise that can be played out in a *becoming*: a becoming of 'who you are' and 'how you evolve' as an individual, a woman, and an entrepreneur. While conscious of the femalization of business culture as a trap that prescribes a normative model of doing business for women (Bruni et al., 2005, p.26), an affirmative perspective can invite not only women social entrepreneurs, but all who desire to create change, to feel free to experiment with different styles of leadership, different business models and different ways of becoming themselves every day.

Entrepreneurial practices of reconnecting, resourcing and recharging broaden the conceptualization of women entrepreneurs as creating a 'gendered' context that, in the examples of women founders of sustainable ventures in Southern Europe, offer some insights into the emancipatory potential of these entrepreneurial practices. And, finally, the nature of blended value (the 3Ps) in sustainable entrepreneurship requires recognition of the need to sustain the person (adding a fourth 'P') in sustainable enterprises. As such, women founders in sustainable enterprises can be sustained through family and community life as they also seek to sustain work, family and community through their entrepreneurial becoming.

NOTES

1.   http://ec.europa.eu/enlargement/pdf/key_documents/2012/package/hr _analytical_2012_en.pdf
2.   http://ec.europa.eu/eurostat/documents/2995521/6862104/3-03062015-BP-EN .pdf/efc97561-fad1-4e10-b6c1-e1c80e2bb582

REFERENCES

Ahl, H. (2002), 'The making of the female entrepreneur: A discourse analysis of research texts on women's entrepreneurship.' Doctoral dissertation. Jönköping International Business School.

Ahl, H. (2006), 'Why research on women entrepreneurs needs new directions', *Entrepreneurship Theory and Practice*, 30 (5), 595–621.

Ahl, H. and T. Nelson (2015), 'How policy positions women entrepreneurs: A comparative analysis of state discourse in Sweden and the United States', *Journal of Business Venturing*, 30 (2), 273–91.

Aidis, R., Welter, F., Smallbone, D. and N. Isakova (2007), 'Female entrepreneurship in transition economies: The case of Lithuania and Ukraine', *Feminist Economics*, 13 (2), 157–83.

Bacq, S. and F. Janssen (2011), 'The multiple faces of social entrepreneurship: A review of definitional issues based on geographical and thematic criteria', *Entrepreneurship and Regional Development*, 23 (5–6), 373–403.

Bird, B. and C. Brush (2002), 'A gendered perspective on organizational creation', *Entrepreneurship Theory and Practice*, 26 (3), 41–65.

Blackburn, R., Hytti, U. and F. Welter (eds) (2015), *Context, process and gender in entrepreneurship: Frontiers in European entrepreneurship research*, Cheltenham, UK: Edward Elgar Publishing.

Bruni, A., Gherardi, G. and B. Poggio (eds) (2005), *Gender and entrepreneurship: An ethnographic approach*, London: Routledge.

Calás, M., Smircich, L., and K. Bourne (2009), 'Extending the boundaries: Reframing "Entrepreneurship as social change" through feminist perspectives', *Academy of Management Review*, 34 (3), 552–69.

Cassar, G. (2007), 'Money, money, money? A longitudinal investigation of entrepreneur career reasons, growth preferences and achieved growth', *Entrepreneurship and Regional Development*, 19 (1), 89–107.

Coleman, S. and A. Robb (2012), *A rising tide: Financing strategies for women-owned firms*, Stanford University Press.

Datta, P. and R. Gailey (2012), 'Empowering women through social entrepreneurship: Case of a women's cooperative in India', *Entrepreneurship Theory and Practice*, 36, 569–87.

De Bruin, A., Brush, C. and F. Welter (2006), 'Introduction to the special issue: Towards building cumulative knowledge on women's entrepreneurship', *Entrepreneurship Theory and Practice*, 30, 585–93.

Dean, T. and J. McMullen (2007), 'Toward a theory of sustainable entrepreneurship: Reducing environmental degradation through entrepreneurial action', *Journal of Business Venturing*, 22, 50–76.

DeTienne, D. and G. Chandler (2007), 'The role of gender in opportunity identification', *Entrepreneurship Theory and Practice*, 31 (3), 365–86.

Eddleston, K. and G. Powell (2012), 'Nurturing entrepreneurs' work–family perspective', *Entrepreneurship Theory and Practice*, 36 (3), 513–41.

Essers, C. and Y. Benschop (2009), 'Muslim businesswomen doing boundary work: The negotiation of Islam, gender and ethnicity within entrepreneurial contexts', *Human Relations*, 62 (3), 403–23.

Fletcher, D. and P. Selden (2016), 'A relational conceptualization of context and the real-time emergence of entrepreneurship processes', in F. Welter and W. Gartner (eds), *A research agenda for entrepreneurship and context*, Cheltenham, UK: Edward Elgar Publishing, pp. 79–92.

Flick, U. (2006), *An introduction to qualitative research*, London: Sage.

Flicker, S. and S. Nixon (2014), 'The DEPICT model for participatory qualitative health promotion research analysis piloted in Canada, Zambia and South Africa', *Health Promotion International*, accessed at: http://heapro.oxfordjournals.org/content/early/2014/01/12/heapro.dat093.full.

Gartner, W. (1993), 'Words lead to deeds: Towards an organization emergence vocabulary', *Journal of Business Venturing*, 8 (3), 231–40.

Gartner, W.B. (2011), 'When words fail: An entrepreneurship glossolalia', *Entrepreneurship and Regional Development*, 23 (1–2), 9–21.

Gherardi, S. and M. Perrotta (2013), 'Doing by inventing the way of doing: Formativeness as the linkage of meaning and matter', in P.R. Carlile, D. Nicolini and A. Langley (eds), *How matter matters: Objects, artifacts, and materiality in organization studies*, Oxford University Press, 227–59.

Gherardi, S. (2015), 'Authoring the female entrepreneur while talking the discourse of work–family life balance', *International Small Business Journal: Researching Entrepreneurship*, 33 (6), 649–66.

Gioia, D.A., Corley, K.G. and A.L. Hamilton (2013), 'Seeking qualitative rigor in inductive research: Notes on the Gioia methodology', *Organizational Research Methods*, 16 (1), 15–31.

Glaser, B. and A. Strauss (ed.) (1967), *The discovery of grounded theory: Strategies for qualitative research*, Chicago, IL: Aldine.

Goodman, N. (ed.) (1978), *Ways of Worldmaking*, Indianapolis, IN: Hackett Publishing.

Goss, D., Jones, R., Betta, M. and J. Latham, (2011), 'Power as practice': A micro-sociological analysis of the dynamics of emancipatory entrepreneurship', *Organization Studies*, 32, 211–29.

Gupta, V. and D. Turban (2012), 'Evaluation of new business ideas: Do gender stereotypes play a role?', Journal of Managerial Issues, 24, 140.

Hechavarria, D., Ingram, A., Justo, R. and S. Terjesen (2012), 'Are women more likely to pursue social and environmental entrepreneurship?' in K. Hughes and J. Jennings (eds), *Global women's entrepreneurship research: Diverse settings, questions and approaches*, Cheltenham, UK: Edward Elgar Publishing, 135–51.

Herman, D. (2009), 'Narrative ways of worldmaking', in S. Heinen and R. Sommer (eds), *Narratology in the age of cross-disciplinary narrative research*, Berlin: Walter de Gruyter, 71–87.

Hockerts, K. and R. Wüstenhagen (2010), 'Greening Goliaths versus emerging Davids—Theorizing about the role of incumbents and new entrants in sustain- able entrepreneurship', *Journal of Business Venturing*, 25, 481–92.

Hoffman, A. (ed.) (2016) *Finding purpose: Environmental stewardship as a personal calling*, Sheffield: Greenleaf Publishing.

Hughes, K. and P. Jennings (2010), The work–family interface strategies of male and female entrepreneurs: Are there any differences?', in C. Brush and A. de Bruin (eds) *Women entrepreneurs and the global environment for growth: A research perspective,* Cheltenham, UK: Edward Elgar Publishing, pp. 163–86.

Hughes, K., Jennings, J., Brush, C., Carter, S. and F. Welter (2012), 'Extending women's entrepreneurship research in new directions', *Entrepreneurship Theory and Practice*, 36 (2), 1–14.

James, A. (2012), 'Conceptualizing "woman" as an entrepreneurial advantage: A reflexive approach', in K. Hughes and J. Jennings (eds), *Global women's entrepreneurship research: Diverse settings, questions and approaches*, Cheltenham, UK: Edward Elgar Publishing, pp. 226–41.

Jennings, J. and C. Brush (2013), Research on women entrepreneurs: Challenges to (and from) the broader entrepreneurship literature? *Academy of Management Annals*, 7 (1), 663–715.

Jennings, J., Jennings, P. and M. Sharifian (2016), 'Living the dream? Assessing the "entrepreneurship as emancipation" perspective in a developed region', *Entrepreneurship Theory and Practice*, 40 (1), 81–110.

Johannisson, B. (2011), 'Towards a practice theory of entrepreneuring', *Small Business Economics*, 36, 135–50.

Jones, C. and A. Spicer (eds) (2009), *Unmasking the entrepreneur*, Cheltenham, UK: Edward Elgar Publishing.

Kelley, D., Brush, C., Greene, P. and Y. Litovsky (2012), *The Global Entrepreneurship Monitor: 2012 Women's Report*, Wellesley, MA: Babson College and GERA.

Langowitz, N. and M. Minniti (2007), 'The entrepreneurial propensity of women', *Entrepreneurship Theory and Practice*, 31 (3), 341–64.

Lincoln, Y. and E. Guba (eds) (1985), *Naturalistic inquiry*, London: Sage.

Manolova, T.S., Brush, C.G., Edelman, L.F. and K.G. Shaver (2012), 'One size does not fit all: Entrepreneurial expectancies and growth intentions of US women and men nascent entrepreneurs', *Entrepreneurship & Regional Development*, 24 (1–2), 7–27.

Marlow, S. (2015), 'Women, gender and entrepreneurship: Why can't a woman be more like a man?' in R. Blackburn, U. Hytti and F. Welter (eds), *Context, process, and gender in entrepreneurship: Frontiers in European entrepreneurship research*, Cheltenham, UK: Edward Elgar Publishing.

Marlow, S. and J. Swail (2014), 'Gender, risk and finance: Why can't a woman be more like a man?' *Entrepreneurship and Regional Development*, 26 (1–2), 80–96.

Marlow, S. and M. McAdam (2013), 'Gender and entrepreneurship: Advancing debate and challenging myths; exploring the mystery of the under-performing female entrepreneur', *International Journal of Entrepreneurial Behaviour and Research*, 19 (1), 114–24.

Marlow, S. and D. Patton (2005), 'All credit to men? Entrepreneurship, finance, and gender', *Entrepreneurship Theory and Practice*, 29 (6), 717–35.

Morgan, D.L. (ed.) (1997), *Focus groups as qualitative research*, London: Sage.

Nicholls, A. (2006), *Social entrepreneurship: New models of sustainable social change*, Oxford: Oxford University Press.

Nicholls, A. and R. Young (2008), Preface to the paperback edition. In A. Nicholls (ed.), *Social entrepreneurship: New models of sustainable social change*, Oxford: Oxford University Press, vii–xxiii.

Nicolini, D. (2009), 'Zooming in and zooming out: A package of method and theory to study work practices', in S. Ybema, D. Yanow, H. Wels and F.H. Kamsteeg (eds), *Organizational ethnography: Studying the complexities of everyday life*, London: Sage, 120–38.

Pacheco, D., Dean, T. and D. Payne (2010), 'Escaping the green prison: Entrepreneurship and the creation of opportunities for sustainable development', *Journal of Business Venturing*, 25, 464–80.

Patton, M. (ed.) (2001), *Qualitative research and evaluation methods*, Thousand Oaks, CA: Sage Publications.

Patzelt, H. and D. Shepherd (2011), 'Recognizing opportunities for sustainable development', *Entrepreneurship Theory and Practice*, 35, 631–52.

Poldner, K., Branzei, O. and C. Steyaert (2011), 'Shecopreneuring: Stitching global eco-systems in the ethical fashion industry', in A. Marcus, P. Shrivastava, S. Sharma and S. Pogutz (eds), *Cross-sector leadership for the green economy: Integrating research and practice on sustainable enterprise*, New York: Palgrave Macmillan, 157–73.

Poldner, K., Shrivastava, P. and O. Branzei (2015), 'Embodied multi-discursivity: An aesthetic process approach to sustainable entrepreneurship', *Business & Society*, 56 (2), 214–52.

Rindova, V., Barry, D. and D. Ketchen (2009), 'Entrepreneuring as emancipation', *Academy of Management Review*, 34 (3), 477–91.

Saparito, P., Elam, A. and C. Brush (2013), 'Bank–firm relationships: Do perceptions vary by gender?' *Entrepreneurship Theory and Practice*, 37 (4), 837–58.

Sarasvathy, S.D. (ed.) (2009), *Effectuation: Elements of entrepreneurial expertise*, Cheltenham, UK: Edward Elgar Publishing.

Schatzki, T. (2005), 'The sites of organizations', *Organization Studies*, 26 (3), 465–84.

Segran, G. (2010), 'Women social entrepreneurs driven by impact rather than scale.' Accessed at: www.knowledge.insead.edu/leadership-management/women-in-business/women-social-entrepreneurs-driven-by-impact-rather-than-scal-717.

Shane, S. (2012), 'Reflections on the 2010 *AMR* decade award: Delivering on the promise of entrepreneurship as a field of research', *Academy of Management Review*, 37 (1), 10–20.

Shinnar, R., Giacomin, O. and F. Janssen (2012), 'Entrepreneurial perceptions and intentions: The role of gender and culture', *Entrepreneurship Theory and Practice*, 36 (3), 465–93.

Steyaert, C. (2007), '"Entrepreneuring" as a conceptual attractor? A review of process theories in 20 years of entrepreneurship studies', *Entrepreneurship and Regional Development*, 19 (6), 453–77.

Steyaert, C. and D. Hjorth (eds) (2003), *New movements in entrepreneurship*, Cheltenham, UK: Edward Elgar Publishing.

Steyaert, C. and J. Katz (2003), 'Reclaiming the space of entrepreneurship in society: Geographical, discursive and social dimensions', *Entrepreneurship and Regional Development*, 16, 179–96.

Steyaert, C. and J. Katz (2004), 'Reclaiming the space of entrepreneurship in society: Geographical, discursive and social dimensions', *Entrepreneurship & Regional Development*, 16 (3), 179–96.

Steyaert, C., Hjorth, D. and W.B. Gartner (2011), 'Six memos for a curious and imaginative future scholarship in entrepreneurship studies', *Entrepreneurship and Regional Development*, 23 (1–2), 1–7.

Strati, A. (2000), 'The aesthetic approach in organization studies', in S. Linstead and H. Höpfl (eds), *The aesthetics of organization*, London: Sage, 13–34.

Tedmanson, D., Essers, C., Verduyn, K. and W. Gartner (2012), 'Critical entrepreneurship studies', *Organization*, 19, 531–41.

Welter, F. (2011), 'Contextualizing entrepreneurship—conceptual challenges and ways forward', *Entrepreneurship Theory and Practice*, 35 (1), 165–84.

Weiskopf, R. and C. Steyaert (2009), 'Metamorphoses in entrepreneurship studies: Towards an affirmative politics of entrepreneuring', in D. Hjorth and C. Steyaer (eds), *The politics and aesthetics of entrepreneurship*, Cheltenham, UK: Edward Elgar Publishing, 183–201.

Williams, C. and S. Nadin (2013), 'Beyond the entrepreneur as a heroic figurehead of capitalism: Re-representing the lived practices of entrepreneurs', *Entrepreneurship and Regional Development*, 25 (7–8), 552–68.

Wu, Z. and J.H. Chua (2012), 'Second-order gender effects: The case of US small business borrowing cost', *Entrepreneurship Theory and Practice*, 36 (3), 443–63.

Yousafzai, S.Y., Saeed, S. and M. Muffatto (2015), 'Institutional theory and contextual embeddedness of women's entrepreneurial leadership: Evidence from 92 countries', *Journal of Small Business Management*, 53 (3), 587–604.

Zahra, S. and M. Wright (2016), 'Understanding the social role of entrepreneurship', *Journal of Management Studies*, 53 (4), 610–29.

9. Reconsidering the practices of home-based entrepreneurs: how mum and dad entrepreneurs manage work time

Stacy Brecht and Séverine Le Loarne – Lemaire

1. INTRODUCTION

This chapter examines how home-based women entrepreneurs balance time in relation to advancing business goals and completing other responsibilities throughout the day. Our research also investigates the differences in how mum and dad entrepreneurs who work from home organize and structure their daily routines, and the correlation between different styles of time management, gender, and the growth of businesses.

There is limited research regarding home-based businesses in the field of entrepreneurship (Anwar & Daniel, 2016). Home-based businesses can be "defined as any business entity engaged in selling products or services into the market operated by a self-employed person, with or without employees, that uses residential property as a base from which the operation is run. This includes two main types of businesses: those where the work (production or service) occurs in the home, and those where the work occurs away from the home with the home serving as the administrative base" (Mason et al., 2011, p.629).

Research shows that women entrepreneurs are more likely than male entrepreneurs to have home-based businesses (Fraser, 2005; Harding, 2006) and to hold relatively low market shares, profits and sales (Carter & Marlow, 2006). However, studies also show that women often create their own companies in order to experience fewer professional limitations, to gain freedom and independence, and to attain a better work–life balance (Brush, 1992; Buttner, 1993; Jennings & McDougald, 2007). Starting a business has been suggested to help women achieve more flexibility when caring for family and earning an income

(Ahl & Marlow, 2021) because the business can be home-based, and work can be adjusted to accommodate household responsibilities (Richomme-Huet & Vial, 2014). However, research challenges this suggestion, as flexibility can have drawbacks (Jayawarna et al., 2019). The demands of operating a profitable venture that replaces previous wage earnings can limit the perceived flexibility regarding how and when business is conducted (Dy et al., 2017), as trying to simultaneously operate a business and fulfill household commitments can cause time-management conflicts. Instead of entrepreneurship accommodating household obligations, it may hinder flexibility (Jayawarna et al., 2019; Werbel & Danes, 2010). Additionally, research highlights that home-based women entrepreneurs can feel like they are "a stay-at-home mom [rather] than an entrepreneur" due to expectations of domestic work being completed in addition to entrepreneurial responsibilities (Nikina et al., 2015). Conversely, Jayawarna et al. (2020) highlight: "For men however, a structural division of labour whereby a female partner undertakes caring labour frees him to prioritise his venture; as such, there is less competition for his time and effort." Yang and Triana (2019) refer to this implicit gendered division of labor in entrepreneurship as the "liability of womanness" (p.24).

There is limited research that explores why women create small business ventures from home; however, there is a common assumption that women work from home for the purpose of motherhood. Also, as noted by Ahl and Marlow (2021), "The assumption that work and family are separate spheres and that women prioritize family reflects the postfeminist sensibility that a retreat to the home is a matter of choice." Thus, the literature regarding women entrepreneurs and work–life balance seems somewhat dialogic: Either you primarily work on developing your business or you spend most of your time caring for family. This is somewhat restrictive. Therefore, there is a need to explore the practices of entrepreneurs in the context of gender as well as to investigate what entrepreneurs do while entrepreneuring from home. Little research has been conducted on the real practices of entrepreneurship (Gherardi, 2015) and how these women manage their time working from home, how they manage their venture and their private life, and how they negotiate time and tasks with their spouse (Nikina et al., 2012). There is a call to study the diverse field of entrepreneurship through an entrepreneurship as practice lens, as "the practice tradition provides a unit of empirical analysis that has thus far been overlooked or marginalized" (Gartner, 2016, p.250). Instead of basing our research question on entrepreneurial phenomena at the individual or organizational level, as scholars often do (Thompson et al., 2020), we based our study on the entrepreneurial practices of home-based entrepreneurs.

As highlighted by Welter et al. (2018), examining entrepreneurship through a contextual lens composed of multiple variables is paramount in establishing richer research findings about the diverse field of entrepreneurship.

Additionally, McAdam and Cunningham (2021) emphasized the need to incorporate context into more gender and entrepreneurship research to progress theory and greater understanding of the field. Furthermore, research emphasizes that the various contexts that affect the study of entrepreneurship are often linked and not independent from one another (Griffin, 2007). Therefore, in this chapter we investigate the contexts of gender, work–life balance, and time management of home-based women entrepreneurs and analyze how these contexts intertwine and, ultimately, affect the practice of entrepreneurship.

To do so, we ground our analysis on four cases of home-based entrepreneurs from Los Angeles (California, USA): two women and two men home-based entrepreneurs in the Los Angeles, California, area who are all married and have toddler-aged children. A careful analysis of their respective timetables and calendars combined with in-depth interviews allows us to reveal the different practices of working from home and what work–life balance really means, across gender, when it is time to work from home. In particular, we show that women and men still have gendered roles, even at home.

The chapter is structured as follows. A literature review on gender stereotypes and role sharing in society combined with the state of the art on gendered work–life balance provides the theoretical insight we use for the analysis. The research design is then introduced, following which our key findings are summarized. Finally, we discuss our results and conclude.

2.   LITERATURE REVIEW

2.1   Gender Stereotypes in Women Entrepreneurship Literature

Women entrepreneurs have some attributes in common, such as operating part-time, home-based businesses, having limited funds and networks, and generating minimal profits (Carter & Marlow, 2006; Fraser, 2005; Harding, 2006). Unfortunately, these combined descriptions contribute to a negative perception of female entrepreneurs, especially in profit-driven economies, and therefore communicate that women-owned businesses lack credibility and underperform (Ahl, 2006).

Research also notes that many home-based businesses are viewed as hobby-businesses rather than a significant source of income (Mason et al., 2011). However, even though home-based businesses are often not perceived to be as credible and as financially successful as traditional, office-based businesses, they contribute substantially to several areas of the economy, representing 50–60 percent of all businesses in the United States, the United Kingdom and Australia (BIS, 2012; Mason et al., 2011). Additionally, not only do these businesses often represent more than half of ventures in these countries, but studies illustrate that home-based businesses in the United Kingdom employ 1 in 6 people and provide £300 billion to the country's economy (Enterprise Nation, 2014). We analyze in greater detail these misperceptions tied to home-based businesses in relation to gender, work–life balance, time management, and financial success.

Women's businesses contribute significantly to economies all over the world. Recently, the Global Entrepreneurship Monitor shared that there are more than 270 million businesses owned by women, and they are represented in 74 economies (Kelly et al., 2017). Regardless of the significant representation of women entrepreneurs and their economic contributions on a global level, negative perceptions of women entrepreneurs not measuring up to male entrepreneurs in terms of revenue, growth of employees, and profit still persist (Alsos et al., 2006; Fairlie & Robb, 2009; Orser et al., 2006).

Gupta et al. (2019) found that implicit gender biases exist when referring to entrepreneurial descriptions such as being highly profitable and owning a social enterprise versus a commercial business. They noted that large-scale commercial businesses were more significantly linked to characteristics typically classified as masculine. Furthermore, Hechavarria et al. (2019, p.12) highlighted that the "perceptions of the ideal entrepreneur, or entrepreneurial team, are influenced by covert sexist attitudes."

Additionally, Bruni et al. (2004) found that male entrepreneurs' private lives are not focused on in the business sphere and are kept separate from "the public arena" to showcase that personal obligations do not conflict with entrepreneurship. However, women's private lives are implicitly intersected with entrepreneurship in terms of family relations and commitments. Moreover, these authors shared, "the implicit sub-text at work in this representation states that family duties take priority in women's lives, and therefore, that women are not trustworthy entrepreneurs" (p.262). We explore how women's entrepreneurship is put into practice with regard to work–family balance and examine if time management in the work and family interface affects the development of businesses, or if perhaps women can indeed "do it all" and successfully manage work and family without sacrificing professional accomplishments.

2.2   Work–Life Balance and Time Management in Practice for Mum and Dad Entrepreneurs

Work–life balance, as described by Clark (2000), is "satisfaction and good functioning at work and at home, with a minimum of role conflict" (p.751). Powell et al. (2019) emphasize that prior research has concentrated more on the balance of work and family responsibilities rather than focusing on the balance of "work–life" or "work–nonwork." However, Greenhaus and Powell (2017) found that initiatives put in place to help organizations provide a balance between work and family also complement the balance of work and other life commitments. In this chapter we examine the balance of work and family and analyze schedules holistically from a work–life perspective consisting of a myriad of life roles entrepreneurs have in addition to their work—"(e.g., nuclear and extended family, friendships, community, leisure, and self-development" (Powell et al., 2019, p.9)—to get a more comprehensive view of their daily obligations.

Although Mattis (2004) notes that greater flexibility and ability to tend to family responsibilities are important reasons why women start their own ventures, there is little research that examines the expectations of women business owners in terms of attaining a greater work–family balance and, furthermore, investigates outcomes (Carter & Shaw, 2006; Dex & Scheible, 2001; Lewis, 2006; Rouse & Kitching, 2006; Williams, 2004). Palumbo et al. (2020) found that "[w]orking from home was found to jeopardize the individual work–life balance. It was positively and significantly associated with work-to-life and life-to-work conflicts" (p.7). Parasuraman and Simmers (2001) highlight that even though female entrepreneurs may experience more independence and flexibility than would be the case if employed by someone else, there is often more conflict between balancing work and family obligations. Additionally, McGowan et al. (2012) found that "for many women, the enjoyment experienced from running their own venture resulting from increased freedom and flexibility was tempered by discontent, in terms of the time commitment, constant work demands and need to balance the interests of children and other dependants with demands of the business" (p.14). Desrochers and Sargent (2004) note that work and family roles and obligations are not mutually exclusive, but they can coincide and result in conflict. However, Shelton (2006) illustrated that implementing "work–family management" strategies such as role-sharing can help mitigate some of these challenges and contribute to greater venture performance and enhance well-being.

When studying the 1998 General Social Surveys in Canada, it was found that mothers were more dissatisfied with their work–life balance than fathers were (Zuzanek, 2000). Additionally, throughout the past 20 years, an increased amount of pressure has been placed on women to measure up to what constitutes as a "good" mother, with women feeling like more attention should be given to caring for children and their activities. This cultural shift to "intensive parenting" (Hays, 1996) "has no doubt contributed to increased feelings of time pressure and time stress among employed mothers" (Hilbrecht et al., 2008).

Arendell (2001) described this change in cultural ideology as requiring mothers to plan, coordinate, manage, and oversee children's activities to provide a more purposeful childhood, thereby increasing mothers' responsibilities. When studying dual-earner couples, she reported that husbands and wives alike supported this parenting movement toward providing children with greater structure, but wives were expected to execute the processes, thus leaving wives with less time to satisfy their own "needs, identities, activities" (2001, p.187).

Furthermore, as studied by McGowan et al. (2012), technology enables "individuals to be always 'at work'" and illustrates how the family and entrepreneurial contexts can easily overlap (p.6). When studying home-based entrepreneurs and work–life balance, Gheradi (2015) found that there was "duality of the meaning of being there" and "the separation between home and work was rather blurred" (p.660). Even though home-based entrepreneurs are physically located in the home, digital technology enables workers to always be "tethered to work," making it challenging to separate the home and work spheres (Ferguson et al., 2016: Gadeyne et al., 2018; Lanaj et al., 2014; Perlow, 2012).

McGowan et al. (2012) found that time management was essential for women entrepreneurs as they juggled several roles in addition to owning and operating a business, such as mother, wife, and caretaker. Notably, this research indicated that "the reality about achieving greater 'flexibility' in the use of time often proved illusory" (p.16). However, Hilbrecht et al. (2008) proposed that men and women may differ in how they define flexibility. The concept of time being differentiated between "masculine" and "feminine" illustrates this idea, as masculine time is associated with linear, monochronic, or industrial time management styles and feminine time reflects cyclical, poly-chronic, or domestic time management approaches (Daly, 1996; Davies, 1990; Sullivan & Lewis, 2001).

Men are also becoming more attracted to establishing a work–life balance and dismissing the conventional masculine role of being mainly work-focused (Ernst & Young, 2015; Galinsky et al., 2011). Thus, how gender roles are actually applied at work and home is becoming more blurred (Greenhaus & Powell, 2017; Powell, 2019). Our study examines how entrepreneurs apply these gender roles from a practice perspective and investigates the similarities and differences as well as evaluates if these conventional gender roles are advancing to become more gender-neutral.

3.   METHODOLOGY

A significant body of literature on women entrepreneurs utilizes an objectivist approach and thus communicates that there are clear distinctions between male and female entrepreneurs, which could be untrue (Hughes et al., 2012). Males and females are often placed in distinctive categories in terms of social behav-ior and cognition, which reinforces the assumption that all men and all women respectively behave in the same ways. Therefore, our methodology investi-gated gender in association with how work is accomplished by using a practice perspective that "forefronts neither positivist nor interpretivist views on knowledge, broadly speaking, but a relational one." We applied a "relational–materialist epistemology [that] views knowledge not as an inert 'entity' or 'resource' nor as individual subjective experience, but articulated in the flow of nexuses of practices" (Thompson et al., 2021, p.1967). Thus, to study how home-based women entrepreneurs with children manage time, we analyzed their scheduled working practices such as business meetings, business development, and administrative work logged in their electronic calendars.

As mentioned earlier, studies show that women entrepreneurs are more likely than their male counterparts to have home-based businesses (Fraser, 2005; Harding, 2006) and generate low market shares, profits, and sales (Carter & Marlow, 2006), but research also highlights that women start their own businesses to experience fewer professional limitations, to gain freedom and independence, and to attain a better work–life balance (Brush, 1992; Buttner, 1993; Jennings & McDougald, 2007). However, studies indicate that home-based women entrepreneurs can feel like they are "a stay-at-home mom [rather] than an entrepreneur" due to domestic responsibilities (Nikina et al., 2015, p.48). Therefore, we explored work–life balance, time management, and gender of home-based entrepreneurs with children to gain more knowledge and insight into the realities of the working practices of home-based women entrepreneurs and to examine how to help provide support for their business pursuits and create more jobs in the process.

3.1   Data Selection

We investigated four case studies through an entrepreneurship-as-practice lens. The case studies consisted of two women and two men home-based entrepreneurs in the Los Angeles, California, area, all of whom are married and have toddler-aged children. The data sample came from business and parental interest groups, and participants were selected based on the criteria of having children of toddler age, being married, and running a home-based business in the Los Angeles area so we could analyze the schedules of comparable cases.

Case #1 examines a woman entrepreneur with a toddler who runs a life coach business from home in the Los Angeles area, and Case #2 and Case #3 highlight a husband-and-wife entrepreneurial team who own a home-based electrical company in the Los Angeles area and have a one-year-old child. Case #4 investigates the schedule of a home-based male entrepreneur in Los Angeles with young children who runs a technology business from home.

In addition to home-based entrepreneurship as a whole being understudied, three out of the four cases we selected represent underexamined facets of "everyday entrepreneurship" conducted by the majority of business owners in the world outside the popular but rare Silicon Valley model consisting of "high-growth, technology-enabled, venture capital-backed businesses" classified as fast-growing "gazelles" or "unicorns" worth at least a billion dollars (Welter et al., 2017, p.312). These four cases enabled us to explore diverse businesses that represent a significant number of entrepreneurs in practice, yet are some of the more understudied contexts in entrepreneurship.

Furthermore, drawing inspiration from implicit entrepreneurial dichotomies highlighted by Welter et al. (2017) such as "opportunity versus necessity-based, venture capital backed versus bootstrapped, formal versus informal, men-owned versus women-owned, innovator versus replicator, growth-oriented versus lifestyle, entrepreneur versus small business owner/ proprietor" (p.314), our cases are represented in these conflicting dichotomies, with three of our four cases—including the life coach entrepreneur and the husband-and-wife electrical entrepreneurs (two separate cases)—fitting on the right side/underexplored entrepreneurial classifications of many of these comparisons. However, the technology entrepreneur is represented on the left side/ more explored facets of entrepreneurship. Therefore, we were able to examine heterogeneous practices of entrepreneurship from a more holistic perspective in relation to gender, work–life balance, time management, and growth of businesses, as well as to help contribute to more practical and theoretical knowledge regarding "everyday entrepreneurship."

Additionally, we selected case studies that align with the entrepreneurial venture typology framework discovered by Morris et al. (2018) that consists of four types of entrepreneurial venture, including "Survival," "Lifestyle," "Managed Growth," and "Aggressive Growth," to ensure we selected a representative sample of the different types of entrepreneurship. However, all four of our case studies aligned with the "Lifestyle," "Managed Growth," and Aggressive Growth" typologies but did not correlate with the "Survival" typology. Case #1 highlights a home-based coaching business that fits under the "Lifestyle" category, having "a local market focus," being a stable operation, and having "limited reinvestment in the business beyond what is necessary to maintain local competitiveness." Case #2 and Case #3 consist of husband-and-wife entrepreneurs who own a home-based electrical company, and align with the "Managed Growth" typology that has "moderate growth" and more of a regional presence. Case #4, a home-based technology entrepreneur, correlates with the "Aggressive Growth" typology that focuses on competing "on a national or international basis" and placing "a strategic emphasis on new products and services." However, the "Survival" entrepreneurial venture is described as having "no permanent premises," and conducts business by means of "local street vendors, informal markets, flea markets, and craft fairs." Therefore, since this typology does not operate from any "permanent premises" or home base, we argue that this typology does not correlate with the home-based context of our study, and therefore suggest that only three of the four typologies can be used as a framework for examining our home-based entrepreneurship study.

3.2   Data Collection Process

We used a qualitative triangulation method consisting of calendar schedules and interviews to explore time management in greater detail. All of the entrepreneurs electronically submitted their daily calendar schedules from the months of December 2019 and January and February of 2020, and all of the subjects engaged in individual online video interviews that were recorded verbatim. The calendar schedules were digital screenshots of the participants' daily schedules that they entered in their online calendar prior to the study. Therefore, to avoid influencing what was submitted, we requested calendar schedules that were published before informing the participants of our study. Additionally, the participants were not instructed on how to structure their schedules and what to label on their calendars, but the electronic calendars used by all of the participants were similar, so we were able to study comparable calendar formats. We used the daily calendars as the foundational, objective part of the study, and then used the interviews as an opportunity to get additional details and clarification as needed. As a study conducted by Sayles et al. (2010) found discrepancies in using "event history calendars and conventional questionnaire interviews," the event history calendar method was preferred "because its use reliably produced more accurate retrospective reports" (p.1).

We conducted interviews in an online video format because it was more convenient for the participants and enabled the interviews to be scheduled in a timely manner, yet still provided rich communication that enabled us to see and speak with the participant in their work environment verbally while also being able to view nonverbal behavior. The interviews were loosely structured and allowed participants to guide the interview regarding their day-to-day experiences and express themselves with less of the potential biases projected by standardized interview questions that could influence how the interviewees "should respond" based on societal norms and/or expectations such as "spending more time at work" or "spending more time with family." The interview consisted of open prompts such as "tell me about your business" and "describe your typical weekly schedule" to decrease potential implicit suggestions in questions regarding how entrepreneurship in practice should be conducted. Additionally, the interviewees provided more information as needed through electronic exchange during the course of the study to help examine the calendar schedules and interviews in greater detail. We chose to collect data for the three-month period of December, January, and February because December consists of holidays celebrated by a significant amount of people in Los

Angeles, such as Hanukkah and Christmas, and the new year is celebrated on December 31 and January 1 by many people in the city. However, the rest of January and February represents weeks that are more common throughout the calendar year. Therefore, we were able to explore schedules more holistically during busy times of the year for personal activities, as well as during times that are more typical throughout the calendar year. Through this process we used calendar schedules as the foundation of the study, and used the interviews as a supplementary tool to better understand how home-based mum and dad entrepreneurs manage time in relation to gender, work–life balance, time management, and business growth through an entrepreneurship-as-practice lens. As similarly applied by Nag et al. (2007), we transitioned the still photographs of each entrepreneurs' monthly schedules into a "movie" that tells a story of the daily lives of the business owners. Additionally, the interviews allowed us to dig deeper and contribute to the narrative of each entrepreneur's perceptions and experiences.

3.3   Coding Process

Based on the electronic calendars, we inductively developed first-order codes such as "work," "exercise," and "study time," as these categories were listed on the participants' calendars. We define "work" as time devoted to work-related activities such as business meetings, business development, and administrative work and define "exercise" as time devoted to physical fitness. "Study time" is categorized by time spent studying to obtain professional licenses or advanced degrees. By applying these codes to each participant's calendar and investigating the repetition or nonexistence of these codes in each person's schedule, we were able to explore work–life balance and time-management styles of each entrepreneur.

Additionally, to help examine our findings from each case, we counted the amount of time each participant devoted to each code over the duration of three months and used the interviews with each participant to help clarify schedules as needed. The first day of the participants' documented electronic schedules was December 1, 2019, a Sunday, and the last day of the three-month documented calendar period ended on Saturday, February 29, 2020. Therefore, we calculated the amount of hours each participant devoted to each code each day for 13 weeks to find the average amount of time that was spent on work, exercise, and studying. Then we examined and showcased the average weekly schedules of each participant.

All of the participants confirmed that time slots not labeled on the calendars typically consisted of time devoted to family (caring for children, tending to domestic commitments, time with spouse, and so on); however, "family time" was not labeled on any of the calendars except in the case of one participant who occasionally listed a few family activities such as picking his son up from school once a week, taking his son to soccer practice twice a week, and attending his son's Christmas party. Since all of the participants' "family time" was unaccounted for on the schedules—such as how much time was devoted to family each evening, or when children and spouses went to sleep, woke up in the morning, awoke in the middle of the night, and so on—we were not able to quantify an average amount of "family time" directly from all of the calendars. However, we received more information about time devoted to family in the interviews we conducted.

Additionally, during the interviews we learned more details regarding each entrepreneur's business, and all of the participants' interviews were inductively coded with themes such as "clear separation between home and work," "degree/licensure commitments," "difficulty separating home and work spheres," "discipline," "exhaustion," "flexibility," "daily childcare," "high stress," "limited childcare," "multi-tasking work and family," and "satisfied with work." We define "clear separation between work and home" as work being clearly differentiated from home and therefore the two spheres not being blurred or competing for attention with regard to responsibilities. "Degree/licensure commitments" indicates participants who devoted time to studying for professional licenses or degrees, and "difficulty separating home and work spheres" refers to participants who found it challenging to focus solely on work while operating a home-based business. "Discipline" refers to the focus and commitment needed to accomplish work tasks when operating a home-based business. "Exhaustion" we define as being worn out and over-whelmed by responsibilities, and we define "flexibility" as participants having the ability to schedule their day to accommodate work and family obligations. "Daily childcare" refers to participants having someone care for their children each day so the entrepreneur can focus on work. "High stress" is defined as one's work being intense and demanding, and "limited childcare" refers to participants having childcare assistance for minimal hours and/or days each week. We define "multi-tasking work and family" as participants managing work and family roles simultaneously throughout the day, and "satisfied with work" refers to participants who described themselves as happy with their work situation.

4.   FINDINGS

4.1   Average Weekly Schedule of "Lifestyle" Entrepreneur

The "Lifestyle" entrepreneur worked less than ten hours per week and chose to devote more of their time to family as well as to personal and professional growth, such as exercising with friends and pursuing more advanced licenses and/or degrees, rather than working at least 40 hours a week, which is what the State of California classifies as full-time work. Even though her business is home-based, she made time to exercise outside of the home and picked up friends to attend workout classes at the gym. Therefore, she was able to focus on health, wellness, and socializing in addition to working on her career and advancing her education. Additionally, the "Lifestyle" entrepreneur found ful-fillment in her work and was able to multi-task with business and family roles frequently; however, she had childcare help for less than ten hours each week. The "Lifestyle" entrepreneur shared, "I am working very part-time. I would rather be with my child."

She also decided to pursue obtaining her professional therapy license while simultaneously working on her coaching business and caring for her child. She said: "I have to study in order to make money. Even with my master's degree, I can't make money as a therapist until I am professionally licensed. Also, I do not like not bringing in income myself (contributing, subconscious or conscious leveling of power in some marriages). Businesses can take time to create, and I really enjoy being fulfilled by my work!" Therefore, in addition to taking a lead role raising her child, she was able to work on her coaching business while also getting licensed as a professional therapist for a second business.

However, even though focusing on family was her choice, she faced challenges in accomplishing family, school, and work tasks simultaneously. She shared: "There is no good time to study when my husband is working overtime. It's getting to the point that I can't work while watching my child." Ultimately, the "Lifestyle" entrepreneur was able to pursue the type of work she desired for the amount of time she chose to set aside without sacrificing as much time with family and personal growth; however, with limited childcare, studying and working on her coaching business was difficult.

4.2   Average Weekly Schedule for "Managed Growth" Entrepreneur #1 and Entrepreneur #2

The "Managed Growth" entrepreneur is represented in two of our cases, con-sisting of a husband-and-wife entrepreneurial team that owns and operates an electrical company. The husband, "Managed Growth" entrepreneur #1, and wife, "Managed Growth" entrepreneur #2, both submitted their individual calendar schedules and were each interviewed separately. The husband shared: "We focus on customer service a lot and make sure that clients are happy and confident with our work. We do the work properly and give affordable prices. We are not greedy. We are just trying to feed our family."

The wife takes a greater lead with the family, but noted that they work together as 50/50 partners to make the business successful. When examining the schedules of the husband-and-wife entrepreneurial team, we found that the husband had a more linear schedule throughout the week. Once he started work, he was typically uninterrupted. Therefore, he was able to focus primarily on his business without other responsibilities unrelated to work incorporated into his weekly schedule. However, while working, he had to go to several sites to meet with various clients, and juggled driving to and from different locations for business meetings and managing his team. He shared, "I run between estimates and service calls. Sometimes I have to go pick up materials for my team and run to the projects they are working on to see what they are doing. I can visit up to ten places in a day. I have to run around like crazy." Additionally, out of all of the participants, "Managed Growth" entrepreneur #1 was the only business owner to work primarily outside the home with clients. Moreover, "Managed Growth" entrepreneur #1 was the only participant who noted that there was a clear distinction between work and home duties.

In contrast, the wife, "Managed Growth" entrepreneur #2, worked from their home office during the day. During the duration of the study, the wife was integrating back into working on the business full-time after having their child, and worked five hours on Mondays, Tuesdays, and Wednesdays in December 2019 and six hours on Mondays, Tuesdays, Wednesdays, and Thursdays in January 2020. In February 2020, she worked nine hours on Mondays and eight hours on Tuesdays, Wednesdays, and Thursdays. Throughout the study, family commitments were mixed in throughout the workdays. For example, while at her desk working on managing the business, she was responsible for pumping breast milk. When asked if she works straight through while pumping, she lifted up the breast pump and said, "Yes, I keep working while pumping. I don't take breaks." Therefore, her schedule consisted of more multi-tasking of work and family activities throughout the day, in which she had to switch back and forth between modes. She highlighted: "Thankfully, my mother-in-law is here to help take care of our child. She is the reason I am able to work." Additionally, of all the participants, "Managed Growth" entrepreneur #2 was the only person who noted she was happy with her work.

4.3   Average Weekly Schedule for "Aggressive Growth" Entrepreneur

The fourth case illustrates the "Aggressive Growth" entrepreneur. While home-based, which is an underexplored segment of entrepreneurs in the context of location, the "Aggressive Growth" typology is more often studied in entrepreneurship research, as it represents an entrepreneur who operates a growing technology company with aspirations to sell the company once it is established. The "Aggressive Growth" entrepreneur shared: "Once this business succeeds, then I want to sell the business and retire. The work schedule is intense."

This entrepreneur did not have to go onsite to meet with clients and had the convenience of working remotely from his computer. His calendar schedule was primarily linear, in which he was able to block out time devoted solely to work on his calendar during the week. He shared, "I operate a start-up business, and it's high pressure. Every day is a grind. My typical schedule is waking up early morning and syncing up with my team in the Middle East, and then I jump on customer calls during the day. I am usually so busy I don't have time to leave my desk for lunch. Sometimes, I also have to eat dinner at my desk." He noted that even though working from home provides him flexibility to help care for children when needed, it is difficult to have children at home while trying to accomplish work tasks. He said, "Family members think you're not working because you're at home. So they will come to you and ask, 'Do you have five minutes to do this, or ten minutes to do that?' Yet constantly, I have to say 'I'm working. I'm home, but I'm working.'"

Despite his work usually starting at 6a.m. and being demanding throughout the day, he was also able to take a lead role with family commitments and pick his children up from school and/or soccer practice as needed, and to attend his son's Christmas party. Additionally, he was working toward his doctoral degree. He shared: "I want to get my doctorate to help me work in high-level consultation for startups and teach college part-time." He added: "It is really, really tough to do both [be an entrepreneur and obtain a doctorate]." Additionally, out of all four cases, the "Aggressive Growth" entrepreneur was the only participant who labeled "fun" commitments on his calendar, such as going on vacations and watching sports games, and he excelled at managing various responsibilities with family, work and school. However, his time was less interrupted during scheduling blocks in which he could typically fulfill one role such as work tasks, family obligations, or studying; thus raising the question whether linear time management enables more efficiency, productivity, and greater work–life balance.

4.4 Time Management Approaches of Home-based Mum and Dad Entrepreneurs

We found that the women entrepreneurs who participated in the study had less linear time management approaches when balancing work and family than the male entrepreneurs, with men primarily focusing on work from morning until evening, and women multi-tasking with work and family more frequently throughout the entire day. One of the male entrepreneurs had no commitments outside work scheduled on his calendar once his workday started, and the other male entrepreneur had minimal interruptions outside work scheduled on the calendar once his workday started. Family commitments were usually scheduled after the workday ended. However, both of the male entrepreneurs' time-management approaches were nonlinear with regard to their work schedules: the "Aggressive Growth" entrepreneur's schedule was "all over the place" and "Managed Growth" entrepreneur #1's "day is crazy." Therefore, when examining the time management of the participants' schedules, it could be seen that both of the male entrepreneurs' schedules were more nonlinear with regard to work schedules, with them managing several work tasks throughout the day; however, work and family were typically not scheduled during the same time blocks. The two women entrepreneurs reported being taken away from business work to care for children often, and managed several work activities and family activities simultaneously, but the "Aggressive Growth" entrepreneur also showed that while he was working from home he was there to step in and care for his children by taking and picking them up from school and extra-curricular activities, and said he often helps his kids with homework.

4.5   Gender Roles of Home-based Mum and Dad Entrepreneurs

The gender roles exemplified were a mixture of traditional and non-traditional. The "Lifestyle" entrepreneur operates a part-time business while also caring for her child, which is a more traditional female gender role, but highlighted that she "does not like not bringing in income." She added, "I like to contribute, and there's a subconscious or conscious leveling of power in some marriages. Also, businesses can take time to create, and I really enjoy being fulfilled by my work," which tends to align with a more masculine gender stereotype. The husband and wife "Managed Growth" entrepreneurial team currently work as 50/50 business partners, but the wife, "Managed Growth" entrepreneur #2, integrated back into work with less time devoted to the busines than her husband due to caring for their child. She was also responsible for getting the child breakfast and dressed in the morning and pumping for breast milk while working; therefore the wife took on a more traditional female gender role, leading the family. However, the "Aggressive Growth" entrepreneur also assisted with his children's school and extra-curricular commitments throughout the day while working, which challenges male gender stereotypes.

Additionally, our data illustrates that even though both of the women entrepreneurs took the lead with childcare activities, they ran viable businesses, with the "Lifestyle" entrepreneur also advancing her professional education to start a second business. The main differentiating factor between "Managed Growth" entrepreneur #2 and the "Lifestyle" entrepreneur is that the wife in the "Managed Growth" entrepreneurial team had childcare for several hours each day, giving her more ability to focus on work. Thus, if given the choice, and childcare support, the data illustrates in these cases that women can be devoted to operating viable businesses while also taking a lead role raising children.

Table 9.1   Code list and meaning from calendars

Work	Time devoted to work-related activities such as business meetings, business development, and administrative work
Study	Time used for studying to obtain professional certifications and advanced academic degrees
Exercise	Time devoted to physical fitness

Table 9.2   Code list and meaning from interviews

Clear separation between home and work	Work is clearly differentiated from home; therefore, the two spheres are not blurred or competing for attention in regards to responsibilities
Degree/licensure commitments	Indicates participants who devote time to studying for professional licenses or degrees
Difficulty separating home and work sphere	Participants who found it challenging to focus solely on work while operating a home-based business
Discipline	Refers to the focus and commitment needed to accomplish work tasks when operating a home-based business
Exhaustion	Being worn out and overwhelmed with responsibilities
Flexibility	Participants having the ability to schedule their day to accommodate work and family obligations
Daily childcare	Participants having someone care for their children each day so the entrepreneur can focus on work
High stress	Participants' work being intense and demanding
Limited childcare	Participants having childcare assistance for minimal hours and/or days each week
Multi-tasking work and family	Participants managing work and family roles simultaneously throughout the day
Satisfied with work	Participants who described themselves as happy with their work situation

Table 9.3   Average weekly time devoted to each code for "Lifestyle" entrepreneur

Codes	Sunday	Monday	Tuesday	Wednesday	Thursday	Friday	Saturday
Work	1 hour	0	0	3 hours, 14 minutes	0	2 hours	0
Study	1 hour	1 hour	0	0	0	2 hours	0
Exercise	0	1 hour	2 hours	0	2 hours	0	0

Table 9.4   *Average weekly time devoted to each code for "Managed Growth" entrepreneur #1*

Codes	Sunday	Monday	Tuesday	Wednesday	Thursday	Friday	Saturday
Work	0	11 hours	11 hours	11 hours	11 hours	11 hours	4 hours
Study	0	0	0	0	0	0	0
Exercise	0	0	0	0	0	0	0

Table 9.5   *Average weekly time devoted to each code for "Managed Growth" entrepreneur #2*

Codes	Sunday	Monday	Tuesday	Wednesday	Thursday	Friday	Saturday
Work	0	6 hours, 37 minutes	6 hours, 18 minutes	6 hours, 18 minutes	4 hours, 46 minutes	0	0
Study	0	0	0	0	0	0	0
Exercise	0	0	0	0	0	0	0

Table 9.6   *Average weekly time devoted to each code for "Aggressive Growth" entrepreneur*

Codes	Sunday	Monday	Tuesday	Wednesday	Thursday	Friday	Saturday
Work	51 minutes	11 hours	7 hours, 26 minutes	6 hours, 46 minutes	8 hours, 30 minutes	8 hours, 41 minutes	3 hours
Study	0	4 hours	0	3 hours, 23 minutes	0	1 hour	1 hour
Exercise	0	0	0	0	0	0	0

Table 9.7   *Code findings from interviews*

Name	Grounded
Clear separation between home and work	3
Degree/licensure commitments	4
Difficulty separating home and work sphere	6
Discipline	6
Exhaustion	1
Flexibility	6
Daily childcare	1
High stress	1
Limited childcare	3
Multi-tasking work and family	7
Satisfied with work	1

5.   DISCUSSION AND CONCLUSION

Based on the findings from our case studies, the stereotype highlighted by Bruni et al. (2004, p.262) that "the implicit sub-text at work in this representation states that family duties take priority in women's lives, and therefore, that women are not trustworthy entrepreneurs" was challenged, as all the women in the study operate viable businesses while simultaneously managing family responsibilities. Additionally, the stereotype that men do not help significantly with domestic responsibilities while having a demanding career was questioned, as the "Aggressive Growth" entrepreneur helped out with the children's homework and drove children to and from extracurricular activities while operating a high-growth firm. Therefore, the findings do not correlate with the gender stereotypes of men and women that are found in the literature, such as women entrepreneurs underperforming as business owners and men entrepreneurs not tending to domestic responsibilities. Furthermore, our findings challenge the stereotype that home-based businesses are underperforming enterprises (Mason et al., 2011), as illustrated by the "Aggressive Growth" entrepreneur, and showcases that businesses do not have to be initiated from a traditional office to be viable, high-growth firms. Additionally, we investigated the study with an underused data collection method consisting of electronic calendars that were published prior to asking participants for their schedules, and hope to illustrate the benefit this method provides in gaining more objectivity for the foundation of a study.

We acknowledge that more case studies should be used to develop further evaluations on how time is managed among mum and dad home-based entrepreneurs to find more generalizable conclusions but suggest our study provides some insight on the working practices of home-based women and men entrepreneurs with children, which can be used as a basis for further exploration. Therefore, we propose a call to evaluate in greater detail home-based entrepreneurial typologies in association with gender. We also propose a call for further studies of home-based mum and dad entrepreneurs from different countries to analyze how the context of location affects work–life balance, time management, gender roles, and business growth.

Additionally, we encourage other scholars to explore if the challenges associated with establishing work–life balance can serve as an impetus for home-based women entrepreneurs to employ more transformative business operating models due to time limitations, thus, requiring home-based women entrepreneurs to reinvent ubiquitous corporate standards such as working long hours to attain professional advancement and enabling them to break free from established corporate practices.

REFERENCES

Ahl, H. (2006). Why research on women entrepreneurs needs new directions. *Entrepreneurship, Theory and Practice, 30*(5), 595–622.

Ahl, H., & Marlow, S. (2021). Exploring the false promise of entrepreneurship through a postfeminist critique of the enterprise policy discourse in Sweden and the UK. *Human Relations, 74*(1), 41–68.

Alsos, G.A., Isaksen, E.J., & Ljunggren, E. (2006). New venture financing and subsequent business growth in men-and women-led businesses. *Entrepreneurship, Theory and Practice, 30*(5), 667–86.

Anwar, M.N., & Daniel, E. (2016). The role of entrepreneur–venture fit in online home-based entrepreneurship: a systematic literature review. *Journal of Enterprising Culture, 24*(4), 419–51.

Arendell, T. (2001). The new care work of middle class mothers: managing childrearing, employment, and time. In Daly, K.J. (ed.) *Minding the Time in Family Experience: Emerging Perspectives and Issues*, pp.163–204. Oxford: Elsevier Science.

BIS (UK Government Department for Business, Innovation and Skills) (May 2012). Make business your business: a report on small business start ups, available at www .gov.uk/government/uploads/system/uploads/attachmentdata/file/32245/12-827 -make-business-your-business-report-on-start-ups.pdf (accessed 23 January 2014).

Bruni, A., Gherardi, S., & Poggio, B. (2004). Entrepreneur-mentality, gender and the study of women entrepreneurs. *Journal of Organizational Change Management, 17*(3), 256–68.

Brush, C.G. (1992). Research on women business owners: past trends, a new perspective and future directions. *Entrepreneurship Theory and Practice, 16*(4), 5–30.

Buttner, E.H. (1993). Female entrepreneurs: how far have they come? *Business Horizons, 36*(2), 59–65.

Carter, S., & Marlow, S. (2006). Female entrepreneurship: theoretical perspectives and empirical evidence. In Carter, N.M., Henry, C., Cinneide, B.O., & Johnston, K. (eds), *Female Entrepreneurship* (pp.27–52). Abingdon: Routledge.

Carter, S.L., & Shaw, E. (2006). Women's business ownership: recent research and policy developments. Report to the small business service, November.

Clark, S.C. (2000). Work/family border theory: a new theory of work/family balance. *Human Relations, 53*(6), 747–70.

Daly, K.J. (1996). *Families and Time: Keeping Pace in a Hurried Culture*. Thousand Oaks, CA: Sage.

Davies, K. (1990). *Women, Time and the Weaving of the Strands of Everyday Life.* Aldershot: Avebury.

Desrochers, S., & Sargent, L.D. (2004). Boundary/border theory and work–family integration. *Organization Management Journal, 1*(1), 40–48.

Dex, S., & Scheibl, F. (2001). Flexible and family-friendly working arrangements in UK-based SMEs: business cases. *British Journal of Industrial Relations, 39*(3), 411–31.

Dy, A., Marlow, S., & Martin, L. (2017). A web of opportunity or the same old story? Women digital entrepreneurs and intersectionality theory. *Human Relations, 70*(3), 286–311.

Enterprise Nation (2014). *Home Business Report*, available at www.enterprisenation .com/homebusiness (accessed 16 February 2015).

Ernst & Young. (2015). *Global Generations: A Global Study on Work–Life Challenges across Generations*. London: Ernst & Young.

Fairlie, R.W., and Robb, A.M. (2009). Gender differences in business performance: evidence from the Characteristics of Business Owners Survey. *Small Business Economics*, 33(4), 375-395.

Ferguson, M., Carlson, D., Boswell, W., Whitten, D., Butts, M.M., & Kacmar, K.M. (2016). Tethered to work: a family systems approach linking mobile device use to turnover intentions. *Journal of Applied Psychology*, 101, 520–34.

Fraser, S. (2005). *Finance for Small and Medium Sized Enterprises: A Report on the 2004 UK Survey of SME Finances*. Coventry: SME Centre, University of Warwick.

Gadeyne, N., Verbruggen, M., Delanoeije, J., & De Cooman, R. (2018). All wired, all tired? Work-related ICT-use outside work hours and work-to-home conflict: The role of integration preference, integration norms and work demands. *Journal of Vocational Behavior*, 107, 86–99.

Galinsky, E., Aumann, K., & Bond. J.T. (2011). *Times Are Changing: Gender and Generation at Work and at Home*. New York: Families and Work Institute.

Gartner, W.B. (2016). *Entrepreneurship as Organizing: Selected Papers of William B. Gartner*. Cheltenham: Edward Elgar Publishing.

Gherardi, S. (2015). Authoring the female entrepreneur while talking the discourse of work–family life balance. *International Small Business Journal*, 33(6), 649–66.

Greenhaus, J.H., & Powell, G.N. (2017). *Making Work and Family Work: From Hard Choices to Smart Choices*. New York: Routledge.

Griffin, M.A. (2007). Specifying organizational contexts: systematic links between contexts and processes in organizational behavior. *Journal of Organizational Behavior*, 28(7), 859–63.

Gupta, V.K., Wieland, A.M., & Turban, D.B. (2019). Gender characterizations in entrepreneurship: a multi-level investigation of sex-role stereotypes about high-growth, commercial, and social entrepreneurs. *Journal of Small Business Management*, 57(1), 131–53.

Harding, R. (2006). *Global Entrepreneurship Monitor UK 2004*. London: GEM UK.

Hays, S. (1996). *The Cultural Contradictions of Motherhood*. New Haven, CT: Yale University Press.

Hechavarria, D., Bullough, A., Brush, C., & Edelman, L. (2019). High-growth women's entrepreneurship: fueling social and economic development. *Journal of Small Business Management*, 57(1), 5–13.

Hilbrecht, M., Shaw, S.M., Johnson, L.C., & Andrey, J. (2008). 'I'm home for the kids': contradictory implications for work–life balance of teleworking mothers. *Gender, Work & Organization*, 15(5), 454–76.

Hughes, K.D., Jennings, J.E., Brush, C., Carter, S., & Welter, F. (2012). Extending women's entrepreneurship research in new directions. *Entrepreneurship Theory and Practice*, 36(3), 429–42.

Jayawarna, D., Marlow, S., & Martinez-Dy, A. (2019). Women's entrepreneurship: Self actualisation or self harm? [Conference session]. Paper to the Babson Entrepreneurship Conference, Babson College.

Jayawarna, D., Marlow, S., & Swail, J. (2020). A gendered life course explanation of the exit decision in the context of household dynamics. *Entrepreneurship Theory and Practice*, 1042258720940123.

Jennings, J.E., & McDougald, M.S. (2007). Work–family interface experiences and coping strategies: implications for entrepreneurship research and practice. *Academy of Management Review*, 32(3), 747–60.

Kelly, D., Baumer, B., Brush, C., Greene, P., Mah, M., Majbouri, M., Cole, M., Dean, M., & Haevlow, R. (2017). *Global Entrepreneurship Monitor 2016/2017 Report of Women's Entrepreneurship*. Wellesley, MA: Babson College.

Lanaj, K., Johnson, R.E., & Barnes, C.M. 2014. Beginning the workday yet already depleted? Consequences of late-night smartphone use and sleep. *Organizational Behavior and Human Decision Processes, 124*, 11–23.

Lewis, P. (2006). The quest for invisibility: female entrepreneurs and the masculine norm of entrepreneurship. *Gender, Work & Organization, 13*(5), 453–69.

Mason, C.M., Carter, S., & Tagg, S. (2011). Invisible businesses: the characteristics of home-based businesses in the United Kingdom. *Regional Studies, 45*(5), 625–39.

Mattis, M.C. (2004). Women entrepreneurs: out from under the glass ceiling. *Women in Management Review, 19*(3), 154–63.

McAdam, M., & Cunningham, J.A. (eds) (2021). *Women and Global Entrepreneurship: Contextualising Everyday Experiences*. Abingdon: Routledge.

McGowan, P., Redeker, C.L., Cooper, S.Y., & Greenan, K. (2012). Female entrepreneurship and the management of business and domestic roles: motivations, expectations and realities. *Entrepreneurship & Regional Development, 24*(1–2), 53–72. www.pure.ed.ac.uk/ws/portalfiles/portal/16500468/McGowan_Lewis_Redeker_Cooper_and_Greenan_Entrepreneurship_and_Regional_Development_2012_for_Open_Access.pdf (accessed 25 August 2022).

Morris, M.H., Neumeyer, X., Jang, Y., & Kuratko, D.F. (2018). Distinguishing types of entrepreneurial ventures: an identity-based perspective. *Journal of Small Business Management, 56*(3), 453–74.

Nag, R., Corley, K.G., & Gioia, D.A. (2007). The intersection of organizational identity, knowledge, and practice: attempting strategic change via knowledge grafting. *Academy of Management Journal, 50*, 821–47.

Nicolini, D. (2011). Practice as the site of knowing: insights from the field of telemedicine. *Organization Science, 22*(3), 602–20. doi:10.1287/orsc.1100.0556.

Nikina, A., Le Loarne, S., & Shelton, L.M. (2012). The role of a couple's relationship in spousal support to female entrepreneurs. *Revue de l'Entrepreneuriat, 11*(4), 37–60.

Nikina, A., Shelton, L.M., & Le Loarne, S. (2015). An examination of how husbands, as key stakeholders, impact the success of women entrepreneurs. *Journal of Small Business and Enterprise Development, 22*(1), 38–62.

Orser, B.J., Riding, A.L., & Manley, K. (2006). Women entrepreneurs and financial capital. *Entrepreneurship, Theory and Practice, 30*(5), 643–65.

Palumbo, R., Manna, R., & Cavallone, M. (2020). Beware of side effects on quality! Investigating the implications of home working on work–life balance in educational services. *The TQM Journal, 33*(4), 15.

Parasuraman, S., & Simmers, C.A. (2001). Type of employment, work–family conflict and well-being: a comparative study. *Journal of Organizational Behavior: The International Journal of Industrial, Occupational and Organizational Psychology and Behavior, 22*(5), 551–68.

Perlow, L.A. (2012). *Sleeping with Your Smartphone: How to Break the 24/7 Habit and Change the Way You Work*. Boston: Harvard Business Review Press.

Powell, G.N. (2019). *Women and Men in Management* (5th ed.). Los Angeles: Sage.

Powell, G.N., Greenhaus, J.H., Allen, T.D., & Johnson, R.E. (2019). Advancing and expanding work–life theory from multiple perspectives. *Academy of Management Review, 44*(1), 54–71.

Richomme-Huet, K., & Vial, V. (2014). Business lessons from a "mompreneurs" network. *Global Business and Organizational Excellence*, *33*(4), 18–27. https://doi .org/10.1002/joe.21550.

Rouse, J., & Kitching, J. (2006). Do enterprise support programmes leave women holding the baby? *Environment and Planning C: Government and Policy*, *24*(1), 5–19.

Sayles, H., Belli, R.F., & Serrano, E. (2010). Interviewer variance between event history calendar and conventional questionnaire interviews. *Public Opinion Quarterly*, *74*(1), 140–53.

Shelton, L.M. (2006). Female entrepreneurs, work–family conflict, and venture performance: New insights into the work–family interface. *Journal of Small Business Management*, *44*(2), 285–97.

Sullivan, C., & Lewis, S. (2001). Home-based telework, gender, and the synchronization of work and family: perspectives of teleworkers and their co-residents. *Gender, Work and Organization*, *8*(2), 123–45.

Thompson, N.A., Verduijn, K., & Gartner, W.B. (2020). Entrepreneurship-as-practice: grounding contemporary theories of practice into entrepreneurship studies. *Entrepreneurship & Regional Development*, *32*(3–4), 247–56.

Thompson, N.A., Verduijn, K., & Gartner, W.B. (2021). *Entrepreneurship-as-Practice: Grounding Contemporary Theories of Practice into Entrepreneurship Studies*. Abingdon: Routledge.

Welter, F., Baker, T., Audretsch, D.B., & Gartner, W.B. (2017). Everyday entrepreneurship—a call for entrepreneurship research to embrace entrepreneurial diversity. *Entrepreneurship Theory & Practice*, *41*(3), 1.

Welter, F., Baker, T., & Wirsching, K. (2019). Three waves and counting: the rising tide of contextualization in entrepreneurship research. *Small Business Economics*, *52*(2), 319–30.

Werbel, J.D., & Danes, S.M. (2010). Work family conflict in new business ventures: the moderating effects of spousal commitment to the new business venture. *Journal of Small Business Management*, *48*(3), 421–40. https://doi.org/10.1111/j.1540-627X .2010.00301.x

Williams, D.R. (2004). Effects of childcare activities on the duration of self-employment in Europe. *Entrepreneurship Theory and Practice*, *28*(5), 467–85.

Yang, T., & Triana, M. (2019). Set up to fail: explaining when women-led businesses are more likely to fail. *Journal of Management*, *45*(3), 926–54. https://doi.org/10 .1177/0149206316685856.

Zuzanek, J. (2000). *The Effects of Time Use and Time Pressure on Child–Parent Relationships: Research Report Submitted to Health Canada*. Waterloo: Otium Publications.

Index